EVERY SINGLE BALL

Brian Corcoran is one of the most respected hurlers and dual players of his generation. He was named Hurler of the Year in 1992 and again in 1999, when he won his first All Ireland senior medal. In the autumn of 2001, he quit both club and inter-county hurling but came out of retirement two and a half years later to win two All Irelands, in 2004 and 2005.

Kieran Shannon is chief Gaelic Games correspondent of the *Sunday Tribune*. The winner of the 2003 GAA McNamee Award, he has co-written two other highly-acclaimed books: *Hooked* with Justin McCarthy and *Kicking Down Heaven's Door* with Mickey Harte. He has previously worked with the *Irish Examiner* and the *Sunday Independent*. Reared in Cork, he now lives in County Clare with his wife, Ann Marie. He also works as a qualified sports psychologist.

EVERY SINGLE BALL

The Brian Corcoran Story

Brian Corcoran
with Kieran Shannon

MAINSTREAM
PUBLISHING

EDINBURGH AND LONDON

First published in Great Britain in 2006 by
MAINSTREAM PUBLISHING COMPANY
(EDINBURGH) LTD
7 Albany Street
Edinburgh EH1 3UG

ISBN 978 184596 200 5 (from January 2007)
ISBN 1 84596 200 1

A catalogue record for this book is available
from the British Library

All internal images courtesy of Brian Corcoran, except where stated

Typeset in Giovanni and Albertus

Printed in Great Britain by
Clays Ltd, St Ives plc

TO MY FAMILY

The greatest memories of my life are when I married Elaine and when she brought our three wonderful kids into this world.

Elaine is the most extraordinary person I have ever met. She has taught me so much about life, about love, about myself. She's so giving, so strong, so fearless, so talented. I aspire to be more like her in so many ways. She is my hero and my best friend. The days we have shared and the dreams we have lived will be with me forever. I will love her until the day I die.

My words can't describe the joy that Kate, Edel and Ewan have brought into my life. When I look at them, I see faces of the past. But they are their own beautiful individuals. They are my now; they are my future.

To my late parents, Nuala and John Corcoran, who have been with me every step of the way. They are never far from my mind and will always be in my heart.

ACKNOWLEDGEMENTS

MY COUNTLESS HAPPY CHILDHOOD MEMORIES ARE thanks to the love and support of my late parents, John and Nuala, my sister, Ann, and my brother, John.

Mam and Dad did everything for us, and it's only as I look back now that I can fully appreciate how much they dedicated their lives to our family.

Hurling has been a huge part of who I am, and I have the people of Erins Own to thank for nurturing the passion within that would become the driving force of my life. I want to say a heartfelt thank you to all the people who got up and went out to train and manage, organise and supervise, provide catering and maintenance, fund-raise and hell-raise for the club. It was a privilege to grow up with the mentors, players and friends I had at Erins Own, and it was a better life for knowing them.

To all the great men that I have played with and all the great men that I have played against. It has been a great pleasure and a fantastic journey.

Thanks to the supporters who were with me on that journey and made it all the more enjoyable and colourful.

To the friends that enriched life along the way.

Thanks to my four personal editors: my brother-in-law Brian Walsh, whom I first met when we played on the Cork Under-14 team together in 1987, my parents-in-law Matthew and

Rena Walsh, who have always been there for us, and my wife, Elaine, who never ceases to amaze me. Their help and feedback were invaluable.

I'd like to thank O$_2$, especially Catherine Tiernan and Pat Madigan for all their help and support, not only with this book but with the Cork team over the last five years. They have been incredible sponsors and have played a big part in our success.

To write a book takes a lot of time and hard work, and when Kieran and I weighed up the pros and cons of writing a book this year, especially with all we had on otherwise, I underestimated the beast that would become this autobiography. Talking into the early hours of the morning about myself is not my idea of fun, but, through the recounting, the disputing, the re-thrashing and the proofing, we had good times and a good laugh. Kieran was always a great person to work with, and I want to thank him for his commitment, his patience and his craft.

During the course of my comeback, when many people around me were questioning my sanity, including myself at times, Elaine was the one person who never doubted I'd make it back and encouraged me to follow my dream and my gut. No one else I know could have done what Elaine has done for me over the years. No one could be more loving, more supportive, more understanding. I will never be able to thank her enough for being the best friend, the best mother, the best thing that has ever happened in my life.

Brian Corcoran
Cork

✳   ✳   ✳

ONE OF THE CHALLENGES OF CO-WRITING THE autobiography of a player of Brian Corcoran's stature is the modesty issue. How can one of the players of his or any generation say he was one of the players of his generation? He can't. And he can't see it as we did either.

There are countless games that Brian Corcoran adorned and dominated that aren't even mentioned inside – such as the Under-15 colleges game in Bansha, when my friend Christy O'Connor was in goals for St Flannan's and witnessed first-hand Brian launch a shot from his own half-back line that didn't just go over the bar but over the netting behind; such as the summer night in 1993 when I sat with my father in the open stand of Páirc Uí Chaoimh and watched him blitz through the Tipperary Under-21 defence for two goals; or the day when Cork played Wexford in a 1998 Oireachtas game against Wexford that he and everyone else has probably forgotten, but I can't because his majesty and brilliance that day were so typical of Brian Corcoran, the Peaceful Warrior.

On the day of the 1989 Munster final, a 15-year-old Christy O'Connor left Clare for Cork at eight o'clock in the morning so he could see Brian Corcoran play for Imokilly in the Under-16 curtain-raiser, before his own brother James played for Clare in the minor final. Bar maybe the great Frank McGuigan, who old men would go all over Tyrone just to see play, who else could have commanded such respect at that age? So, here in this book, when Brian does occasionally admit to playing well, or cites a cutting from some of the scrapbooks his late mother Nuala kept, to give the reader a sense of how he was faring at certain points in time, know this: he was that good and more.

The other big challenge in this book was writing it in a year when I was also completing my Masters in Sports Psychology. But I got by with a lot of help from my friends. First and foremost, I am extremely grateful to my wife, Ann Marie, whose support, love and good humour were invaluable. Thanks, too, to Tommy Conlon for his advice and his peerless wit. To Christy O'Connor and Damian Lawlor: respect, boss, and thanks, friend. Thanks to my *Sunday Tribune* colleague, Malachy Clerkin, for his feedback and suggestions; to our empathetic and supportive editor, P.J. Cunningham; to my college course leader in Waterford IT, Gerry Fitzpatrick; to the Mainstream Publishing team of Kevin O'Brien, Bill Campbell and Graeme Blaikie for their vigilant editing, patience and support; to Brian's family for their endless suggestions and insights; to my journalistic colleagues and friends Enda McEvoy and Michael Foley for helping out on more than a few queries; to Paddy Heaney for introducing me to Jerry Kramer's book *Instant Replay*; to Michael Hearn for insisting I do this book; to my brother Simon, who was mighty persuasive with his immortal text message: 'Carlsberg don't do autobiographies, but if they did, they'd do Corcoran's'; to my brother Damien, whose courage and dedication inspires me; and, especially, to my parents, Brendan and Rosaleen, for being there always.

Finally, I would like to thank Brian Corcoran. Ever since I started as a journalist with the *Evening Echo* and the *Examiner* in Cork in 1995, Brian was always very courteous and cooperative with me. I don't think there's another person I would have done a book with this year, and I don't think I could have found another player with the intelligence and honesty to do the kind of book we did this year. What I've always admired about Brian Corcoran is not so much what he won but how he won, how he played the game. How he wrote this book was just as impressive. His attention to detail, sincerity and openness in this project at times staggered me, and I will always appreciate that.

Kieran Shannon
Ennis

CONTENTS

CHAPTER ONE

HEAVEN

'I firmly believe that any man's finest hour, his greatest fulfilment of all he holds dear, is the moment when he has worked his heart out in a good cause and lies exhausted on the field of battle – victorious'

VINCE LOMBARDI

IT'S A SUNDAY IN SEPTEMBER, AND I'M IN A WARM-UP room in the bowels of Croke Park, standing in front of a wall with a ball and hurley in hand. I feel good now. A few hours ago, I couldn't eat our pre-match meal. Every other game this year I could – big games such as the Munster semi-final and All Ireland quarter-final against Waterford, the Munster final against Tipp, last month's All Ireland semi-final against Clare – but today I just couldn't get that chicken and pasta down. Now I'm fine. I'm settled. I'm comfortable now that I have a ball and hurley in hand.

This time two years ago, I didn't feel comfortable with them. I hadn't held a ball or hurley in two years. I was finished with hurling, had been finished ever since that summer of 2001. I preferred to play golf. Sometimes, in the season or two before I retired, I even preferred to stay on in work than go to training. As a kid, I loved nothing more than striking a ball, off the side wall of my parents' home in Glounthaune, through the open window of an old derelict cottage at The Cross just down the road or over the bar in our club pitch with Erins Own. But, as the years went on, I found hurling had less and less to do with striking the ball. It had to do with running laps and up hills and through valleys. It had to do with ploughing through the mud for seven months to play maybe seventy minutes in May. It had nothing to do with fun and was all about winning, because, if you weren't winning, you weren't even playing.

But then I went to the 2003 All Ireland final and went over to see the lads in the Citywest Hotel. The following night, I met up with them again at the homecoming in Cork. And I just knew from the hurt they were feeling from losing that game that they were going to win the 2004 All Ireland. I just knew it, and I wanted to be part of it. So, that Wednesday evening, when I got back from work, I went out to the garage and found a sliotar and the hurley I used in the 1999 All Ireland final. Donal Óg Cusack could never understand why I used that hurley, with the top of it chipped off, but, as I used to tell him, I never needed that top part hitting a ball. That Wednesday night in our kitchen when I picked up my hurley again, I was no longer that player of '99, and, as I bounced the ball up and down, the hurley felt totally alien to me. A few weeks later, I went up to the ball alley in Erins Own, and it was as if I had never played the game. Even six months later, when I had just got the call to go back and train with Cork, a few clubmates pulled me aside and warned me that I could be setting myself up for a massive fall with this comeback.

Now, an All Ireland medal, Munster medal and an All Star on from that night in the kitchen, the hurley again feels like an extension of me. I hit the ball off the wall, control it and hit it back. Now I catch it. My eye and touch is in. I feel at ease, at home, as if I'm back outside my parents' house in Glounthaune.

This room is beginning to fill up now. I was the first one in here today – just like, I suppose, I was the first one in our dressing-room years ago. My first All Ireland here was as a minor in '88. I was 15 back then. John Gardiner beside me here would have been five. My first senior final was in '92. Every other player in here hadn't even sat their Junior Cert by then. But they've seen and been through a lot themselves, this bunch. They've won minor and Under-21 All Irelands together. They've lost together. They've gone on strike and challenged the whole way the GAA runs and thinks together. Last year, we won a senior All Ireland together. Now we want to win another one.

It's nearly time to go out. First, our manager, John Allen, asks us to form a circle, from twenty-nine down to one, and presents a jersey to each of us. Everyone claps. Everyone's upbeat. Donal Óg, the last man to receive a jersey, says with a smile, 'It's good to be here.'

A steward outside shouts, 'Walk, lads, walk!', afraid we might slip, but we always walk out of this room now. It goes back to that 2003 final. The lads were too revved up that day: Diarmuid O'Sullivan tugged his hamstring sprinting out onto the field. The morning of the 2004 final, our trainer, Seanie McGrath, suggested fellas should just jog out of the dressing-room, and Donal Óg said, 'We'll walk out if you want.'

I remember a club championship game in '99 down in Cobh. We were playing Donal Óg's and Sully's club, Cloyne. Our coach, P.J. Murphy, was just about to give his speech but suddenly paused; there was no point competing against the racket from next door. We just stayed there, listening and stretching, as Cloyne went about raving and ranting and flaking each other. When they finally went out, taking the door with them, we said a few quiet words, and for the first 15 minutes just watched my brother John point free after free after free. He ended up with eleven points that day, nine from frees, and we won well. Now Cloyne go for the more relaxed approach – and are enjoying the most successful period in the club's history. It works for them, and it works for Cork.

I've seen the old Cloyne way in old Cork dressing-rooms. When I close my eyes and picture us back in the good old days of the great Canon Michael O'Brien, I see warriors like Pat Hartnett shouldering the wall and banging fellas on the chest, inviting them to bang his, Tomás Mulcahy in the centre of the huddle, shaking his fist, and Denis Walsh beside him, nodding furiously, while John Fitzgibbon and myself are standing at the back, detached from it all. Every fella has his own way of getting into the zone. Some fellas possibly need to shout or be shouted at. But, for a lot of other fellas, a more low-key style works best. This Cork team appreciates that. There's no point leaving our energy, the game, in the dressing-room.

We come out of the tunnel and onto the grass, and see the Liam McCarthy Cup on a podium in front of us, a reminder of what's at stake. I throw my ball onto that grass, just to get a feel for it. I pick it up, hit it on, pick it up, hit it on, then pick it up again. In the old days, I'd have lashed it by now. But Donal O'Grady, our manager in 2004, used to tell us, 'Lads, run into the 21 and knock it over the bar. Start off positively.' So I run in, take my point, run back down for the photograph, then run back up towards the goal, and we all pair off. Sully pucks a few balls out to me in between putting on his Vaseline, and I keep hitting them over.

I've hardly felt as relaxed in my whole life.

And then, after the warm-up, meeting the president, and the parade, the 2005 All Ireland hurling final is on. In the first 15 minutes, a lot of ball comes our way in the full-forward line. At a team meeting last week, we told the lads the ball could have come in quicker than it did in the semi-final against Clare. Today, Donal Óg is looking for me from his puckouts, our half-backs are looking to hit us first time rather than go through our half-forwards and it's working. A ball comes over the top, and I control it. I slip but get up quickly, and, just as I'm looking to pass off to someone, I notice my marker, Tony O'Regan, is standing off me. I shoot, and it goes over. I lay off another ball for Niall McCarthy to pop over for a point. And then Ben O'Connor latches on to a ball in acres of space and blasts it past Liam O'Donoghue. Croke Park explodes.

We will never trail in this game. There will be some nervous moments, such as the few frees and points Galway string together before half-time. Damien Hayes will score a goal midway through the second half that cuts our lead down to one. But we withstand it all. Donal Óg has the presence of mind to take 33 seconds to puck the ball back out after that goal. John Gardiner points a massive free to extend the lead to two. All the work, all the science, Seanie and John have put in with us over the year kicks in, as we click into fifth gear. The game enters injury-time, and the PA announces there'll be two minutes. I look up at the scoreboard. We're five up. I've looked up at that scoreboard before, or at least the hand-flicked one that used to be there in '92, and known what imminent defeat is like. It's awful, and when the whistle goes I commiserate with Tony Óg. But winning, winning is heaven. Winning is why I play: for moments like this, as I hug Cian O'Connor, my clubmate; for moments like embracing Timmy McCarthy, the silent soldier from Castlelyons; for moments like watching Seán Óg Ó hAilpín, who's come from Fiji to Corcaigh to Páirc an Chrócaigh to lift the Liam McCarthy Cup, fulfil a childhood dream up here on the Hogan Stand.

This smile can't leave my face. It's as if someone has

passed me happy gas. It's as if we're all having this one big team wedding day. We're in the dressing-room now, and Liam McCarthy is sitting on a table in the middle of the room. Fellas run up and kiss it. Others hold it. Our logistics manager, Jimmy McEvoy, is standing by it, getting photos of him and all the lads with it. Last year, Jimmy wished he had brought his digital camera, but he's got it now. John Allen thanks us for all the work we've done this year, says it's the proudest moment of his sporting career and that Seán Óg is the greatest sportsman to ever come out of Cork. And he's right. Tomorrow morning, Seán will get up at seven o'clock to go on a six-mile run to get ready to win next year's All Ireland. He has been booked only once in his life – when he was 13. Four years ago, we all feared he'd never play again after that car accident, and yet here he is, the captain of this group of men. It's as good, as special, as any other win. After all those years of trying and trying, 1999 was incredible. So was 2004, after all those years away. But to win back-to-back is just as satisfying. As Michael Jordan said, 'To win one takes talent. To repeat takes character.'

We go up to the players' lounge, but, as there are no spare chairs and our legs are tired, Donal Óg and myself get on the bus and just sit at the back, taking it all in. Then the rest of the lads get on, and Jimmy has 'We are the Champions' playing on the CD system. Because that's what we are, the champions. We are the best team in Ireland.

This team can continue to be that for years to come. I don't know if I can. Today was probably my last game for Cork. I came back to win one All Ireland, and I've now won two. Michael Jordan won three consecutive championships when he came back from retirement, but he got $31 million for the privilege. My comeback has worked out even better than I could ever have dreamt. I'll probably leave it at this. Right now, I just want to take all this in. I won't drink a drop. I want to remember it all. This is a special time. Thirty-one million dollars can't buy you this.

The problem is the price you have to demand of yourself to win. Because to win in September you have to suffer in January. It's why this is probably the end. It's probably why this is so sweet.

CHAPTER TWO

PURGATORY

'The fight is won or lost far away from witnesses;
behind the lines, in the gym, out there on the road,
long before I dance under those lights'

MUHAMMAD ALI

MONDAY, 16 JANUARY 2006

I don't know if I'm mad or what.

Tomorrow night, I'm going training, back to the muck, the dark and the hurt.

Last Friday, in the Cullinan Hotel in Cape Town, I was all set to tell the lads I was retiring. I'd be starting a new job – as an information-technology manager – in Cashel, 60 miles away from Elaine, the kids and Cork. I hadn't trained with the rest of the lads on the holiday; in fact, I hadn't togged off since the GOAL charity match the Wednesday after last year's All Ireland. The past few months had been magical, not having to worry about training, not having to watch what I ate and instead just being able to spend time with Elaine and Kate and Edel and baby Ewan. My mind was made up; almost 15 years after it all started, my senior inter-county career was over.

Just as I was about to head out the door and tell the group, I started to have second thoughts and chose to hold off making any decision until I knew more about the job. It had been pushed back already. Maybe it would be pushed back some more. Maybe I would find I could combine both.

I still mightn't hurl this year. I told the lads that in the meeting downstairs. John Gardiner looked stunned when I said it. Some people knew all right – John Allen, our trainer Seanie McGrath, Tom Kenny, Donal Óg Cusack and my clubmate Peter Kelly – because I had mentioned the new job to them over the winter, but most of the lads were like Gardiner. Afterwards, in the hotel bar, a few of them came over to me. I had a particularly good chat with Pat Mulcahy. He's probably going to be captain this year, and he's keen the group stays intact.

'Even if you can make training one night a week,' he said. 'Even if you could be an impact sub.'

John Allen is on the same wavelength. Realistically, with the backdoor system, we're already in the All Ireland quarter-final, and he feels if I can even aim to be back as late as that it could make all the difference.

We talked about much more than my situation in that meeting. We'd heard word that we were getting some flak for not going on the All Stars trip to Singapore and that the media would be waiting for our response when we got back. The feeling in the room was that the criticism was neither fair nor valid. For starters, it would have been a bit rich to ask our employers for another week off after being away in South Africa for close to three weeks. For most guys, it would mean all their annual leave would be used up by the end of January. Some fellas take a day off before big matches to rest, while others take a day off after games to recover. That's just the way this group is. In South Africa, most of the lads worked out every day on top of the four official training sessions.

It's some difference from when we won the All Ireland in '99.

That year, we were on holiday in Thailand and went jogging on a skyscraper in 40° heat after being on the lash all night. Some lads could barely walk; others had to be sent back to bed. It's a lifetime ago now. All in the past. And that's where we're putting all the jibes about us not going on the All Star trip. The group has no case to answer to any commentators, so we're not answering it.

There's no escaping Fermoy, though. We're only back in the country two days and already the Cullinan seems a long time ago. So does the stunning sight of Table Mountain, the views from Cape Point, the pool and playground the kids loved in Sun City, Knysna, the safari in Pilanesberg. Because the muck and the dark and the pain are now so close.

My biggest fear is fatigue. I'm asking myself, what are the chances that I won't be tired when I'll be up at six every morning and making a three-hour round trip every day? You can't perform at your best if you're tired. In March, I'll be 33. To even compete with the younger lads, I can't be tired.

If you could look into a crystal ball right now and tell me that Cork will not win the three in a row, I would retire this second. No Munster team in sixty-two years has reached four consecutive All Ireland finals. No team in twenty-eight years has won three in a row. We were nearly caught by Clare last year. On any given day, anything can happen. It's not like the Premiership, where the best team is chosen over 40 games. Once you reach the quarter-final, it's knockout. Other teams will have the hunger. Will we? Kilkenny thought they had it in 2004, but, when it came down to it, they couldn't match ours.

The only reason I'm even considering playing is because I believe in this group of players. If any team can win three in a row, this team can. This is a chance to become the best team of recent times, one of the best of all time.

That's what's driving me to Fermoy tomorrow. History and madness.

TUESDAY, 17 JANUARY

It's definitely madness. I'm definitely mad. I'm here in the car on the way back from Fermoy and I don't know if I'll be able to stay awake to get back to Glounthaune.

I was struggling right after the warm-up. Then the shuttles began.

Eight forty-metre runs.

Then six two hundreds.

Out to forty and back.

Out to thirty and back.

Out to twenty and back.

Out to ten and back.

All that stopping, turning, starting again; it nearly killed me.

By the time it came to do some hurling, I could barely make it up the little incline that divides the main pitch and the training pitch. My legs were like jelly, my calves felt like they were about to rip, my stomach was in knots and I couldn't breathe.

Then, when I did manage to stagger up the bank, I was straight into a drill, with Tom Kenny and Neil Ronan feeding balls to me from either side. I could barely see a thing. I was so dizzy from the workout that the drill with Tom and Neil began to look more like a game of dodgeball.

And then it was into more shuttles.

Eight forty-metre runs . . .

The moment the session ended, I headed straight for the rub from Chris O'Donovan. More torture. But at least I was lying down.

Every part of me is still aching. Why didn't I do some training over the winter? Why? Nearly all the other lads were flying. Diarmuid O'Sullivan and Niall McCarthy struggled, but at least Carthy has been in the Silver Springs gym and Sully's played some soccer. His problem is that he's even worse than me when it comes to the food. We're going to have to cut down on it now. They say fitness is something that you use or lose. Well, I've lost it. As I wobbled up that incline tonight, Donal Óg was passing. 'Think of a sunny day in Thurles,' he said, patting me on the back.

Even in '99, when we'd be pounding and groaning around the tunnels of Páirc Uí Chaoimh, he'd pep us up with that.

It's a great line, but all I can think of right now is bed.

TUESDAY, 24 JANUARY

More torture tonight, this time in Castlemartyr. I was wearing a thermal top and pants, and the investment made a difference on a bitterly cold night, but it couldn't stop me from keeling over after the two one-hundred-metre shuttles and the press-ups in between. Seanie McGrath told me to skip the third one. I told him I wanted to do it. 'Trust me,' he said, so I did. The five eighty-metre shuttles weren't much better, but they'd have been worse if I hadn't trusted Seanie.

He's earned that trust. On Sunday morning this weekend, we did some Fartlek training in my alma mater, Midleton CBS. Basically, it was interval running around a square; you jogged the sides then sprinted the diagonals. There were only four of us, because all the other lads were involved in games over the weekend; well, five when Joe Deane showed up. Joe thought training was at half-ten instead of half-nine. What did Seanie do? He stayed on to do the full session with him. But then this is Seanie McGrath, who, as a child, had his leg amputated from the knee down and bounced back to compete in the Olympics in swimming and sailing.

Lou Holtz, the former Notre Dame football coach, once said life is 10 per cent what happens to you and 90 per cent how you react to it. If that's the case, then, from reacting to amputation to reacting to Joe Deane being late, nobody's got a better take on life than Seanie McGrath.

THURSDAY, 26 JANUARY

In Fermoy again tonight. The pitch is heavy and sticky and the lights are so weak most of the lads struggle to see the ball, but it's worse for me. Tonight, I may as well have been blind.

I was born with a lazy right eye. It meant a lot of visits to the Eye, Ear and Throat Hospital on Western Road as a kid and having to wear these bloody thick-rimmed brown glasses with a big elastic band around the back that I absolutely detested. In the summer of '81, we were having a family picnic in Farran Woods when a wasp got inside my glasses. I jumped up and down, trying frantically to get the glasses off, but the wasp stung me, and by the time we got to the hospital my eye had swollen to the size of a sliotar. Another day, I was hurling in the field behind our house with my brother John and our cousin John Kelleher. Just as my brother was taking a shot, I walked straight into his swing. I wondered where all the blood was coming from, then realised it was pouring from my eye. When my mother dashed to the scene, she was sure I had lost my eye. I was rushed to hospital and my eye was saved. But whether it was the wasp, walking into John's swing or a defect from birth, I've had defective vision in my right eye for as long as I can remember.

I can read fine, as my left eye is 20:20. The problem begins when I have to judge distances and moving objects – problems, in other words, like tracking a sliotar flying at you at 70 miles an hour.

You often hear hurlers talk about getting their 'eye in'. Well, it's particularly true for me. Now, when I was a kid, getting my 'eye in' wasn't a problem: I had a hurley in my hand morning, noon and night. But, as I got older, that wasn't possible. I played Fitzgibbon Cup games when I might as well have been on a rugby field. I've come back from injury or a winter break and looked like a novice.

Sometimes, I got hooked or blocked because I've little

peripheral vision in that eye. In the 1999 All Ireland semi-final, I was having a stormer when I picked up a ball and looked down the field to see who was free. But, just as I threw up the ball and swung, John Troy came up literally on my blind side, flicked it away and scored a point. To this day, I still get slagged about it. If I go back through my career, I've rarely got blocked or hooked off my left. But if opponents knew about my bad eye, I'd have been blocked or hooked a lot more often.

That's why I've told no one.

SUNDAY, 29 JANUARY

Groundhog Day in Midleton. Again, we were there this morning; again, numbers were low with all the trial and club games going on. There were only five of us for Seanie to work with: me, Joe, Neil, Timmy McCarthy and Jimmy McEvoy.

Jimmy's our logistics manager. If we've a problem, Jim'll fix it. This morning, he trained with us too as he's running the Rome city marathon. He also mentioned that Seán Óg is after tearing his hamstring training on his own. I find that a bit worrying. We've been lucky with injuries this past two years and can't afford to be missing the likes of Seán Óg in the summer. His dedication to training is phenomenal. He actually enjoys it. When we're doing our warm-downs, we're meant to jog, but Seán Óg can't. It's got to the stage that when we're doing them, fellas are shouting, 'Lads, make sure Seán Óg isn't at the front!' His jog is like a three-quarters run for the rest of us. Even back in '99, he had to zigzag his runs to stay back with the rest of us. He's an incredible athlete. But sometimes the fitter you are, the more injuries you sustain.

Larry Tompkins was one of the best footballers that ever played for Cork, yet we probably didn't see the best of him. One night, I was walking from college on my way down to the Park when Larry picked me up in his car. I hadn't seen him in months because he had been out injured, but the championship was only weeks away and he was feeling great. 'I'm over that, all right,' he said. 'Sure I trained there in the Mardyke earlier on.'

We togged off and were out kicking a ball around when Billy Morgan came out and said, 'Right, lads, warm-up – two laps of the field.' We hadn't even got to the top corner when Larry was on the ground, clutching his torn calf. I felt for him that night. He had no luck in the second half of his career when it came to injuries.

It was injuries to the likes of Larry that scuppered the footballers' tilt at a three in a row back in '91. I hope we don't have any injuries that scupper ours.

THURSDAY, 2 FEBRUARY

Tonight's the best I've felt all year.

I found the 15-minute warm-up hard enough but stayed up with the guys at the top for the 160-metre shuttles. Then, when Seanie put us through 12 40-metre sprints with a ball-pick in the middle of each, I might have been out of breath but I didn't feel dizzy or sick. In fact, I felt so good I was able to sprint after the warm-down and be the first in line for a rub.

Normally, Seán Óg is at the top of the queue, and when he is, you're there for the night, the Adonis needs such attention. Tonight? Not only was Seán Óg not there but neither was Chris, while Dave Pyne had hurt his ankle playing soccer with his son, Ted.

The one night I was first . . .

THURSDAY, 9 FEBRUARY

Peter Kelly had some news when he collected me for training this evening. I'd missed Tuesday's session with a cold, and the panel for the league had been announced then. Three of last year's panel won't be there this year: John Browne, Jonathon O'Callaghan and Ronan McGregor. I feel bad for all three. Poor Johnny Cal's constantly injured and hasn't had any luck. McGregor is the same. I'll miss him, and I'd say Seán Óg will miss him even more. Ronan's also from Na Piarsaigh, and everything he does is Seán Óg-esque. He goes to the gym with him; he wears the socks up like him; he even talks like him. Seriously, the guys on Today FM's Gift Grub should get onto him for the way he has Seán Óg down. He has Stevie Gerrard to a T as well. The place will be duller for not having him around.

I knew John Browne the best of the lot. Everyone raves about the back line we have now, but that was a serious unit we had in '99 too, and John was a key man in it. You could always rely on John Browne. He was more shocked than anyone when they brought him on in the 2004 All Ireland after Brian Murphy got injured. The selectors were going, 'John! You're on!', and John was like, 'What? Shit! Where's my helmet?' He hadn't even brought it, he was that sure he wouldn't be playing. The joke afterwards was that he was lucky he even had his hurley. In truth, we all were.

Another year of possibly being on the bench could hardly have appealed to John, though. Not after all he's won with Cork. Not when he and his fiancée Yvonne have just started a dental practice in Douglas. That's the way hurling and life goes, I suppose. People move on and people move in, like this year's newcomers Killian Cronin and Conor Cusack from Cloyne, Dara McSweeney from Inniscarra and Ronan Conway from Bishopstown.

Tonight, we trained in the Cork Institute of Technology. The facilities there, especially the lights, are excellent, and it was an enjoyable session, mostly working on our striking. Management kept it to 45 minutes to keep us fresh, and they were right. Tomorrow night, we have a fitness test. On Saturday, we train and have an all-day health workshop, and on Sunday we have a game.

I'm going to play for Erins Own in the East Cork championship on Sunday instead. I suggested it to John after he named a team for the challenge game against Limerick, and he agreed I'd be better off getting a game under my belt than sitting on the bench in Bruff. He also asked about the job and told me not to pull out, no matter how tough it gets. I said I'll have to see how it goes. If I'm not fit to play in the summer, then I'm not going to play.

It'll be my turn to slip away.

FRIDAY, 10 FEBRUARY

Tonight, we had the fitness test, and I found I had to drag myself to it. I spent most of last night choking and coughing and keeping the whole house awake, and my mood was bad all day. When I finally did garner the energy to drive down the road to Glanmire Community College, I was late, which meant I had to go with the fit guys.

Ever since '99, I've been a valued member of the Fat Club. That year, our membership included Joe Deane, Kevin Murray, Alan Browne, Mark Landers, Fergal McCormack, Fergal Ryan and Sully, and for our sins we'd have to do special training. By the end of the year, we were all either All Stars or All Star nominations, and in the Burlington that night we joked that we could eat as much as we liked while the rest of the lads could train as much as they liked.

I ended up having a good laugh tonight, as well. Before the bleep test, we had the dreaded fat test, with our dietician Ann McKiernan having the glamorous task of pinching the fat of various parts of our bodies and measuring it with callipers. So we're all lined up, and one by one Ann takes the measurements. While Kelly and Kevin Hartnett fly it, the rest of us are struggling with that delicate art of keeping ourselves semi-tensed in the hope that it doesn't all fall out without being too tensed and too obvious.

First up is Mickey O'Connell, standing straight as an arrow, chest out like a peacock. We all start sniggering: you're overdoing it, Mickey, boy; forget it! But, as it turns out, he hasn't. He's in good shape, and it's even better to see him back on the panel.

I'm next. Ann starts with the arms, moves to the waist and calls out the readings. '11.4 . . . 12.5 . . .'

I'm thinking, 'Right, either those callipers are dodgy or you're not in bad shape at all, Corcoran, boy!'

Unfortunately, it's the former. Seanie notices a problem with the callipers, sorts it and tries again. '18.4 . . . 19.5 . . .' That's about right. Now Seanie's chuckling. 'Too many ice creams over the winter, Corcoran!'

I have the best score of the night when it comes to the hamstring-flexibility tests, though. Graham Callinan can't get over it. 'Whaaa? There has to be a retest!' This time, there's no need. One thing I've always had is flexibility, probably from the martial arts I did as a young fella. Then it's height and weight. Brian Corcoran: 1.85 m (6 ft 1 in.) and 93.0 kg (14.5 st.). Seanie reckons my fighting weight should be 89 kg, so I haven't that much to lose. I have a good bit of work to do on my speed, though. I'm behind the group average in the 20-metre sprints and well behind the panel's best of 2.7 seconds, set by young Shane O'Neill.

Finally, it's the worst test of them all, the bleep test: two lines, twenty metres apart, the tape recorder and those bleeps. In case you've been spared the ordeal, basically the test measures your body's capacity to take in oxygen by having you run back and forth from one line to the other, keeping in synch with the bleeps. Every minute, the bleeps get more frequent, and you have to run faster. When you fail to get to the line before the bleep, that's when you drop out.

I'm not confident starting off. I've had a chest infection all week. My aim is to get to level 12, but at around 8 I start to feel the pinch. I dig in, vowing not to give in until I physically can't go any more. As level 11 starts, my thighs are burning, my legs feel like lead and my lungs are gasping for air. I'm on the verge of level 12, but then the bleepin' bleep beats me to the line. I'm out, the first in our group to go. My head spins, my legs wobble and I can't get in enough air, but Seanie insists that I keep walking around. As I do, I watch the rest of the lads fall out, one by one. Kevin Hartnett is the last man running. We all roar him on. At 15.5, he calls it quits. The most I have ever done is 14.5.

It's a pity we only do it in the winter. I'd love to know what I could have done in the summer, when I was in my prime. Now, I'm just about fit to crawl into bed, knowing we're training in the morning.

SATURDAY, 11 FEBRUARY

Sometimes you've just got to choose your attitude.

When the alarm went off at quarter past seven this morning, I couldn't believe it was time to get up. I looked outside. It was dull and miserable, and because of that I was fairly miserable myself. Then, an hour later, I pull up outside the Ballinure pitch in Mahon. Seanie pulls up behind me, jumps out and is in great form. Then I see Timmy McCarthy strolling onto the pitch in that carefree way of his. Timmy's been up since half-five milking cows, and there's not a bother on him either. He's chosen his attitude; why shouldn't I? I end up having a decent session.

Then it's off to the Rochestown Park Hotel for the day. We start off by giving a few middle-aged female members of their leisure centre a bit of a mid-morning thrill when 27 of us jump into the pool and start jogging laps of it. Then it's breakfast and a two-hour workshop with Ann. We have an interesting discussion about how it's a bad idea to drink after a match because it inhibits recovery. Jerry Wallis points out that in some cases the odd drop can help, and tells us the story of the African athlete who'd drink a bottle of Heineken the night before a big meet to help him sleep; the guy won three Olympic silver medals. Quick as a flash, Wayne Sherlock jumps in: 'Yeah, well maybe he'd have won three golds if he hadn't bothered with the Heineken.'

Being a virtual teetotaller, I found Ann's dietary tips had more relevance to me. From here on, it's porridge, porridge, porridge, maybe oats and muesli now and again, and a lot more fruit and smoothies too.

I'll also have to cut down on my portions. After lunch, I outlined to Ann what I had for breakfast and the number of sandwiches I ate at lunchtime. Turns out I had already eaten my recommended calorie intake for the day. I've always had a ferocious appetite. When I was in college, my mother used to give me a sliced pan of sandwiches and they'd be gone before 11. The night before the 1991 All Ireland minor football final, we were staying in the Marino Institute of Education, and when the quantity of food wasn't to my satisfaction I headed down the road to the shop. One of our selectors, Pat O'Donovan from Bantry, thought it was hilarious when he saw me arrive back with a sliced pan, a packet of ham and a litre of milk. It isn't exactly what Ann is prescribing now.

After Ann's presentation and workshop, we caught a bit of the France–Ireland rugby game on the television. France ran riot in the first half, but in the second half Ireland came right back at them and ultimately just ran out of time. They could have thrown in the towel after 50 minutes but they didn't. They chose to keep at it, to keep playing. They chose their attitude.

We got a further insight into the mentality of some of those players this evening when Jim Williams, a former teammate and current coach to the Munster contingent, came in to us. He spoke about preparation and lifestyle, Munster's desire to win the European Cup, but above all he spoke about attitude. He admitted he was a limited player, but he had made a career out of the game and played for Australia ahead of hundreds of more talented players because of his attitude. Attitude, he said, was the mother of all success. 'Be responsible for your own attitude.'

SUNDAY, 12 FEBRUARY

I've played my first game of the year. We beat St Catherine's by two points down in Ballynoe, but as I walked back to the dressing-room our coach Sean Prendergast was laughing at me struggling up the hill. 'Was that your first game since the All Ireland?'

I just about mustered the strength to say, 'Was it that obvious?'

Hurling-wise, my touch was poor. Physically, I was sluggish. When I crawled through the door, Elaine asked me how I got on.

'I'm so far off the pace,' I said, 'I'm going to need a miracle to be right in three months.'

TUESDAY, 14 FEBRUARY

Valentine's Day, and yet I'm in a different country to my wife. I suppose it doesn't make that much of a difference to Elaine; I'd have been training tonight anyway. It's only February, and already I've missed important family events this year, such as our youngest daughter Edel's ballet debut in the Everyman Theatre. Last year, I missed Kate's. The problem on training nights is that, by the time I get home, the girls and

Ewan are already in bed. I get plenty of pats on the back for my contribution to Cork, but Elaine's only reward is to see me achieve my dream. So what do you give a woman on Valentine's Day who has shown you infinite patience and love? More apologies for not being there.

I'm over in Belgium on work, in a place called Beerse, 40 minutes from Antwerp, as part of my IT job. Seanie wanted me to bring my hurley over, but there's no place to use it. I've just come from a workout in the pool and about 30 minutes on the treadmill. I had porridge this morning too and managed to pass all the duty-free shops without indulging myself. I just want to get home now to see Elaine and the kids.

THURSDAY, 16 FEBRUARY

I'm going up with the lads to Offaly on Sunday for our first league game. A few hours ago, I'd have thrown an expletive into that sentence, but something Kelly said has changed that.

John had planned to give me the weekend off, but tonight he came up and said, 'Look, we're fairly stuck with injuries; would you mind coming on Sunday?'

And I said I didn't, but when we were having our grub afterwards I sat next to Kelly. 'Pete, I'm after getting feckin' caught to go to Offaly.'

He looked at me. 'Would you listen to yourself? "Poor me, I have to go to Offaly!" Here I am bursting my bollicks to get to Offaly!'

And, of course, he was right. I am lucky. Most fellas would be honoured to be on that bus on Sunday. When I was a kid, all I'd have wanted was to be on that bus to Offaly.

I don't think there's anyone who is more thrilled to be on it than Kelly himself. Last year was his first year on the panel. He was 26. He never played minor for the county; he never played Under-21; he was going grey, for God's sake. Even up in the club, when John Allen called him up to the panel, some fellas were surprised Kelly made it. A year on, and everyone in the club looks up to him. The way he works, the way he carries himself, the way he plays, his attitude: he's our Jim Williams.

Everyone in the Cork set-up loves him too. He wasn't on the panel a month and he had the numbers of all the lads on his mobile. Sully and Niall Mac are always calling up to his house. It's the most open house you'll ever come across. I know; it's only two doors up from me. His mother, Mary, used to bring me into college every morning. I bought my first car from his father, Ray. They have this lovely way of making you feel at home in their house.

Kelly's made himself feel right at home with Cork. We mightn't start training until quarter past seven, yet he'll be down an hour early to get a rub and the scandal. Then, when we're finished, I might be ready to go home with him and next thing he's only coming out of the shower, yapping away with everyone.

But I'm happy to put up with it.

And, thanks to his kick in the ass, I'm happy to put up with Offaly on Sunday too.

SUNDAY, 19 FEBRUARY

So, it starts here, our first league game of the year.

'My 31st league campaign, Corky!' Dr Con Murphy proclaims loudly as I join him near the back of the bus.

I can't let him away with it, not when Con barely turns up for home games. 'Your 31st league game, you mean!'

Con's buzzing. Mickey O'Connell appears on the bus, and Con lets out a big laugh. 'Great to see you, Mickey! Are we opening a pitch or something? Is Jimmy Barry coming too?

Christ, there won't be a dry eye in the place when you run out today!'

Behind Con, the card school has gathered, and Joe, Niall, Callinan and Ronan Curran are trying to clean out the rookies. Elsewhere, papers are being passed around. There's a lot about the Clare controversy, with Ger Loughnane as usual in the middle of it. With other counties, it could have a negative impact on the team, but Clare seem to revel in it. That might come against us when we meet them in Thurles on 28 May.

We arrive at the Rackethall Hotel in Roscrea for our chicken and pasta three hours before the game. In the team meeting, John wishes the new guys – Ronan Conway, Killian Cronin and Shane O'Neill – all the best on their debuts. He says that, realistically, most of last year's team will be there come summertime, but there are definitely one or two places available. The chance is there for them to claim those spots.

He then addresses all of us. 'Lads, there are 31 counties that want to see us beaten this year. We can't expect any favours from referees; we can't expect favours from anyone. We must be prepared for intimidation. We need to match aggression with aggression but in a controlled, disciplined way. We play within the rules but must be ready for teams that don't. Discipline is everything.'

We get back on the bus, and I'm sitting next to Donal Óg. He's listening to his iPod, and, as I can clearly tell, Mel Gibson's *Braveheart* speech: 'They make take our lives, but they'll never take our freee-dommm!' That's Donal Óg, the most intense and passionate man you'll meet. When I started working out for my comeback, he'd invariably be in the Silver Springs gym before me. We began lifting weights together, and, as I'd been out of the game for over two years, he was lifting more weights than me. After a few weeks, I started to edge ahead, which was only natural; I'm the bigger man. Donal Óg wouldn't accept it and trained even harder. He just refused to give in; he refused to come second.

He was under a lot of pressure that autumn. After the 2003 final, people were saying he should be dropped. Now there's no question who should be number one in Cork. And even though it's the golden age of goalkeepers, I wouldn't want any other goalkeeper in Ireland but Donal Óg Cusack.

I've been told I'll probably come on for the last ten minutes today, but I still haven't shaken the flu, so when we hit the dressing-room I put on a polo neck inside my jersey along with a sweatshirt and jacket and tracksuit pants. I go around wishing the new lads well, but I sense, as they run out to Offaly's guard of honour, that most of the other lads aren't fully tuned in.

It shows. After twelve minutes, Offaly are three ahead. Sully brings us level by going up to bang home a penalty, but then their tall new full forward Joe Bergin has the ball in our net. It shouldn't count – he was in the square – but to Ógie's disgust the umpire raises the green flag. Moments later, Offaly hit over a perfectly good point, which us subs, warming up, have a clear view of. The umpire waves it wide. And that annoys me. I know it's a break for us, but it annoys me. The linesman had a clear view of it, yet he was powerless to do anything. To think an All Ireland final could hinge on something like that . . .

It's nip and tuck in the second half as well, and the home crowd love it. They sense victory; Offaly are staying that point or two ahead. John, sensing defeat, brings Tom Kenny and John Gardiner on. Then Ger Cunningham tells Conor Cusack, Kelly and me to get ready. I have so many clothes on it's like I'm doing a striptease in the dugout, but finally I run into the full-forward spot.

A few balls come down in quick succession, and I win them, but the ground is heavy and the belts are hard. After five minutes, my legs are dead and my lungs feel ready to explode.

Timmy scores a great point to earn us a draw, but as I struggle through the warm-down I feel as if I've played 70 minutes, not 15.

By the time I reach the showers, they're cold. That's all I need now, to be covered in mud from here to Cork. It's a bloody long way from Birr to Cork, and clearly it's a long way from Birr to Croke Park, too.

That's not why I'm feeling so low now, though. It's that I myself am light years from Croke Park.

I remember being interviewed a few months after the 2004 All Ireland. We talked about my comeback, and I said one of the reasons I'd returned was because it'd bugged me that my last game in Croke Park was losing the 2000 All Ireland semi-final against Offaly. We didn't do ourselves justice that day. I didn't do myself justice that day. That's not how I'd wanted to leave it, I said.

And the reporter said, 'If that's the case, why are you staying on for 2005? You've got your dream end in Croke Park. Would you not do what [Donal] O'Grady's done and get out now at the top?'

I stayed on. And thank God I stayed on. But now, am I pushing my luck going for another year? Today, I was spluttering for air against Offaly. Do I want to humiliate myself up in Croke Park again? Is that how I want this to finish? Will it even be my choice? Up to now, I haven't been sure if I'm even going to play this summer, but if I don't get my act together fast, John might make the call for me.

That's it. I either commit to getting fit or I pack up now.

CHAPTER THREE

ROOTS

'A quick temper will make a fool of you soon enough'

BRUCE LEE

BACK WHEN I PLAYED SENIOR FOOTBALL WITH CORK, one of the game's greatest warriors offered me some advice. 'You have to become more ruthless, boy!' Niall Cahalane said to me. I knew what Niall was getting at: that inter-county football and hurling were cut-throat games. One winter's day in Navan, I was marking Niall's old friend, Colm O'Rourke, and every time I seemed to go up for a high ball I'd be greeted with an elbow across the face. I was taken aback; O'Rourke was probably the best corner-forward of his generation. Then I realised: maybe he felt that was the only way to survive and thrive in a jungle of Cahalanes. Yet all the digs did was to make me even more driven to get out and up for the next ball.

I suppose I've always been like that. I remember playing for Midleton CBS in the 1989 Dean Ryan Under-16½ Munster Colleges final against North Monastery. I played with an injured ankle that was heavily strapped, and, just after half-time, some of the Mon lads tried to break a few hurleys off me. During the break, our coach Mick Hennessy had said that if I was to play senior for Cork it would be on days like this that I'd have to prove myself. Between Mick's bollicking and the Mon's belts, I got into such a rage that I couldn't even feel the ankle. I went on to dominate the rest of that game, and we went on to win. Afterwards, I almost felt like going up to the Mon lads and thanking them for giving me the boost I needed. I've always been able to channel my negative anger into positive energy to fuel my game. Why get even when you can try to get ahead?

Winning the game is what it has all been about, but not at all costs. I've always felt that I can outplay my opponent, and if I have to resort to bullying or intimidating him then I've been defeated, irrespective of the result of the game. If someone tries to provoke me, I take that as a sign he can't handle me. If I can't beat a guy playing the game, then I don't want to beat him.

In Killarney in July 1998, I played my first game of football in three months. I had been focusing on hurling during that time. It was costly. I was given a torrid time against Kerry that day, first by Mike Frank Russell, then by John Crowley. I could have indulged in damage limitation; I could have grabbed Mike Frank's and Crowley's jerseys and held them to a point or two. But I didn't. They weren't the problem. My lack of ballwork and preparation were. The ball was my enemy, not Mike Frank or Crowley.

I've found that, most of the time, if you play the ball, your opponent tends to as well. When I've had to deal with provocation, I've always kept my discipline. Except for on one occasion. It was with the Cork footballers, the year I played centre-forward in the league, and the centre-back had been niggling at me all day. Eventually, I'd had enough and swung back my arm. The centre-back collapsed to the ground. I stepped back and braced myself for the imminent volcanic eruption. This wasn't any centre-back on the ground. This was Cork training. This was Niall Cahalane.

And Cahalane did jump up and thump me – on my shoulder with the palm of his hand.

'About fucking time for you!'

As much as I laugh now when I remember that day in Ballygarvan, it wasn't a turning point; it was the exception. From that game to this, I've never been booked, and I've never been sent off in my career, either.

We all have our own ways of playing, of winning All Irelands. A few months after we won the 1999 All Ireland, my direct opponent, John Power, said that he was totally thrown by my attitude that day. He came out psyched, ready to take me on physically, and I just ignored him. I play my own game and leave everyone else to theirs. That's just the way I am.

My brother John was the same. Growing up, I'd watch him playing and notice he would never get caught up in any cheap shots yet would almost always end up being the best player on view. We're the sons of John 'Jack' Corcoran and Nuala Sheehan. They never put any pressure on us to be the best. They were just happy for us to compete – fairly. They'd never have tolerated John or myself hitting a fella with a hurley or our fists. It just wouldn't have been fair. It wouldn't have been right.

I WASN'T SO MUCH BORN INTO MY FAMILY AS WHIPPED out and into it, and I've the birthmark to show for it. That scar on the top of my head isn't a hurling wound; I've had it from day one, 23 March 1973. At one point, my mother lost so much blood my father was told she wasn't going to make it. But Mam was strong, physically and mentally, something she'd prove to me from my first day to her last.

Home was next door to my father's old house in Caherlag. It

was a wonderful place to grow up in, a small, close community of about twenty-five houses seven miles east of Cork city in the parish of Glounthaune, overlooking Little Island.

Dad worked for Bord Gáis and then on Saturdays for a horse veterinary surgeon whose stables were just a couple of hundred yards down from our house. Mam ran her own sewing business at home, knitting and curtain-making, altering pants and suits. It was a house with a strong work ethic. Sick days or owing money were not an option. If you wanted something, you had to work hard for it. When my class was going on a school trip to Moscow, I didn't even ask my parents if I could go. It wasn't that I thought they would refuse; I just didn't think it was fair to ask. I didn't even contemplate going to University College Cork (UCC), because I didn't want my parents to feel under pressure to pay the fees. Instead, I applied for a computer course at Cork Regional Technical College, where the grant would go some way towards meeting the costs.

Yet we never went without. My parents were kind-hearted, generous people who worked tirelessly to provide for us. I suffered from eczema until my mid-teens, and during the summer I'd get a bad rash right up my arms and legs. The doctor recommended goat's milk as a form of treatment. What did Mam and Dad do? They bought three goats for me. It was a house full of love and full of life, with the kettle always on and people always streaming in, collecting or handing in some fabric or just for an old chat.

They were also good-living, God-fearing people, and they'd a strong desire for us to be the same. At six o'clock every day, the television would be switched off and we'd say the rosary. Each morning, before work, my father would go to mass in St Patrick's. Mam would walk the three-mile round trip to mass every day of Lent. She even had hopes that I'd become a priest, and for a while I probably believed it myself. For all her attempts to change the television channel at the remotest hint of romance, by my teens I knew enough to know I wasn't going to be a priest and assumed my mother had given up all hope too.

Then, one day, I brought a pot of tea into the front room for my mother and the ladies from the ICA. One of them asked if I had any girl on the scene. 'Not at all!' my mother interjected. 'Brian has no interest in girls.' I was 16 by then and to this day cringe at the memory. It would take her a bit longer to finally concede defeat, but the faith she instilled in me and the discipline that came with it serve me well to this day.

My father was a quiet, unassuming, forever-pleasant man. I can still see his smiling face when John, myself and our sister Ann would walk along the road each Friday to meet him coming home from work, as he'd always have a few sweets for us. As long as we all kept out of harm's way and he had his pint on a Sunday night in John Joe's after a day's coursing, he was happy. I was easily pleased, too. I'd play cowboys and Indians in the fields that surrounded us, make tree-houses and hurl. Come Wimbledon, we'd take out some chairs from my mother's kitchen and use them as our makeshift tennis net, and then, when the Aga Khan at the Dublin Horse Show was on, we'd jump those same chairs like the carefree eejits we were.

As much as I enjoyed hanging out with friends like Mick Hanratty, Paul and Pat Hickey, Kieran Murphy, Ed Kenny and Ronan and Shane Aherne, I loved the freedom of doing my own thing too. I'd often go down to the pitch to practise or go to Cork Golf Club in Little Island and either caddie or look for golf balls. During the summer, I'd often hitch a ride into town or go in with my father on his way to work and spend the whole day in Cork. I might go to mass in the morning, and then, when Eason's opened, read the golf or wrestling magazines there until the staff hunted me out. Then I'd maybe pop over for some snooker in the Victoria club, or The Vic, as it's known. When I was asked in an interview in 1991 what I'd like to have been if I wasn't a GAA player, I answered a professional golfer or snooker player. I was a long way off being a snooker player, but I was handy at it; my highest break was 56. After The Vic, it would be off to the old Pavilion. These days, it's a HMV record store, but back then it was a cinema. I might have been the only one in it sometimes, but I didn't mind.

Energy wasn't an issue either. In my teens, I'd walk two miles to the bus stop with a golf bag on my back, get off in Midleton, walk another three miles to East Cork Golf Club, play thirty-six holes, walk back into Midleton, get the bus, walk the final two miles up the hill before probably finishing the day by going training. I loved golf, as did all of my mother's family, and every April Mam and myself would sit, almost vigil-like, watching the Masters. On Christmas Day, locals could play for free in Cork Golf Club. So every Christmas morning John and myself would play a round with our uncle D.D., and as soon as I'd finish my dinner I'd be at the front door waiting for my father to drop me down again so I could play a round by myself.

Other than that, I didn't have access to a course as a kid, so we'd improvise, hitting shots with our nine irons up and down the hurling pitch. Tom Aherne, the teak-tough captain of our hurling intermediate team who worked – and still works – as a subeditor in the *Examiner*, was the worst culprit. Tom was married with kids, but when it came to golf, Tom was as big a kid as the rest of us, and after a few months a 'No Golfing' sign had to be erected to deter the little rascals and their considerably older ringleader.

I was 22 when I finally got to join a golf course. It took that long to buy a car to drive to one. I now play off four. As for Tom, he's as handy and as boyish as ever.

✳   ✳   ✳

I KNOW THIS WILL SURPRISE SOME PEOPLE, BUT MARTIAL
arts and fight sports were another passion of mine. Bruce Lee
was as much a god to me as Jimmy Barry-Murphy. I'd go into
Cork City Library just to read up on his art of jeet kune do
and his one-inch punch. Jean-Claude Van Damme was another
idol. I must have watched him as Frank Dux in *Bloodsport* 50
times.

When I was 14, I took up the Korean art of tae kwon do
– the art of hand and foot. Unfortunately, just as I was one
grading away from getting my black belt, I had to pack it in.
College and GAA commitments were piling up, and, with the
other people my age falling by the wayside, the notion of being
a hairy 18 year old sparring 12 and 13 year olds didn't appeal.
Even now, I regret I had to finish up, but I'm grateful I did it at
all. The importance of respecting yourself, your opponent and
the code itself – values I'd learned from Mam and Dad – were
reaffirmed by the martial arts. It's only in the last few years
that even the top GAA teams have started to practise dynamic
stretching; in tae kwon do, we were doing it all along. To this
day, I've yet to suffer a hamstring or muscle injury, and I put
that down to those tae kwon do classes in Little Island.

American wrestling also enthralled me. I knew it was
all fixed, but I just loved its razzmatazz and flamboyant
characters. Me and my buddies would imitate their moves.
That was, until the day we were out on the road and I picked
Tony Hickey up into a suplex position. I had Tony upside
down, his head on my shoulder and legs straight up in the
air, when I dropped him backwards, onto a hedge, to cushion
his fall. The Undertaker would have been proud of that one,
right? Great laugh, what? It was, until we looked back and
saw Tony getting up, looking as white as a sheet. He'd just
missed a two-foot steel bar sticking out of the ground. When
I hear Al Pacino's famous *Any Given Sunday* speech on the
Cork bus and how life is a game of inches, I sometimes

think of that day and how Tony was six inches from meeting another undertaker.

I had to abandon another fighting gimmick of mine around that time. I used to do a lot of sit-ups and for a laugh let friends punch me in the abs to see if they could wind me. I even charged some fellas to have a go – a handy way to feed my chocolate habit. One day, this guy with a black belt in karate tried his luck. The only rule I had was that the punch had to be above the belt and below the chest. He ended up hitting me on the pelvic bone and breaking his knuckle. At that, my little earner came to an end.

Fortunately, I've only ever had to call on my martial-arts training once – an incident old football teammates still remind me of. The Thursday before the 1995 Munster final, I was making my way to Jury's Hotel in the lashing rain for a team meeting when I was jumped by two fellas. I managed to kick them off and cross the road, but when I looked back one of them had picked himself up. Then, as he went to follow me, he was hit by a car. He just bounced back up, like some character from *The Terminator*. The next second, we were wrestling. I punched him, but, as he fell, so did my hat. I dashed off then looked back. The lads were gone, my hat was still there, so I did a U-turn. But, just as I picked it up, the boys appeared again at the corner – and the first guy was heading across the road.

'Right,' I thought, 'until you put this guy down for good, he's not going to stop.' So that's what I did. As he folded to the ground, moaning, I picked up my hat. Finally, that was the last of that lunatic. As I made a mad dash for Jury's, though, I noticed the two sleeves of my jacket had been ripped off and this white foam was hanging out under my shoulders. When I walked in the door in Jury's, the lads could all see the state I was in.

'Jesus Christ, what happened to you?'

'Some fella wanted my hat.'

✷　　✷　　✷

I TRIED OUT OTHER, MORE CONVENTIONAL, SPORTS growing up. I couldn't wait for the annual schools' Cork City Sports every year. It was a chance to perform in Páirc Uí Chaoimh, and, being the grandson of Bill Corcoran, a well-known national runner and cyclist, I considered myself a bit of an athlete. I'd usually do well, too, in the eighty-metre sprint, and the one year I didn't win a medal I was disgusted. I hardly talked to anyone for the rest of the day and didn't feel like talking to anyone for the rest of the week, either. The desire to win was something naturally in me. Playing well and losing wasn't enough; I had to win.

I'd soon learn it wasn't possible to always win; in fact, throughout my career I've lost more than I've won. I came to adopt Vince Lombardi's less famous line, 'Winning isn't everything, but trying to win is.' It would annoy me seeing lads with lots of talent not willing to train or practise, or, if they did, not caring enough on the day of a game and just giving up. The way I saw it, things could happen that were out of my control, but I had full control of my work rate. I might pace myself in unimportant games or take the foot off the pedal if we were well ahead, but I can honestly say that every time I competed when it counted I gave it 100 per cent, and the same applies today. The performances may have varied greatly but never the effort. That allows me to sleep easily at night.

I dabbled a bit with soccer as well. It was the game at breaktime in school, and a classmate convinced me to play competitively for Leeside FC. They put me in midfield, and it wasn't long before I was scoring regularly. Opposing teams would call me King Kong – for some reason, the lads playing soccer seemed smaller than the lads playing hurling and football – but at times they could have called me Kevin Kehily. A couple of times, I jumped in the air to compete for a high ball and, instead of heading it, instinctively caught it, just like Kevin would do on the edge of the square for Cork.

My father would have preferred it if I was handling it all the time. Mam and himself would go to every GAA match I played but never to the soccer. One day, there was a clash of games. Leeside had an Under-11 game, Erins Own an Under-14 game. I wanted to play with my own age group, but Dad insisted I go to the football. It was the only argument that I can ever remember having with Dad. And I had plenty of time to reflect on it while I sat on the bench, watching the Under-14s play.

Ultimately, though, I was just like him. As much as I enjoyed my two years with Leeside, GAA was my life.

IN THE SPRING OF 1985, TWO SPECIAL VISITORS CAME TO our primary school in Glounthaune. Jimmy Barry-Murphy was one, with the other, Liam McCarthy, in his hand. After Jimmy said a few words in the main hall, our principal, Mr O'Neill, asked a few of us to play a little hurling game on the little pitch behind the school. I tried my heart out to impress Jimmy. A few minutes later, Mr O'Neill called me over. 'Jimmy, this is Brian Corcoran. Some day, he'll play for Cork.'

Years later, I'd read how a six-year-old Tiger Woods played Sam Snead in a two-hole tournament and lost by only one shot. When Snead offered Tiger his autograph, Tiger reciprocated by offering Snead his. I wasn't that cocky, but, as I bashfully shook Jimmy's hand, inwardly I had no doubt that Mr O'Neill was right. Some day, I'd play for Cork. Every night, as I'd say my prayers in my bed, surrounded by *A-Team* posters, I'd ask God to help me win an All Ireland senior hurling medal. I never doubted, though, that I'd make the Cork team. Nobody, I believed, could do something with a hurley and a sliotar that I couldn't do.

That confidence came from the gable end of the house. My father used to park his car at the side of the house, which blocked my path, so I'd have to use the three feet between the sitting-room window and the side of the house. That was my target. If I missed, I was in big trouble, but I never did. I always believed I could put the ball through the eye of a needle, left or right, and that belief was strengthened from hours wearing out that gable end with my sliotar.

I'm convinced that when you're young you have gifts, or ways, which you lose when you're older. As a kid, I thought an Under-12 goal was huge; hitting a sliotar between the posts was like landing it in the ocean. As I got older, the posts were wider but seemed much smaller. It was as if the mind began to complicate things, while as a kid I just looked at the goals and hit the shot; free taking was easy. As an adult, the only time I have a hurley in my hand is at training or on the day of a game; as a kid, I had my hurley in my hand every free moment I had.

A few years ago, I read Bob Rotella's *Golf is a Game of Confidence*, and on the very first page he defined confidence as 'playing with your eyes':

> The brain and the rest of the body simply react. The basketball shooter doesn't give herself a lecture on the mechanics of pushing a ball through the air. The trap shooter doesn't ponder how to coordinate the movements of his torso and his trigger finger. Confident athletes let their brain and nervous systems perform the skills they have rehearsed and mastered – without interference from the conscious mind.

That's what I was like as a kid. I didn't lecture myself or ponder my technique. I'd rehearse and master, and when I'd shoot there was no interference from the conscious mind.

Over the years, I began to realise that, as an adult, the conscious mind gets involved in your game, be it hurling or golf. The key is how you use it.

My good friend Donal McSweeney gave me a great quote of Henry Ford's: 'Whether you think you can do a thing or think you can't do a thing, you're right.' Or, as my buddy Bruce Lee put it, 'As you think, so you become.'

One day, I was playing a foursomes match in Bandon for Harbour Point and had just sunk two key putts to leave us one down with two to play. The last putt had been a tricky left-to-right ten-footer that I had to get. As I lined up my putt, I pictured it dropping into the centre of the cup. It did – so, with a spring in my step, I stepped up to the 17th tee and surveyed the scene. There was out of bounds all down the right, with a galvanised shed the other side of the ditch. But it was still a very drivable hole, and I had been driving down the middle all day, so I took out the driver. Just at the top of my backswing, the shed came racing into my head. You can guess what happened next.

Whoosh!

Bang!

Straight into the shed.

Because, unwittingly, that's what my mind had programmed my body to do. And what I've learned is that the subconscious mind is like a little child. You must tell it what you want it to do, not what you don't want it to do. As the great athlete Michael Johnson used to say, instead of giving it negative commands, flood it with positive ones.

The night before Erins Own played Avondhu in the 1993 county championship replay, I slipped a Michael Jordan tape into our video player at home. I'd scored the point to get us that replay, but my performance that day had been average enough. Watching Jordan fly and dunk and talk about how 'on my game, nobody can guard me; I'll control you like a puppet', I was floating myself. The next day, we lost to Avondhu, but I had the consolation of playing one of my best games ever for the club. I put that down to watching Jordan. As he'd say himself, 'The process of seeing success before it happened put me in a positive frame of mind and prepared me to play the game.'

I've continued through the years to create 'future histories', as Ali called them. In the first half of the 2005 Munster semi-final against Waterford, I had barely touched the ball. John Allen could see what had happened. 'Corcoran's in there at full-forward and only one ball's been hit into him! Get it into him!' When I ran towards the full-forward spot for the second half, I pictured the net dancing and the mass of red behind it jumping. A few minutes later, that's exactly what happened. I got a ball out on the wing, took on Fergal Hartley, worked my way past and next thing that net and that mass of red were jumping. Success isn't always guaranteed, but being aware of your thought processes and having the discipline to think positively can convert potential failure into success.

One story Rotella tells sums up the power of the mind for me. One day, he hosted a seminar on confidence in sport and asked the former NFL player Stuart Anderson to share what went through his mind when he was thinking confidently. Anderson recalled that he was a very good shooter in high-school basketball, nearly 50 per cent from general play. One night, they had a play-off game, and he couldn't buy a basket. He must have put up fifteen shots, and only two of them had gone in. With a minute to go, his team was still in the game and only a point down. The coach called a timeout and drew a play for one of the younger players. Anderson went, 'Wait a minute! I'm the guy who shoots. Give me the ball.' The younger player didn't want the pressure anyway, so the coach reluctantly called a play to get Anderson the shot. He sank it. His team won, and the next day the papers headlined his winning shot.

'How did you stay confident after you missed all those shots?' one of Rotella's students asked.

'I was a shooter. Fifty per cent from the field. The more I missed, the more likely I was to make the next one.'

'OK,' the student said, 'so what do you think when you've knocked down the first five?'

And Anderson said, 'You decide tonight's my night. I'm on a hot streak, and I'm going to make everything I look at.'

That's the kind of reality I created for myself against Waterford that day in Thurles.

That's the kind of one I'd create as a kid. I was the Stuart Anderson of east Cork. I was Brian Corcoran, the best underage hurler in the county.

IF, AS SPORTS PSYCHOLOGISTS SAY, CONFIDENCE IS LIKE a table, then I had all the required legs to sustain it. All those hours down in the field or hitting that gable wall were the greatest pillar of strength, but all the social support I had was invaluable too. I shudder at how many penalty points that mentors and parents like Colman and Margaret Dillon, Humphrey Collins, Eoghan O'Connor, Timmy Buckley, Martin Bowen and Billy Hegarty would have accumulated on their licences for squashing seven or eight of us into their cars to bring us to Erins Own games.

Then there was family. Dad didn't play the games, but he was passionate about them, while Mam's family was steeped in the GAA. Her father, Tim, played for Little Island and was the first chairman of Erins Own. Her brother D.D. played and to this day is a hugely active member of the club. He was honoured by the club in 2004 with a lifetime's achievement award. The biggest influence of all, though, was John. He didn't coach me or tutor me, but he paved the way for me. The moment I walked into Midleton CBS as a first year, I was known. I'd be making my way down the corridor and I'd hear people say, 'That's him, that's John Corcoran's brother.'

Off the field, we were opposites. I was always quiet, private, reserved. John was more outgoing, into the girls and, by his late teens, liked his few pints. On the field, he was calm, clean, honest. He was a brilliant colleges player. He was the main man on the school's first Rice Cup title in '83, captain of the school's first Dean Ryan winning team in '85 and playing for the Cork minors by '86. That year, he literally brought the family places we'd never been. In the Munster final in Killarney, he scored a late goal to earn Cork a replay. After they won it, we were off to Croke Park for the All Ireland final. I'll never forget the excitement of walking in, finding our seats in the Hogan Stand and looking down on a pitch I'd only seen on TV. That day, I sat and wondered how long I would have to wait to play in Croke Park. I figured it would be four years, never thinking it would be just two. As it turned out, Cork lost that day to Offaly, but a year later John was back, this time with the footballers. They lost as well, to James McCartan and Down, but in '88 he finally got his hands on an All Ireland medal when he played with the Under-21 hurling team that slaughtered Kilkenny.

Then, one day, I returned home from one of my missing days playing golf to find my parents distraught. 'Where were you?'

'Why, what's happened?'

'John and his bike were in a crash.'

The good news was he was alive and kicking. The bad news, he'd completely shattered his left elbow. The doctors said he would never hurl again. It was like the end of the world for us.

The following year, John was back playing with the junior Bs. The year after that, he was back with the seniors as we shocked the whole of Cork by winning the county. He even played for Cork that year in the league. Even now, at 37, he's still out there, swinging that arm and hurley with the junior Bs. I know I won't be playing when I'm 37.

AS MUCH AS JOHN'S NAME HELPED MY STANDING, I'D built up a bit of a reputation in my own right. I was on a couple of Erins Own teams that had won East Cork Under-12 and Under-14 titles in hurling and football. My mother would cut out any newspaper write-up that featured my name or John's, and soon she was buying a new scrapbook every few months. In an Under-12 league game against Carrigtwohill in which I broke my nose but still managed to score 2–6, the *East Cork News* wrote, 'Brian Corcoran saved the game with two final magnificent points, the latter in the depths of injury-time from the halfway line, his face stained with blood.'

In 1987, my profile went to another level. In the East Cork Under-14 final, I scored 6–5 from play from midfield against Midleton. We lost that same game by a point, and that night I was devastated. A few days later, the *Examiner* had a big write-up about how 'players, mentors and supporters from both sides marvelled at this quite extraordinary display'. It described how we'd been six goals down just after half-time and how we'd clawed our way back, but to me the first paragraph said it all: 'Imagine scoring six goals and five points in a match and still ending up on the losing team!'

I still had a lot to cheer about that year. I captained the CBS to the Rice Cup, just as John had four years earlier. Then I made the Cork Under-14 team to play in the Tony Forrestal tournament in Waterford.

The following year, things got even better. First, I made the school's Harty Cup team, and in a hurling-mad school like ours that carried certain privileges. One day, a teacher was checking our homework. 'Sorry, Sir. I had a game yesterday evening. I didn't get a chance to do that.'

'I understand, Brian. No problem. How did ye get on, by the way?'

'We won, Sir.'

'Good stuff! Well done.'

He moved on to the fella behind me. He hadn't done his either. 'What?' said the teacher. 'For tomorrow, 50 lines . . .'

Those of us from the Harty class of '88 didn't have to worry about lines. We practically had the freedom of the school – because that year we became the first team in the college's history to finally land the Harty.

I played at corner-back, not the last time I'd break onto a team in that position. After beating St Colman's of Fermoy, we faced the other kingpins of Munster colleges hurling, St Flannan's of Ennis, in the semi-final. Flannan's had beaten the CBS in the final the year before and, with seconds remaining, were four points up. Then we won a free out around midfield. Our mentors sent instructions for the ball to be dropped in, but Peter Smith ended up striking it off the upright. The ball broke and our full-forward Paudie O'Brien latched on to it to send it flying past a certain goalkeeper called Davy Fitzgerald. Seconds later, our sub Con O'Regan belted another ball over the bar. We won the replay by four points and then, in the final at a packed Mitchelstown, beat Thurles CBS by four as well.

We had a very strong team. Our captain and my clubmate John Dillon had been described in the papers as another Charlie McCarthy. Timmy Kelleher was another clubmate who would play for Cork. Another Erins Own man, Eamon Coughlan, was full-back. We had Peter Smith, David Quirke and, upfront, Paudie, who'd scored 1–4 in the Harty final. It was going to take a special side to beat us in the All Ireland final.

St Kieran's, Kilkenny, had a special side. D.J. Carey wasn't even considered their best forward: that's how special. Adrian Ronan enjoyed that status. In the Leinster final, he'd scored

4–9. We'd hold him to 1–3, but in the end that's what Kieran's would win by. With ten minutes to go, we were a point up, but a couple of goals in a couple of minutes transformed what is now considered a colleges classic. We'd bounce back, though. Four months later, half our team would play half theirs in the All Ireland minor final, including, amazingly, me.

A few weeks after the Harty final, I was invited to a trial for the county minors. I refused politely. I didn't think I'd make it. I was only 15. No one, not even Ring, had played minor for Cork at 15. When they beat Waterford in the Munster semi-final in Midleton, I was just a spectator in the stand.

The following week, Erins Own played Midleton in the East Cork minor championship. I was centre-back on David Quirke, who was centre-back on the county team, and I played very well on the night. When I got home, D.D. called and said that he'd been talking to Christy Kidney, one of the minor selectors, at the match and that they again wanted me to try out for the team. This time, I reluctantly agreed. I went down on the bus to Limerick, where the team were having a trial run for the Munster final. They stuck me in at corner-back in the trial game. I played reasonably well but didn't expect anything to come from it. The team had been good enough to beat Waterford by 19 points. My time would come the next year or the year after.

It came the next night. D.D. burst into the house; I'd been picked at midfield for the final on Sunday. I went into a state of shock. I'd been picked? At midfield? I'd played there for about 20 minutes at the end of the colleges final; now I was expected to play there in front of 40,000 with the county?

I was a placid kid at the time – an earthquake wouldn't wake me – but I didn't sleep much that night. My brain kept racing back to watching John in all the big games in '86. I'd been shaking like a leaf in the stand; imagine the nervous wreck I'd be when I'd have to play myself.

I needn't have worried. The next night, training with Cork was like being back training with the college for the Harty. Seven of the other CBS lads were in the panel. Together, we'd be all right. By the time I ran onto the field, I was as relaxed as I'd been playing for Erins Own just a fortnight earlier against Midleton.

Marking me was Michael Ryan, who'd later play senior and win an All Ireland for Tipp. He was 18 and I was 15, but the way I was now looking at it I'd played and outplayed 18 year olds with the college and club before. I worked hard, hit a lot of ball and was very pleased with my performance, and even more so when, by the end, we'd beaten Tipp 5–7 to 1–2. When the whistle went, one of my immediate thoughts was that we were heading for Croke Park.

I was like a child on Christmas Eve the night before we played Antrim in the All Ireland semi-final, up in my room in the Lucan Spa Hotel, wondering if tomorrow would ever come. When it did, it was even better than I imagined. The dressing-rooms might have been cold and dark, and there might only have been a few hundred people in the stadium, but I'll never forget running down and out of that tunnel for the first time. Once we were out on the field, I couldn't help looking up towards the upper deck of the Cusack, where I had sat with my father two years earlier. That day, I'd looked down at the tunnel, wondering when I'd get to run out through it. Now I just had. A dream had come true.

In the final, we were again up against a Kilkenny side and an exceptional full-forward line. If anything, it was better than that of St Kieran's. In one corner, there was Ronan, at full-forward there was Charlie Carter and in the other there was D.J. There's probably never been a better underage full-forward line, and in the final they'd show why. Quarter of an hour in, D.J. caught a clearance from his clubmate Pat O'Neill and laid off to Charlie, who buried it in the net. Ten minutes after half-time, Brian Cunningham put us a point up, but then D.J., Charlie and Ronan started to cut us up. By the time I was switched back onto Ronan, it was too late.

The whole weekend had been an adventure, though: getting our gear bag and jumper with '1988 All Ireland minor hurling final' inscribed below the crest; playing in front of 60,000; scoring my first point in Croke Park; rubbing shoulders with the Galway and Tipp seniors at the reception in the Burlington on the Monday; and seeing Frank Murphy's reaction when one of our lads, with a few drinks in him, asked Cyril Farrell, the Galway manager, what he'd made of his performance in the minor match. Then there was the homecoming at the train station, our little parade around town and sticking in the video and seeing ourselves on the box for the first time.

It would have been much better if we'd won, but, as everyone kept reminding me, I was 15. I'd another three years to win one. I was bound to win one.

And, naturally, I agreed.

I was the Stuart Anderson of Ireland, and one day I'd be champion of it too.

CHAPTER FOUR
MINOR MATTERS

'To win, you have to lose and then get pissed off'
JOE NAMATH, 1969 SUPERBOWL MOST VALUABLE PLAYER

HAVE YOU EVER GOT UP IN THE MORNING WONDERING if you've just had a nightmare or if that really did happen the previous day? On the morning of 20 April 1989, I woke up with the scoreline Clare 7–8 Cork 0–7 engrained in my brain. Surely it didn't happen. Surely it was only a bad dream. I got the *Examiner* and went straight for the sports pages. There were those numbers again, and, just below them, the immortal line, 'No, that scoreline is not wrong!' It hadn't been a bad dream. It had actually happened. We'd actually been four goals down fifteen minutes into the first round of the Munster minor hurling championship, and I had actually been switched from centre-forward to centre-back after Clare scored a fifth.

Something else happened that night in Kilmallock. As I was getting onto the bus, someone tapped me on the shoulder. It was Mick O'Loughlin, the minor football coach. I had declined to play football for Cork earlier in the year; did I want to play for them now? I decided to give it a go. The club might have treated football as a bit of a joke, and in the CBS we didn't take it too seriously either, but earlier that year we had rattled Colin Corkery's Coláiste Chríost Rí in the Cork Colleges and then Billy O'Shea's Killorglin in the Corn Uí Mhuirí, and I had played very well in both. Now that the hurlers were out, there was nothing better to be doing for the summer. Three weeks after the kick in the hole and the tap on the shoulder in Kilmallock, I was playing in the full-forward line alongside Corkery. We won, and I went well. But then I got a knock in training and was deemed unfit to start in the Munster final. It was a killer. The sun was blazing and the terraces were heaving in Killarney, and, though I came on at corner-forward near the end and scored a goal, Kerry held on to win by a point.

The following year, I was sure we'd take them. I was fit, we had them down in the Park and we had this whiz-kid from Nemo upfront called Joe Kavanagh. But Kerry had this whiz-kid from Glenflesk in midfield called Seamus Moynihan and ended up hammering us by ten points. Later that same day, the Cork seniors hammered Kerry's, but as the whole of Cork seemed to stream out of Páirc Uí Chaoimh on a high, I was with our coach, Fr Donncha MacCarthaigh, in his car, trying to fathom what had happened to us, wondering would we ever beat Kerry.

Two weeks later, the whole of Cork was floating out of Thurles, and this time I was floating with them. The Canon's donkeys had beaten Babs's thoroughbreds in the Munster senior hurling final, while in the minor final we'd avenged the Kilmallock debacle by beating Clare by a goal. Suddenly, the county could sense a possible senior double. And we minors, with the semi-final against Derry surely a formality, were dreaming of an All Ireland of our own.

The Derry match, as it turned out, wasn't straightforward. They had the Collins brothers and big Geoffrey McGonigle on board, while I couldn't play because of a hand injury, and a few minutes after half-time we were a man down and only a point up. The lads pulled through, and I was back for the final. Once again, we faced Kilkenny, and at half-time we were ten points down. When we got back into the dressing-room, I looked over at our coach, Denis Coughlan, and he was shell-shocked. We all were. We were finished. Before he threw in the towel altogether, though, Coughlan threw in a sub, Damien Fleming, and by the end of the game Damien had scored two goals. Then, with time nearly up and Kilkenny a point ahead, Kevin Murray turned the full-back and passed to Fleming, who billowed the net for the third time. And for a split second we were ecstatic; we had won the All Ireland. Then we were brought down to earth. Willie Barrett had blown his whistle for a foul on Murray as he was offloading to Fleming. Instead of being two points up with time up, we were now a point behind with a twenty-metre free. We had no option but to take the point and take the replay.

Years later, I read an interview Willie gave in which he said that his two biggest regrets were failing to spot Tomás Mulcahy juggling the ball before his goal in the 1992 Munster senior final and costing Cork the 1990 minor All Ireland by blowing up when he should have played advantage. At the time, we were just thrilled to have another chance, and that night, as we basked in the seniors' glorious win over Galway and our own prospect of skinning the Cats in the replay in Thurles, Coughlan was the happiest man in Ireland.

Denis and myself hadn't started the year on great terms. I showed up for a trial game in Rathcormac without my gear, having picked up a knock from a game the day before, and Denis wasn't impressed. 'Just because you've been on the team for the last two years, doesn't mean you're going to automatically be on it this year. I wasn't involved the last two years. You have to prove yourself to me!' I was determined to prove myself to Denis and, by the end of the drawn game, I had. I had been centre-back, marking Andy Comerford, back when we both were much leaner and had way more hair than we do now.

Unfortunately, there was quite a gap between the drawn game and the replay, because of the footballers' successful completion of the Double, and I was coming under ferocious pressure to play for Erins Own. Because I was still only 17, I had taken my father's advice not to play with the seniors that year, but now the junior championship was on and their trainer was begging me to play. I didn't want to, but, after coming under severe pressure, I said I would. And so, days after playing in front of 70,000 in Croke Park in an All Ireland final, I was in midfield against Lisgoold in the Junior B championship out in Watergrasshill, in front of 30 diehards and a dog. The price of allowing the club to twist my arm was to twist my ankle ligaments. I was marking a lad who must have been 18 st., and inevitably that 18 st. fell over and landed on my leg.

The following night, I had the delightful task of breaking the news to Coughlan at training.

'Whaaat? You're going to miss an All Ireland final because of some bloody Junior B game?'

And, of course, he was right to go spare. My father hadn't wanted me to play; I hadn't wanted to play; it made no sense to play.

The following Sunday week, myself, Coughlan and a doctor were in a field not far from the one in Semple Stadium to gauge what state my bandaged ankle was in. I went for a run in a straight line, stopped, turned 180° and sprinted back. Coughlan didn't buy it. 'Press off now while you're running.' And, of course, the ankle couldn't take it, and Coughlan couldn't play me.

Kilkenny won by 14 points. In desperation, the selectors brought me on three minutes before half-time, but by then we were already 2–11 to 0–4 down. As I hobbled off, I was gutted. After '88, everyone had said, 'Not to worry, sure you've another three years.' Suddenly, two of those years were gone, and I'd lost another final.

A certain county board protocol darkened the mood even further. You could only keep a Cork jersey if you reached an All Ireland final; even if you won Munster but lost an All Ireland semi-final, the jersey had to be given back. After the drawn game in Croke Park, a few of the fellas swapped jerseys with the Kilkenny lads, while I wrapped mine up and put it in my bag, with its number six on the back and the threading '1990 All Ireland minor hurling final' on the front. The next thing, our county secretary, Frank Murphy, came into the room demanding that we give our jerseys back. Fellas were wondering why; sure, weren't we allowed to keep them, it being a final? No, no, no; those jerseys would be needed for the replay. So around Frank went, gathering every Kilkenny jersey that was in the room before returning with all the Cork jerseys that had been in Kilkenny's. It all meant that on that day in Thurles, Peter Smith was the one who left with number six and I was left with number twenty-three.

A little less than a year later, in a dressing-room in Cusack Park, Ennis, it was even more farcical. Even though I was still minor, I was on the county Under-21 team, and that summer we had blazed through Munster. Our run finished against Galway, however, and though we'd contributed to a classic, we were asked to hand back our jerseys as it had only been an All Ireland semi-final. Just as fellas had finished changing and were getting up to leave, we were all told to sit down. A couple of jerseys were still missing, and we weren't going anywhere until those jerseys were forthcoming. For the next ten minutes, there was just one big stand-off. Officers told us they'd go through our bags to look for them if needs be. Eventually, the lads each walked up with a jersey in their hand and threw it into the bag. I watched on, inwardly livid, but I was only a player. What was I going to do?

One of our selectors did something about it. At the next county board meeting, Seanie O'Leary kicked up stink about the incident, and a month after Ennis every player who had been locked in that dressing-room was sent out a Cork jersey by post.

By then, I had another All Ireland-final jersey, though. And a winners' medal to go with it.

EARLIER THAT SAME SUMMER OF '91, THE SUMMER THE Tall Ships came to Cork, the Dubs and Meath couldn't stop playing and Bryan Adams wouldn't get off number one with 'I Do It For You', I played my first senior championship match with Erins Own. It was out in Riverstown, in the first round against Glen Rovers, and after a few minutes the selectors switched me from centre-forward to centre-back to mark Tomás Mulcahy. Tomás had just won and lifted the All Ireland for Cork the previous September, but I did well on him, and when the Glen then moved John Fitzgibbon out onto me, I held him too. Days after that senior debut with the club, my sister told me that one of the senior selectors had just rang, wanting me to make my senior debut with Cork, in a challenge game against Dublin.

I was a bit startled when she said that. I was still only minor, and they were still the All Ireland champions; wasn't it a bit early to be considering me? Before I knew it, I was playing centre-forward, calling Tony O'Sullivan for a pass and hitting it over the bar. 'Wow,' I thought, 'Tony O'Sullivan passed me a ball!' I hadn't expected such an experienced player to be passing it out to the kid, but Tony and Kevin Hennessy and the rest of the lads continued to, and by the end of the game I had scored 1–3 off John Twomey, an All Star nomination.

That night, Frank Murphy gave me a spin home and told me that he and the selectors had been impressed. 'We'll probably be in contact with you again,' he said as the car pulled up outside my house, but as I hopped out and the car pulled away I was thinking, 'Probably next year, you mean.' It had only been a challenge game, after all; it had only been against Dublin. A few nights later, though, I was in Páirc Uí Chaoimh training with Tony, Teddy McCarthy and other legends, and Canon Michael O'Brien was telling me he was thinking of playing me in the Munster final the following week against Tipperary.

As things transpired, he didn't. I was disappointed when I didn't get the chance to play, but in hindsight I probably wasn't ready for it. I had only played one senior championship match for the club and one senior challenge game with Cork. It's sometimes hard to remember and believe now, but that was the first time RTE televised live a championship match between Tipp and Cork. Uninitiated viewers couldn't have got a better premiere. The previous day, the dramatic conclusion to the epic Dublin–Meath saga had been screened live too, yet somehow this was even better. Cork had been ahead by as much as six points after one brilliant groundstroke of John Fitzgibbon's, but then Fox took over to leave it Cork 4–10 Tipp 2–16.

There was a lot of speculation in Cork over the following days that I'd be playing in the replay. Mark Foley was struggling with his form, and there was a sense that Cork needed to throw something different, something unexpected, at Tipp; what could be more different and unexpected than a kid still playing minor? The Canon told me he was definitely thinking of playing me this time; indeed, he was thinking of starting me, at centre-forward. The problem was that the Munster football finals were fixed for the same day at a different venue. That triggered more talk, with me playing in the football in Killarney then jumping into a helicopter and flying to Thurles. But that wasn't realistic; in trying to be everywhere, my head would be nowhere. It had to be one or the other.

The following Tuesday night, the hurlers were training in the Park. As I was going in, the minor football coaches, Fr MacCarthaigh and Eamonn Ryan, were outside waiting in a car, saying they really needed me in Killarney. Then I was called up to see Frank. Eamonn and Fr MacCarthaigh had just been in to him to make representation on behalf of the minors, and, in fairness to Frank, he now wanted me to make a representation on behalf of myself.

'To be honest,' I told him, 'I think I should be going to Killarney.'

Later that night, after I'd finished training with the hurlers, the Canon called me over. My request had been granted. I'd be going to Killarney.

It was the right call. I preferred hurling to football, but I was still only minor. With the footballers, I'd be certain to start, playing with my own age group. After four years on the minor hurling team and three years on the football team, this was my last chance to win that minor All Ireland medal I'd been craving since '88.

I'd also become very fond of the footballers. Some of them I'd known a while. I'd first come across Joe Kavanagh at the trials the previous year out in Ballincollig. Normally when you go for those trials, fellas just pass the ball to buddies from their own club or school and those of us from a small club or non-footballing school have to nearly kill someone to get our hands on the ball before doing something spectacular with it. With Joe, there was none of that old boys' network stuff. He was full-forward, I was centre-forward and the first ball he got, he passed to me. 'Fair dues to him,' I thought. 'He could have given that to one of the Nemo lads instead of the junior footballer from Glounthaune.' From that moment on, Joe had a fan.

I'd got to know and like the rest of the panel too. Podsie O'Mahony from Ballincollig was a gas character. Paul O'Rourke from Roscarberry was another looper you couldn't but love. Kevin O'Dwyer was as solid a fella as he was a goalkeeper, while our two midfielders, Pat Hegarty and Fachtna Collins, were class fellas as well as class players. Everyone was sound. We'd had the odd weekend down in Bantry to ease the travel for the west Cork lads and had bonded brilliantly. It showed on the field. We had to go down to Killarney and face a Kerry team that had the already legendary Seamus Moynihan on their side. But this time we weren't going to be stopped, and we won, ten points to eight.

On the way home, we were singing on the bus, but I wasn't as jubilant as the rest of the lads. A few hours earlier, while Kerry and Limerick had been playing out a fine game of football in front of my eyes, my ears had been tuned in to the radio for news from Thurles. Shortly after half-time, Cork had been nine points up, in control, and visions of us playing Galway in Croke Park raced through my mind. But then Jim Cashman got that belt on the hand, Pat Fox sneaked in for another goal, John Leahy seemed to be everywhere and suddenly Tipp were Munster champions. There would be no day against Galway now. A year after the Double, my own little Double had been smashed. At least, though, I had one All Ireland semi-final to look forward to.

Things were hectic for me around this time. Ten days after that win over Kerry, I was out with the Under-21 hurlers in their Munster final against Limerick. I started the game at centre-forward and managed to score three points off Ciaran Carey before being switched back to wing-back to face the wind for the second half. Then, the Sunday after that seven-point win, I was out with the minor footballers again, in Croke Park. It was typical of the time. It was manic and it was tiring, but it was great. All I could see was the next ball, the next game, the next win.

With the minor footballers, that next ball was more often

than not the high ball. By now, I was full-back, my third year playing in a different line of the field for them. Years later, the full-back spot became a position I detested, but as a minor I was comfortable there. Teams of that age, level and time did not yet play in 70–30 ball for the forward; instead, they'd just lump in the 50–50 kind, which, with my height and strength, suited me.

Leading into that semi-final against Donegal, though, I had my doubts whether the high ball would favour me. The word was that the Donegal full-forward was 6 ft 6 in. The night before the game, I worked it out in my own head. 'Right, if he's 6 ft 6 in., he can't be that fast, so try and play him from the front, and anything that comes in high, just punch it away; you're hardly going to outfield the guy.' As it turned out, James Ruane was about the same height as myself. Later, we found out he wasn't expecting it either. The story round the Glenties had been that the Cork full-back was 6 ft 6 in.

The following Sunday didn't go as well. It was that day with the Under-21 hurlers in Ennis and the stand-off over the jerseys. It was a great game, as good as the 2–19 to 4–10 scoreline suggests, but it was crushing to be on the wrong side of it.

But again there was another ball, another game, another win to chase. And, this time, another All Ireland.

While I had gone into the semi-final against Donegal with a false impression of who I'd be marking, the scouting reports before the final were more detailed. Fr MacCarthaigh and Eamonn had been up to the Connacht final to see Mayo, and the Thursday before the final they handed us each a card on the man we'd be marking. I was on a Tony Walkin, but that day it didn't matter who I was playing on. Never before had I been so focused or keyed up for a game. That morning, there was no banter with the rest of the lads at breakfast or on the bus; I just kept quiet and to myself, thinking, 'We're going to win, we're going to win, we're going to win.' After

John's heartbreak of '86 and '87 and my own in '88 and '90, this was the last chance to bring a minor All Ireland medal to the Corcoran household. Defeat was not an option.

The following day, a few papers described my performance as the best ever by a minor footballer in Croke Park. Mayo pumped a lot of high ball down around my square, and that was always going to suit me. One of my strengths has always been my ability to read a game. On one occasion, when the ball was played out in front of Walkin, I could tell that the hard ground and hop was going to beat him, so I just stood back, waited for the ball to bounce over him, collected it and drove out to set up another attack. That day, though, was all about the result, not my performance, and when a Ronan Golding shot thumped off the post and into the net with ten minutes to go, the result was in jeopardy. Even when we came right back at them with Seanie Barrett, who'd scored a goal in the first half, soloing through to fist over a point, Mayo levelled it again with a point from Kevin O'Neill. But then Fachtna and Pat won some crucial ball around midfield, Joe swung over a point with that left foot of his and I won a vital ball to set up a move that ended with Mark O'Sullivan scoring the insurance point. Before we knew it, the ref was blowing the whistle, the scoreboard was saying Cork 1–9 Mayo 1–7 and our subs and mentors were sprinting onto the field.

There's a photo I still have at home of that day. I'm up on the steps of the Hogan Stand, looking down to some of my teammates below, giving them the thumbs up with a huge grin right across my face. For years, I had pictured making that walk up those steps but in '88 had seen Kilkenny boys make it instead and then watched on the telly Offaly, Derry and Meath boys do the same. Now we were the ones making that walk, and it felt incredible.

The best moment for me, though, was doing the lap of honour, running up towards Hill 16 along the Cusack Stand side. Though it was full, I could still pick out my parents jumping and waving up in the top deck. They'd shed sweat and tears for this moment too.

That sense of contentment lasted for months. Watching Down spoil Meath's incredible ten-game season and end Ulster's twenty-three-year wait without Sam Maguire; meeting that game's man of the match, James McCartan, in the lobby of the Burlington that night; the flags and families at Kent Station; the open-top bus over to the Imperial Hotel; then, on the Tuesday, visiting the schools of Ballincollig with the lads and the cup, dreaming the girls' screams were for us when they were really just for Podsie: all were moments to treasure and savour.

And then there was coming home to Caherlag and seeing the banner 'Well done, Brian!' hanging across the road and up to 40 neighbours out to greet me and celebrate. That same week, our close neighbours Edwin and Jo Kenny, Tom's uncle and aunt, had a barbecue in my honour, inviting the whole neighbourhood.

Their generosity didn't end there. They also gave me a bottle of champagne. I didn't open it, though. Instead, I decided to keep it until I'd won a senior All Ireland. I'd got a taste of winning All Irelands in Croke Park, but now I wanted more. The champagne could be put on hold. Hopefully for just a year.

CHAPTER FIVE

GETTING STRONGER

'I have seen, to my disgust, the players draw the crowds, make the money and lose their sweat at many a hard hour's game, while those gentlemen at the head of affairs take charge of the bag and jump into their cars again before the match is over – off to their hotel to count the coins made by the rank and file. They will scoff at the application from injured players for compensation . . . [The official] never caught a hurley in his hand, never felt the sting of the ash on his shin bones, does not know what it's like to be laid up . . . The governing body has been captured by non-players, and the players themselves – the men who pay for the freight – seem to have no direct representation on it'

JAMES KELLEHER, CORK AND DUNGOURNEY HURLER, 1908

THURSDAY, 9 MARCH 2006

Maybe I'll make it for the summer yet.

Tonight, for the first time this year, I felt good for a full session. Towards the end, we were doing ten consecutive sixty-metre sprints. I was running with Joe Deane and Niall

McCarthy, and Joe said to me, 'Corcoran, you're getting faster with age!'

I smiled back, 'I'd say it's you're getting slower with age,' but earlier Seanie had also remarked on how fresh I was looking.

It's a strange thing to say about a game against Down, but Sunday's a big game for us. We're not pushed about winning the league, but we'd want an extra game or two before the championship, and, with Waterford blowing us off the field the other day, we have to beat Down to have any chance of reaching the quarter-finals. We struggled to beat Down up there last year, and the word is they're coming down tomorrow night, 36 hours before the game. We'll be taking it seriously too, especially our warm-up. Our first night back after the Waterford game, Jerry Wallis brought us through a new warm-up that himself and Seanie have devised to liven things up. They plan to video our warm-up on Sunday, because they feel the Waterford game was further proof that fellas who under-perform tend not to have warmed up properly.

On Sunday, I must literally start as I plan to go on. Big Brother is watching.

SUNDAY, 12 MARCH

We had an unusual breakfast this morning: chicken and pasta. The routine is to eat our pre-match meal three hours before throw-in, so a half-one throw-in meant a half-ten pre-match meal.

The game ended up being a formality, 3–25 to 0–9, with our full-forward line of Joe, myself and Conor Cusack scoring a goal each. My goal came with 15 minutes left when my clubmate Kieran 'Hero' Murphy offloaded to me. I could hear the footsteps behind me, so to avoid being hooked I batted the ball when I reached the edge of the square. Graham Clarke wasn't expecting it, which is another thing that shot has going for it.

The first time I scored a goal like that was in my first championship game back in 2004 when I came on as a sub against Kerry. The following week, O'Grady had us practising it in training and then for the entire year. He never mentioned what inspired the idea, of course; it was just another ingenious drill he'd devised. I should have patented it.

I also scored three points today. Better still, I was able to run without being out of breath, while my touch was the best it's been all year, even if we did have more time on the ball than normal. I left Páirc Uí Rinn feeling upbeat, and my form's even better now that I've heard Midleton CBS beat St Flannan's in the Harty final. It's only the third time Midleton have won it. The last time was in '95, when Donal Óg, Sully, Joe and Mickey O'Connell were on board; the first time in '88, when yours truly was there. Half a lifetime ago now. Frightening.

TUESDAY, 14 MARCH

It was a mad rush to make training tonight. I started the job in Cashel last Monday, which meant all last week I was leaving there at about quarter to five to make training for seven. Tonight, training was at six, so I had to put the boot down to get to Nemo Rangers. It was worth the rush and, since I hadn't seen their new complex before, worth the wait. The large AstroTurf is top-notch, the lights state of the art and the clubhouse like a hotel.

The thing is, we only had an hour there. At seven, we had to get off the pitch because there were five junior soccer clubs coming on after us. It's a pity that we haven't got facilities like this every night. When we train in other fields other nights, we're doing drills where we can barely see the ball. It was a pleasure to train in a place like Nemo tonight. At this time of year, we should train there more often.

FRIDAY, 17 MARCH

I was gutted for Pat Mul and the O'Connors today. Newtownshandrum lost the All Ireland club final to Portumna. Ben's been restricted by a groin injury for a while now, and today it told. We'd want to have him fit for the summer. It's not just Newtown who aren't the same without a fit Ben and Jerry; neither are Cork. It was inevitable that one of them would get injured; with all they've won with Newtown and Cork, they've been on the go for four years non-stop. I've often been amazed by how they maintain that intensity.

The twins were 14 when I first heard of them. Even then, there was a lot of talk about these wizards from Newtown. Ben was the first to break onto the senior panel, in '99, and I don't think we'd have won the All Ireland that year without him. In the closing minutes against Kilkenny, when we were barely holding on, Ben was back in our half-back line to get on and bring out ball. I couldn't get over it, that a 20 year old had the awareness to know exactly what we needed at that moment.

Jerry had to wait a good bit longer to establish himself. Why, I don't know, but then it was only towards the end of 2004 that Seanie McGrath could tell the difference between the pair of them. He'd be there talking away to one of them, then go, 'Well, see you on Tuesday, Ben!' only to be told, 'Actually, Seanie, it's Jerry.'

Seanie apart, the rest of us have found it easy enough to tell one from the other. Jerry's haircut is tighter. Ben mightn't shave for a few days; Jerry, being a Garda, shaves every day. When it comes down to it, though, they're the same. Droll out, level-headed, grounded. Last year, when I stated in a newspaper article that I would trust every one of the Cork team with my life, a few friends questioned this remark. Surely, they said, there were a few among them who, if you were blindfolded in a game of Trust, would leave you balls-naked in the middle of Patrick Street. And, of course, there were and there are. What I meant was that they were all men who'd have my back in war and I'd have theirs. But Ben and Jerry, I'd trust in a game of Trust – and I trust they'll bounce back from today's heartbreak too.

TUESDAY, 21 MARCH

I'm in Switzerland and will be again tomorrow, but I'd like to think I've made up for the session I missed at home with the workout I've just had in the pool and gym here. Big Brother was not watching tonight, but, if I am to have any hope this year, I need to be my own Big Brother.

SUNDAY, 26 MARCH

Today was a bit of a waste. We were meant to play Wexford away, but just as we arrived at their ground we could see supporters leaving, and then we learned that the referee, Barry Kelly, had deemed the pitch unplayable. How they couldn't have told us that earlier in the day or even earlier in the week beats me; the forecasts and weather have been dreadful all week. Most of the lads were disgusted. They'd travelled down last night and were all psyched for this game.

After a while, we started to see the funny side of it. I suggested that, instead of coming back in a few weeks' time, we should take Wexford on in a five-a-side indoor game for the points.

'Nah,' said Sully, 'I'll go three rounds with one of them.'

THURSDAY, 30 MARCH

We were back in Fermoy tonight, and my fitness is definitely improving. Unfortunately, the showers aren't. I was getting a rub when Seán Óg came in, and he was livid. Fred Sheedy, one of our selectors, asked what the showers were like, and Seán Óg fumed, 'They're cold again! And people are wondering why we're going to Portlaoise on Saturday!'

That's where and when the Gaelic Players Association's (GPA's) AGM is. There's a motion to go on strike on 9 April because of the GAA's refusal to officially recognise us. Its perceived failure to properly engage on the grants-scheme issue, which proposes that each county player be given a government grant of a couple of grand for their contribution to Irish life, has also irritated the membership.

I'm all for players' rights. I was the first Cork hurler to join the GPA, and for a few years I was about the only one. I didn't push it; I just asked fellas did they want to join. I went around the entire dressing-room.

'Nah, it's all right, Brian.'

'Don't see what it'll do, boy, to be honest.'

I came to Donal Óg. 'I'll join.' And for the next few years it was just the two of us.

Then, in the early spring of 2002, a few months after I'd announced my retirement, some documentation from the GPA executive landed through my door. I forwarded it on to Donal Óg, with a note: 'Don't know if you want to keep this up, but as you're the only other member . . .'

Keep it up? By the end of the year, virtually the whole panel were subscribed GPA members, had gone on strike and steamrollered a series of reforms that would ensure they were the most professional and organised team in hurling history. More than half those 30 players will be in Portlaoise on Saturday. All because of one man: Donal Óg Cusack, the rebel's rebel.

SATURDAY, 1 APRIL

I'm on the road to Portlaoise. Kelly and myself left Cork there at two o'clock. It's meant missing the Munster–Perpignan European Cup quarter-final, which is a shame as a former clubmate of mine, Tomas O'Leary, is playing.

We meet the rest of the Cork lads outside Portlaoise for some grub, which the county board has arranged for us; John Allen has been anxious, with the game tomorrow, that we get a decent meal. We then head to the Heritage Hotel for the meeting. Most of us are wearing hoodies, and since it's raining some of us put our hoods up. As we approach the door, we notice the television cameras, and inside we joke that people must think we're trying to conceal our identities.

The meeting starts. Here in Portlaoise at the top table there's our chief executive Dessie Farrell, our chairman Donal Óg, Kieran McGeeney and our president D.J. Carey. Up in Belfast, to where we're connected via a live video feed, there's Donal O'Neill and Fergal Logan, two of our longest-serving and most valued advisers. Dessie and Donal Óg speak first. They've drafted a list of demands and concerns that the GAA must address: formal recognition of the GPA; the government grant scheme; better player entitlements; the fixture chaos; the advertising ban on Club Energise. Then they open it to the floor.

McGeeney speaks first, and suddenly we're all in one of those Armagh huddles. 'Whatever's decided here,' he says, 'we all stick together. Even if the same fella kicked the shit out of you last week, you back him up here. It's all for one and one for all.'

Some people are mad for a strike, saying that it's time we did something about the lack of respect the GAA has shown towards us. Sulphur is in the air as a number of players air their grievances. I listen to their arguments, but I don't believe that going on strike is appropriate at this time.

I ask for the microphone. 'Lads, I'm all for some kind of action, and, if we decide to go on strike, I'll go on strike. But, to be honest, I don't think we can go on strike next Sunday. I don't think we'll be seen to be reasonable. We haven't told the GAA what we actually want, yet we're going to tell it that, if it doesn't give it to us, we're going on strike.

'We have to say what we want and what we're about. You go into any decent company up and down the country and the first thing you'll see in reception is a mission statement. We have to have a mission statement, let the GAA know what we're about. And we have to go even further. We have to say what we're *not* about. Because the first thing anyone cynical about the GPA is going to say is, "Right, where's pay for play hidden in here?" I look at this draft here: "Better player entitlements". That could mean pay for play. If we're not for pay for play, we should state we're not about pay for play. If, ten years down the road, that changes, we can change our mission statement then. I agree it's scandalous that the GAA doesn't recognise us – that's the big one here, as far as I'm concerned – and if they don't do something about that, we should act. But if we're threatening strike on Sunday week, I don't think we'll be seen to be reasonable. I don't think we'll have given the GAA enough time.'

I sit down, and a voice from the back of the room can be heard. 'I wouldn't agree with that there now. We've given them seven fuckin' years; isn't that enough time?'

A few more fellas stand up to echo similar sentiments. Glenn Ryan's more on my wavelength, though. Strike action, he says, is the ultimate weapon. If we use it first time out, we don't have anything else left in the arsenal. Now's not the time to press that button.

It strikes a chord with fellas. A few more proposals are suggested from the floor, more moderate in tone. Someone suggests that every game next Sunday be delayed by 15 minutes, and it's agreed by all. And that's all we have time for. The video link to Belfast expires at eight o'clock, and it's nearly that already. Dessie will hold a press conference in Dublin on Monday explaining the list of demands and where we're coming from, and next Sunday we'll have our 15-minute protest. After that, the ball's in the GAA's court.

As we file out, I get talking to David 'Doc' O'Connor, the Wexford corner-back, asking him for directions to Wexford, and, being the honest guy he is, he resists sending us on a wild goose chase. As we follow his instructions on the way down, we hold a teleconference with Donal Óg. He isn't happy and wishes we had more time to take a vote to clarify we don't want pay for play.

The fourteen of us arrive at the Ferrycarrig Hotel and head straight to the team room for tea and sandwiches. We can hear the roaring and taunting from next door: Callinan, Curran, Martin Coleman, Carthy and Hero are playing poker, and Hero is cleaning up. A few minutes later, a couple of girls pop up, asking if some of us would go into the bar to put a garter on a girl who's on her hen night. Seán Óg asks for volunteers, but there aren't any. 'Look,' he says to the girls, 'we'll be in after.'

'Yeah, right. Jesus, ye're no *craic* at all.'

'Look,' I say, 'if he says he'll be in after, he'll be in after.'

And a while later, when we're about to go up to our rooms, we remember our promise to the girls. We head down, and Seán Óg duly, if bashfully, plays along and performs the duties to a symphony of screaming laughter from the ladies. True to his word: that's Seán Óg. Then, when we head back upstairs, I meet Donal Óg in the corridor, and another half-hour GPA discussion ensues; and that's Donal Óg.

SUNDAY, 2 APRIL

Last Sunday, in his hotel, when we were having what we thought was our pre-match meal, former Wexford manager

Liam Griffin quipped that we should take it easy on his lads. At the time, I thought he was only joking. Right now, I'm thinking he was only half-joking. Wexford were very poor today, and, because we didn't follow his request, we won by nineteen points to seven. Our backs were excellent, forcing their forwards to shoot a pile of wides under pressure. Seán Óg was tried out in midfield and was outstanding. It could have been the hurley he was using: it was the same one Setanta played with in the 2003 All Ireland final. This morning, he told me that he rang Setanta during the week to ask if he could use it, and Setanta told him it was fine but to get some copies made.

I'm happy with my own performance. I scored four points from play, set up a few others and felt full of running. I actually enjoyed myself out there.

There's no doubt in my mind now. I'm with the team for the year.

MONDAY, 3 APRIL

Dessie, McGeeney and D.J. had that press conference in Dublin this morning, and, from what I can gather from the telly and radio, it's been well received. The demands are reasonable, and so is the 15-minute delay next Sunday. Some protest had to be made. These past few weeks, the GAA excused its absence at our recent meeting with the government because president-elect Nickey Brennan won't assume office until Congress in three weeks' time. Yet Nickey met up with the Australians over the International Rules and went to New York to discuss the stadium there. The reality is that we just haven't been a priority.

We've had to put up with this apparent status since the GPA was formed. I was one of the players up at the launch of the Marlborough deal in 2000, along with the likes of Brian

Lohan, Peter Canavan and Ja Fallon, and at the time it was considered groundbreaking that players should be involved in an endorsement deal without approval from Croke Park. GAA regulations at the time also demanded that we should hand 50 per cent of any endorsement money back to the GAA. That regulation is no longer there, because it proved to be totally impractical, but even at the time my thinking was, firstly, no way should the GAA dictate to me what money I make from someone external to the GAA, and, secondly, no way should it get any of it. The money was pittance, but it was more to do with the principle of the matter.

People said, 'You can't say the GAA has nothing to do with it; you got that deal because you're a hurler.' But who made that person into a hurler? Croke Park didn't do it. Myself, a ball and that wall outside my parents' home made me a hurler. Then people said, 'Ah, but what about the quiet, effective corner-back? He never gets any endorsements.' Just because not everyone gets endorsement deals it doesn't mean no one should. Some quiet, effective corner-backs have got sales jobs because they've played for their counties. Should Croke Park ask for some of their wages too?

We keep hearing that all the gate money goes back to the clubs. What do Erins Own get from Croke Park or Munster Council? Not a penny. We've clubmen having to run lottos and draws every week, organise golf classics, practically beg to keep the club going, and then in the summer the GAA will ask them to pay up to a hundred quid to go and see the county with their family. That is if they can get a ticket at all. The whole way money in the GAA is distributed needs to be completely re-examined. The Longford County Board shouldn't have to be fund-raising like they are to get some tracksuits for their county hurlers; that should come straight from Croke Park. More money should be going into teams and coaching instead of being ploughed into white-elephant stadiums. There's talk that Ennis is going to have a brand-new 40,000 capacity stadium, and that Fitzgerald Stadium in Killarney is going to be upgraded to 55,000. How often do they expect to half-fill it, let alone fill it? Is it to house Gooch or is it to house Eminem? You don't get 55,000 at any county final.

And yet it seems that every time players' issues are raised the GAA gives out sound bites about how pay for play will be the ruin of GAA and the values it embodies. While I'm sure there are players who would like pay for play, and while I'm sure it would make my life a lot easier if I was sleeping in, training in the afternoon and spending the evenings with my family, I am not for pay for play, and I believe the GAA uses this argument as a red herring every time players look for status.

Let's look at what the GAA does value. Elaine would have liked to have brought the three kids to watch me play in the 2005 All Ireland final, but, as Ewan was just a baby, a seat in the stadium with all the noise and crowds was just not an option. Those not in the know might assume that, for the big games, the wives and girlfriends are wined and dined in a private viewing booth during the game. The reality is that, in 2004, Elaine had to drag a buggy and two kids up countless steps to her seat, had to fight her way with the kids through the crowds and an unforgiving Garda line after the match to congratulate me, and finally was asked to leave the empty stadium before I rushed from an interview to verify her identity and accompany her to the players' lounge. Last year, she decided that watching the match from a comfortable seat in the Burlington Hotel was a far more attractive prospect. A seat in one of Croke Park's private boxes, which are reserved only for VIPs (people who contribute to the GAA in the way that the GAA values – that is, financially), would have solved the first problem. An ID card to state that she was allowed certain access rights as an assigned member of the Cork team would have solved the others. Such a card could have made the difference between my mother and father seeing me win the Liam McCarthy Cup at Croke Park and watching me win it on the telly.

Croke Park will argue that they need all those private booths to provide income to sustain the stadium. So we, the players, are not to be afforded the same privileges and comforts as those who 'sustain' Croke Park? And therein you have the crux of the problem: we, as players, are not seen as contributing financially to the GAA and therefore are not valued or respected.

Not only are we not respected, but, in my opinion, our rights as players and people were violated when our image rights were sold to a company without our permission. So now we are in a position where a corporate body who need never have seen a game of hurling can come along, sell and profit from the hurling images we've grafted long and hard to build with our blood, sweat and tears, and they throw a few coppers into the Croker fund for the privilege. This is not right. It is not fair play. And it is not respectful.

This is why the GPA was formed. Most players' associations are funded by the governing body of their sport, but the GAA does not recognise the GPA, let alone fund it. The GPA so has to rely on fund-raising and innovative initiatives such as the partnership with Club Energise to survive. Members of the GPA found the time to attend the meeting with government officials to discuss the Government Grant Scheme for Players. The GAA did not. The scheme is only worth a grand or two a year to the players, but it is a compensatory gesture for the loss of earnings we accrue, for the effort we're putting in and for the contribution we make to the image of sport in Ireland. It's not about money; it's about respect.

SUNDAY, 9 APRIL

We're out of the league. After observing the 15-minute delay, we lost, 18 points to 16. We had our chances, but Clare deserved to shade it. We're not going to lose any sleep over it, even if seven weeks without a competitive game now is quite a wait. We were seriously depleted again. Last week, Pat Mul had to travel to Wexford as we needed cover in the forwards, and he eventually came on at centre-forward. Two hours before the game today, John asked me if I wanted to take the frees. In the end, Tom did, even though he doesn't take them for Grenagh either.

I'm a bit disappointed with myself. I started brightly on Frank Lohan and was unlucky to have a batted shot come off the post, but, as the half went on, I began to feel dizzy. That's what you get when you don't pay enough attention to your hydration over a couple of days. Seanie often tells us that if you're not hydrated properly, you're working off 70 per cent straight away, and that's about all I was operating on today.

I could tell this morning I hadn't drank enough water. Your urine should be clear and odourless. Mine wasn't. I tried loading up after that, but it was too late. At least it's underlined to me now the importance of hydrating myself. From here on in, it's five litres of the stuff every day.

Hydration was something that was never mentioned in the old days. You might take a sip in the dressing-room or when someone was down injured; that was it. I look back at a game like the first round against Clare in '95 and now know I didn't just feel lethargic that day because I had been studying for my finals the previous week; I would barely have had a drop of water that week. These days, if we're on the bus to Thurles or on the train to Dublin, the place is stacked with water and energy drinks. If, on 28 May, a Clare runner delivers a drink to a Clare player and that Clare player offers me a drop, I'm not to take it, because I don't know what's in it. We're only to take what our lads send in.

We also all have to bring a new bottle to training every night. Two years ago, a few fellas started getting throat infections, and Seanie reckoned it was because we weren't able to rinse out some of the concentrated sugar from the energy drinks properly, causing bacteria to develop. Now I bring a new plastic bottle to training every night.

These inches all add up. With about ten minutes to go in last year's semi-final against Clare, Sully and Jerry O'Connor were seriously wilting when Jerry Wallis ran out, opened their mouths and rammed a fistful of Fruit Pastilles in, knowing it would give them a sugar boost and that they wouldn't hit the wall until the game was over. In the parade before the final, Jerry noticed that, while we were all passing water back to each other, the Galway lads were looking around, shouting, 'Give us some water!', but none came.

Today, I was those Galway lads. I can't and won't be on 28 May.

CHAPTER SIX

1992

'Brian Corcoran was a great minor but he has to go through a championship campaign. Whether he's the type of hurler that's going to survive Munster championship hurling against the likes of Fox and English, I have to wait and see'

MICHAEL 'BABS' KEATING, JUNE 1992

WE WALKED INTO THE ROOM, AND UP AT THE TOP WERE two chairs, one with the Cork jersey draped over it, the other with Tipperary's. It was Jury's Hotel, Cork, 7 June 1992, hours before the two teams who'd won the previous three All Ireland titles met in a do-or-die Munster semi-final.

'Can anyone,' asked Canon Michael O'Brien, 'tell me the difference between those two jerseys?'

We looked at each other. Where was the Canon going with this one?

'I'll tell you the difference!' he finally answered. 'See that one? That's the blood and bandage of Cork! See that other one? It has a big yellow streak running through it!'

After the roars of laughter subsided, and he'd given the rest of his team talk, the Canon had a few words with me. Though

I had been named to play at right corner-back, I was going to be playing over on the left. Instead of taking up Nicky English, I'd be marking Pat Fox, the reigning Player of the Year. I was fine with that. It wasn't going to be much tougher or easier than English, who, just two years earlier, had been Player of the Year himself. The main thing for me was that I was playing.

Shortly after I'd joined up with the Cork seniors at the start of that year, something became clear. It wasn't a case of whether I'd make my senior championship debut, or even a case of when; it was a matter of in what position.

In a tournament game against Waterford, I'd scored three points from wing-forward. Then, a couple of weeks later, I was moved to corner-back and in successive weeks kept Wexford's Martin Storey and Galway's Cathal Moran scoreless. I even played minutes at full-back in the league quarter-final against Waterford, and after surviving that ordeal there was a school of opinion that I was the man to play there come the championship. Richard Browne had retired, and while Denis Mulcahy had just come back, at 34 years of age some punters thought he should quickly rejoin Richard in the stands. The options were to persist with Denis, try Teddy McCarthy or Pat Hartnett back there or go with the kid who played there in the football.

Thankfully they didn't play me there in the league semi-final. Instead, I lined out at left wing-back and did well. Then, for the first round of the championship against Kerry, I was at corner-back. Now I was going to be in the corner against Tipp too. After the nomadic experience of the previous six months, I could live with that.

What made it even more tolerable was that they had persevered with Denis. It was always going to take him a few games to get back to the pitch of the inter-county game, having been away from it for three years. He was a great man to have beside you, reassuring you. He could have said to me, 'Listen, young fella, you mark your man and don't leave him come anywhere close to my patch, all right?' Instead, he went, 'Brian, play your normal game now. Feel free to go along the line. Don't be afraid to make a mistake now, you hear me? Try to play from in front, and, if you miss it, I'll be there to cover for you; I'll look out for your man.'

In the other corner, Seanie O'Gorman was just as supportive. I had licence to sweep behind him if I felt the need for it. And then behind us was Ger Cunningham, the best and soundest keeper in the business. Fox was going to be a handful all right, but, if he got past me, he'd still have Denis, Seanie and Cunningham to deal with.

More than a Munster final – and, in all likelihood, an All Ireland final – was at stake that day. In a way, the previous year's was being contested too. Tipp had won that All Ireland, but in Cork the thinking was that they never would have if Jim Cashman hadn't been taken out of it under a dropping ball in Thurles. There was no love lost between Seanie McCarthy and John Leahy. Pat Hartnett was all revved up to come on and bang shoulders off Declan Carr and Joe Hayes. If there was a yellow streak running through Tipp, then by God we were going to be the ones to reveal it.

The Canon had us just right, though: focused and fired up, yet loose and relaxed. On the bus from Jury's to the Park, he kicked off 'The Banks' himself. And even though Páirc Uí Chaoimh was heaving and buzzing with 45,000 people who'd been waiting for this day since the draw had been made, I ran into my corner and shook hands with Fox feeling as calm and composed as could be.

OVER THE LAST FEW YEARS, I HAVE ALWAYS GIVEN SOME simple advice to newcomers making their debut for Cork: 'The first few balls you get, let them off. Keep it simple.'

I remember watching Andy Cole's debut with Manchester United against Blackburn, and in the opening two minutes he was put right through on goal. He fluffed it, and it would take him more than two years to feel at home with United. What if he had scored that first day? Would it have taken two years then? The reason I give that advice is that, on my debut, it worked for me. I didn't have to wait two years to feel I belonged in that shirt. I felt I belonged from the moment I stuck in my hurley to intercept the first ball and just let fly on it as it bobbled out towards the sideline. Once I saw that ball fly 50 yards up the field and heard the crowd roar, my confidence soared.

I was on the long-range frees, and, while my first one, into the Blackrock End, dropped short, it was deflected out for a 65, which I put straight over the bar. I was winning and clearing a lot of ball in a great battle with Fox. Pat was like myself: only interested in playing ball. There were a lot of physical exchanges going on around us, though. Their full-forward Cormac Bonnar was running through when Denis came right back at him and hit him a fierce shoulder. The whole of Páirc Uí Chaoimh shuddered, while poor Bonnar shrivelled. It was as if he'd been torpedoed.

Soon, the same applied to Tipp. After they'd shaded a tense, scrappy first half six points to five, John Fitz nipped in for a goal, and then so did Tomás, either side of a few more points from Tony O'Sullivan and a ninety-yard free from me. Tipp did score a goal themselves, in the last minute through Declan Ryan, but it was too late. We'd won 2–12 to 1–12. I don't know about Tipp showing a yellow streak, but we'd shown the blood-and-bandage spirit of Cork. Before I knew it, I was thrown in front of a camera and presented with the Man of the Match watch. The Canon was hugging me and the crowd were on the field as if we'd won an All Ireland.

The next day, we won Munster. Again, it was in the Park, just this time it was sun-drenched, not overcast, and this time it was Limerick, not Tipp. Limerick were coming off winning the league, but for 60 minutes you'd never have known it as we blew them off the field. I was doing well on Shane Fitzgibbon, Jim Cashman was dominating Gary Kirby, Cathal Casey was clipping over sideline balls for fun, Seanie Mac and Pat Buckley were totally on top at midfield, while upfront another rookie, Barry Egan, and Tony Sull were destroying Limerick. Even if you'd taken Tomás's infamous goal out of it, we'd have been seven up at half-time, and entering the last ten minutes we were ten ahead. Even when they reeled off three goals in the final minutes, we were never in any danger, and after Ger Manley had come off the bench to score three points, people were wondering was there anyone or anything that was going to stop us winning an All Ireland.

The team itself wasn't getting carried away. I certainly wasn't, even if Limerick's coach, Eamon Grimes, would say in the dressing-room that day that I'd 'probably become one of the greatest hurlers of the '90s'. After about half an hour at the reception in Jury's, I slipped away, phoned my father to collect me outside Jury's Hotel and by eight o'clock was back home having a packet of crisps and a bottle of Coke, pucking around on the road with my friends. I didn't want to be stuck inside on one of the most beautiful days of the year. I preferred hanging around with my friends to being stuck inside in the bar. Apart from Barry and my clubmate Timmy Kelleher, the lads were all much older, all had wives or girlfriends and all drank.

That's not to say I didn't enjoy their company. A conversation with Pat Hartnett could go anywhere, from the martial arts to, next second, the meaning of life. His Midleton clubmate Kevin Hennessy was another gas character, constantly hopping balls off everyone, the Canon included. Tomás Mul and Tony Sull were others never short of a wisecrack. I just watched and enjoyed. Trying to exchange one-liners with the likes of Hennessy would have been like exchanging punches with Mike Tyson. You'd have been destroyed, embarrassed, floored.

THE DAY OF THE 1992 ALL IRELAND HURLING FINAL against Kilkenny, Canon Michael O'Brien had another motivational gimmick and a late positional switch for us. Unfortunately, neither was as inspired as those deployed for the Tipp game.

John Fitzgibbon from the Glen was totally geared for that final. I'd marked him in training in the weeks leading up to it, and when the ball would be down the other end he'd be saying, 'Christ, I can't wait to get at them! I remember coming down through there after '83. They had the bonfires out and were laughing at us. Laughing at us!' I liked John. He was an absolute artist who never seemed to get excited or agitated about anything.

That was, until the Thursday night before the final, when the Canon asked John and Hennessy how they would feel about swapping positions. They both thought it was a crazy idea. Yet, a few hours before the final, the Canon announced at our team meeting that John Fitz and Hennessy would be switching spots, with Hennessy going into the corner and John Fitz moving in on the edge of the square. I looked over at John, and, while he said nothing, his facial expression said everything. 'What in God's name are ye doing?' Hennessy would now be on a whippet in Eddie O'Connor, while Fitzgibbon was now on Pat O'Dwyer, the kind of player Hennessy would have had the strength and guile for. The pair of them hadn't even switched spots in training; why now, on the morning of an All Ireland final?

Then there was the Canon's pep talk. Normally he'd know the right thing to say at the right time, but that day, just before we went out, he went down on one knee and called us in. Outside, the stewards were banging on the door, while inside fellas were after banging every wall with their shoulder; surely these words of wisdom from the Canon would be worth the wait. So we gathered around and looked down on the floor. Then, after what seemed an eternity, he looked up with tears flowing down his face and, in the softest voice we'd ever heard from him, said, 'Lads, do it for me!'

Now, as much as we liked and respected the Canon, we had plenty of other reasons to win this one: doing it for our parents; doing it for the club; doing it for ourselves. As for the tears, the joke months afterwards was that the Canon must have had an onion hidden in his hand.

As we took to the field, I was in my own zone, where everything felt nice and relaxed. Naturally I'd been nervous in the morning, but a few one-liners from Hennessy at breakfast and my old routine of going straight to the dressing-room showers and hitting the ball off the wall had made the butterflies disappear.

I'd been assigned to Eamonn Morrissey, who had been flying all summer. He'd scored six points from play in that year's Leinster final and a couple of points in every other game, and with D.J. playing out on the wing that year Morrissey was seen as the main threat. But again I made a good start. Though Morrissey was slightly ahead of me for the first two balls, I ended up dispossessing him both times and driving the ball up the field to a chorus of cheers. After that, Morrissey's head seemed to drop.

I started well on the frees, too, putting the first 65 straight over the bar. Then it began to rain. Before we'd gone out, Cunningham had told me to change the grip on my hurley, but at the time I'd figured that I didn't need the hassle of running around looking for some tape. But, of course, Cunningham was right; I should have changed my grip. When I was taking another 65, my hurley slipped in my hand and the ball went wide. And then there was the famous ball I won out on the wing, when, just as I cleared it down the field, my hurley went flying into the stand. I've met a thousand people since who claim I hit them with that hurley. At the time, though, all that mattered to me was that one of them threw it back in.

In general, the team had started well too. Hennessy and Fitzgibbon and Ger Fitzgerald mightn't have been as cohesive or as effective as they'd normally be, but Seanie Mac was on top in midfield, Teddy Mac and Tony Sull had popped over a few nice points from the wings, while at the back we were holding our men and our discipline. Then, just before half-time, the game changed. I've always had great time for Denis Walsh, one of the steadiest and most consistent defenders ever to play for Cork, but just when it looked as if their corner-forward, Jamesie 'Shiner' Brennan, was going nowhere, crouched over the ball with his back to goal, Denis pulled and, instead of hitting the ball, ended up hitting Brennan's ass. Penalty.

I was part of our goalline team and was fully tuned in for this shot. If there was something I'd learned earlier that summer, it was to be fully tuned in for a penalty. One night in training, Seanie McCarthy was practising penalties, and, because he was left-handed, the first nine shots were all aimed towards Jim Cashman's side. As he wound up to take the tenth shot, I thought I'd be just an ornament again. Instead, I was nearly hospitalised. Again, Seanie had rifled it but this time aimed the bullet for my side, and because I'd switched off it caught me right where it hurts. The next thing, I'd been lifted off the ground and was curled up in a little ball in the net. I'll never forget that dreadful sensation for as long as I live: the cold sweat pouring out of me, the pain down below and this awful longing to get sick. Suffice to say, when D.J. Carey stood up to take that penalty, I was on full alert.

Again, though, I was an ornament. Like Seanie, D.J. opted

to go to his left. There was little that Jim could have done with it. Although it wasn't the hardest shot, it was deceptive, as D.J. decided to avail himself of the wet surface and skid the ball off it. It meant that instead of being 0–7 to 0–2 up at half-time, we were now only two up, and Kilkenny had the wind for the second half.

They had an inspired John Power and Pat O'Neill too. O'Neill had hardly been in the game at the start but then got split and all bandaged and fired up after an innocuous clash with Tomás Mul. Power also came thundering into the game. Three minutes after the break, he tore through the middle and managed to kick the ball to the net. For the second time in five minutes, they'd scored a goal, and now they were ahead.

They'd stay ahead for the rest of the game. Michael Phelan had moved from midfield to full-forward, and when he half-hit one ball it went straight through the hands of Liam McCarthy, bounced off me and right back to McCarthy, who pulled and drove it past Cunningham. A Ger Manley goal cut the deficit to just a goal. But, when Adrian Ronan got a ball out on the wing and shot over his shoulder and over the bar, I muttered to myself, 'Today is not our day.'

I looked up towards the Canal End. The scoreboard read Kilkenny 19 (3–10) Cork 15 (1–12), and by my calculations the clock was saying there were just two minutes left. Those minutes were a countdown to misery, and when it ended all the Kilkenny fans up in that Canal End started streaming towards us. I looked at that big clock again. Some day, I thought, I want to see you once more on All Ireland final day and we'll have a countdown to victory. Then I looked up at the podium. And just like in '88 there was a Kilkenny man with the cup. Again, I had played very well, but again I was on the losing side. When, I thought, is the day I'll be up there with it?

The other lads were also devastated. Hennessy was particularly distraught. When John O'Shea of GOAL came in looking for volunteers to play the GOAL game in Kilkenny for the following Wednesday, Hennessy momentarily took his hands from his head. 'John, could you give us a few minutes, please? We've just lost an All Ireland final.' John slammed Kevin for that in the paper, saying there were worse things in life than losing All Ireland finals. But Kevin's despair was understandable. Deep down, he knew he wouldn't be back.

As it turned out, Cunningham and myself came around enough to play in that GOAL game. On Sunday night, though, I wasn't in the mood for anything, certainly not the banquet. As much as I was proud of my own performance, I kept thinking, 'Eamonn Morrissey was taken off, but he's got an All Ireland and I haven't.' The following morning, the mood was even worse. Tony O'Sullivan and his wife have reminded me since of how suicidal I looked. But later that morning, in the lobby of the Burlington, an Erins Own supporter, a Mrs McGregor, saw me going around with my pout and said, 'Look, the All Ireland is gone. But there's still a county for Erins Own there.'

She was right. One adventure had ended but another was about to start.

THE NIGHT MIDLETON WON THE HARTY CUP IN 1988, a local video cameraman, Brendan Barry, went around the table as we were having our meal in the Midleton Park Hotel, asking us each to say something to the camera. I referred to my club, saying that hopefully we'd win a senior county in the next couple of years. There were giggles all around me. Erins Own? Win a county? Was I joking or what? And I suppose I was. The club had just won the intermediate championship the previous autumn, but we were light years away from winning a senior.

At the start of '92, we weren't even dreaming of winning one. In fact, we were seriously considering dropping back to intermediate. We'd only won one championship game since coming back up in '88 – mere cannon fodder for the likes of Blackrock, the Glen and, most galling of all, Sars. It was even put to a motion at the club's AGM at the end of '91 – intermediate was our level, our grade.

Ultimately, it was defeated. A few weeks earlier, we'd won the East Cork Under-21 final, beating our old rivals Midleton. Our group of young fellas had been deprived of playing in the county championship because Midleton had already been nominated to represent East Cork, and the feeling in the club was that they shouldn't now be denied a shot at senior. So, we stayed senior, but by April that decision was looking foolhardy. In a league game that month, St Finbarr's destroyed us 3–20 to 1–6. The first round of the county against the Glen was fast approaching. Another humiliation seemed only weeks away.

Somehow it was averted. Instead, we were eight up at half-time. Once the second half started, though, the Glen clawed their way back, and, as the game entered the closing seconds, they were back on level terms. Then Christy Ring junior was straight through on goal. The easy option, the obvious option, would have been to take his point, but Ring, being a Ring, was thinking only goal. He let fire a bullet, one I'm convinced only two men in the county at the time could have stopped, and thankfully one of them was in goals for us that night. Somehow, Raymond 'Razor' O'Connor, Cian's uncle, deflected the shot, the ball was cleared and the ref blew the final whistle. As I walked off the field, one of the Glen selectors came out roaring at Christy for not taking his point. 'You should be glad you have your draw,' Christy said back to him. 'We didn't even deserve one, let alone a win.' Christy was right. But so was the selector. In the replay, we again built up a decent lead, and this time didn't let it go. We'd dumped the mighty Glen out of the championship, the biggest win in the history of the club.

After that, we hurled without a worry or care in the world.

THIRST FOR SUCCESS
With the East Cork Under-12 Cup in 1984

BROTHERLY DISPLAY
My brother John and myself, showing off our
medal and trophy collection in 1984

THE WONDER YEARS
Away from it all in 1985 – and yes, I did set him free again

AMONG MY OWN
Down in the Erins Own club pitch with Timmy Lambe, Shay Bowen,
Martin Bowen, Christy Twohig, Humphrey Collins, Eoghan O'Connor,
Sean Twohig, Brendan Lambe, Tim Sheehan and Kieran Murphy
(courtesy of *Imokilly People*)

CLASH OF THE TITANS

Playing Seamus Moynihan (above) in the 1990 Munster minor football final (courtesy of *Southern Star*), while (below) myself and Pat Fox watch Denis Mulcahy and Cormac Bonnar square off in the 1992 Munster semi-final (courtesy of *Irish Examiner*)

CLASS OF '92
The men I won my first Munster senior medal with (above), and the men I
won the 1992 Cork senior county championship with (below)

FOR THE PRIDE OF THE PARISH
Scrambling for possession in Erins Own's historic 1992
county final win over Na Piarsaigh (above), and clearing our lines
in our 1994 junior county football final win over Kiskeam (below)
(both photos courtesy of *Irish Examiner*)

ALL STARS
Receiving my All Star in 1992 from the then Taoiseach Albert
Reynolds and GAA president Peter Quinn (courtesy of Sportsfile)

MORGAN'S ARMY
The Cork football team that played Derry in the
1993 All Ireland final (courtesy of Sportsfile)

BRINGING IT ALL BACK HOME
John and myself holding the 1994 Cork junior football title,
with our sister, Ann, my father, John, and mother, Nuala

STAR IN THE MAKING
With my good friend and future teammate
Tom Kenny in 1995, when he was 14

GAME FACE
With the Cork footballers in 1996
(© INPHO/Lorraine O'Sullivan)

BREAKTHROUGH
Nothing was going to stop me from winning my first
All Ireland medal in 1999 – not even D.J. Carey and John Power
(courtesy of *Irish Examiner*)

It was never as if we were on a mission, just one big, happy, exciting adventure. In the next round, we brushed aside the challenge of UCC, setting up a semi-final against the East Cork divisional team, Imokilly. Joe Deane, Donal Óg, Timmy and Sully were still a few years too young to play for them, but by this stage Seanie O'Leary had started to organise them into a serious unit, while they could call on county players like Cathal Casey and Denis Walsh from St Catherine's as well as players from every junior and intermediate club in the division. And, just like the first game against the Glen, it was desperately close, with us two points up in the closing seconds when their full-forward Philip Cahill hit a rasper of a shot only for it to come back off the crossbar. Again, we'd survived, and now all of a sudden we were watching Fr O'Callaghan standing on top of the dressing-room table, proclaiming, 'We're on our way to the county final!' – the cue for a roar that shook the room.

No one was as surprised as ourselves to be on that journey, so, while we were there, we soaked it all up. Looking back on the build-up to that final, it was a wonderful, innocent time, full of days to be treasured: the lads smiling and talking away while being interviewed and photographed at the press night; the buzz in our own house, with mum making the flags and woollen wristbands around the clock; the other mothers and neighbours making sure there was tea and sandwiches for the media that night and for us after training every other night; going around to the primary schools with their flags and songs.

No one was enjoying the adventure as much as I was. As well as I had hurled with Cork, I'd felt confined, restricted, stifled at corner-back. With Erins Own, I was back up in the forwards, and it was almost as if I was playing another sport. I no longer had to be watching or stopping someone else; I just had to watch the ball and dare someone to stop me. I was thriving in it and, heading into the final, was averaging nine points a game.

The rest of the team was an intriguing mix of ages, standards and personalities. In goal was Razor, a pure natural. He'd played centre-forward for Cork in the '77 All Ireland minor final against Kilkenny. Over the years, he started to put on a few pounds, but even when he hit his 30s he was too gifted not to be accommodated. When his older brother Mickey O, the sub keeper to Martin Coleman on the Cork All Ireland winning team of '76, retired in the winter of '91, Razor took over between the posts. He was a revelation there. He mightn't have held a hurley from the end of one championship to the start of the next, yet in his first night back training you still couldn't get a ball past him.

Outside him was Brian O'Shea, our full-back. Brian was one of the wonders of the world. He could get cleaned out in training, and get cleaned out in league games, but always rose to the challenge in championship. It helped that he had Colman Dillon and Damien Long alongside him. Colie was a fantastic, tidy hurler and did a lot of sweeping up, while Longy was a teak-tough corner-back who never gave an inch.

I'd say we had the smallest half-back line in Ireland that year, but also the best. Timmy Kelleher was in the centre. On one wing, we had Tony O'Keeffe, who'd played with John on the Cork minor team of '86, while on the other we had Colie's brother John. In midfield, we had Frank and Kieran Horgan, with Paul Geasley alongside me and John in the half-forwards. Matt Nicholl had played all his hurling either at full-back or corner-back, but now he found himself up at corner-forward. In the other corner was one of our selectors, P.J. Murphy, who was 35 by this time. Alongside him, we had big Barry O'Neill, whose first sport was rugby.

Na Piarsaigh, meanwhile, had Tony O'Sullivan and Mickey Mullins and a glut of other players who'd either played or would play with Cork at some grade or another, such as Chris Connery, Paul O'Connor, Mark Mullins and Leonard Forde. Together, they'd won the county in 1990 and, after missing out the following year, were expected to walk it again now in '92. No one was giving us a chance, ourselves included.

If no one was tipping us, everyone was cheering for us. When we ran out that day, I was more taken by the crowd than by the previous month's in Croke Park. The whole place seemed to be a sea of blue and red. Normally, you'd get ten or twelve thousand at a county final, but there were at least twenty thousand here.

People say that I was totally in the zone that day, just because I finished with ten points, five from play. But much of the game bypassed me, and, at the start in particular, the ball seemed to go everywhere I wasn't. Then, when I did finally manage to get my first touch and first point from play, I missed two frees. When we won another a few minutes later, one of the lads suggested that I should maybe leave it to my brother John. I decided to chance it, though. It was from the exact same spot as the previous two, sixty yards out, slightly right of the goal, into the Blackrock End, and I knew it was just a matter of slightly readjusting my alignment. That third free did go straight over, and after that I didn't miss another one.

Shortly after that free, I won a ball out on the right wing, out by the covered stand. Running at speed, I shot over my shoulder, off my right, without looking at the posts. It was one of those moments when everything around you seems to be in slow motion. It's like you have all the time in the world to shoot and you know exactly where the posts are. Denis Walsh, the prominent hurling writer, would say it was the kind of shot 'a bad player would have been killed for trying and a good player would have too much sense to contemplate'. Jimmy Barry-Murphy would state I'd been 'mad' to go for it, but once I did I didn't even have to look up to know it was going over the bar. I finished crashing into the wired perimeter, and when I looked up in the stand I could see an old schoolmate, Seanie Barry, from our old east Cork rivals Carrigtwohill, and the rest of the stand on their feet.

Midway through the first half, big Barry at full-forward had given them something to shout about when he got in for a goal to put us three points up. All of a sudden, it was as if you could hear everyone in the Park thinking, 'Erins Own are in with a shout here.' At half-time, our trainer Billy Hegarty and P.J. and Ned Flynn drilled it home that we could win and should not be afraid of or surprised about winning. At half-time the first day against the Glen, we'd nearly been in a state of shock that we were so far ahead and duly invited the Glen to come back and very nearly win. We weren't going to make that mistake again here.

Instead, Na Piarsaigh were the ones who were stunned. They'd obviously never envisaged being behind to Erins Own after half-time. You could tell because they started to panic. Even though they were only a few points behind, they began to go for goals from way out the field when there was still a good quarter of an hour to go. They laid siege to our goal in those closing minutes. Balls were landing down and being dropped and then cleared off the line. Big Brian O'Shea would go to pick a ball and it would hang in the air, as if in slow motion, and, just as four Na Piarsaigh hurleys would go in to flick it away, Brian would catch it and clear it down the field. What seemed like an eternity later, with us clinging on, 1–12 to 0–12, nearly the whole ground was whistling, urging the ref to do the same, and the supporters were climbing over the wire, ready to sprint onto the pitch. And then the ref finally took their advice, and all hell broke loose.

My immediate feeling was one of delight, but it wasn't any more moving or intense than, say, a Munster or Harty Cup with the minors or Midleton CBS; it was just another cup to be won. But then, when I got over to the stand side, it hit me what this all meant. Razor was being hugged by his brother Mickey O, Cian's father. Mickey O had played senior with the club for 20 years. Now, the one year he had packed it up, we'd won the county, with his brother wearing the jersey he used to wear. I saw other retired players, hardy boys like Tom Aherne, who'd captained the club when we'd won the intermediate in '84, hugging and crying in each other's arms. My uncle D.D. came running out, tears pouring down his face, to hug me.

Then I was hugging John. John my brother; John who the doctors said would never hurl again. A moment like that, you can't put into words. I'd say we must have been on that field for half an hour, going around hugging everyone and them hugging us back. When I say all hell broke loose, I should really say heaven did. There's a great picture we have at home of my uncle D.D. and Billy Hegarty out on that pitch. D.D. and Billy would have had a few run-ins over the years, but in this photo the two of them have an arm around each other, with the other arm out giving a big thumbs-up. All is forgiven; all is forgotten; all is fine in the world.

When we finally came out of Páirc Uí Chaoimh, an open-top bus was outside. Na Piarsaigh had booked one, and now it was all dressed up with nowhere to go. We hadn't even thought of organising one, for the simple reason we hadn't even thought of winning. All we'd organised was for a meal in the old Ashbourne Hotel. As it turned out, I didn't even get inside the Ashbourne that night. The whole of east Cork seemed to be crammed in there, while I was perfectly happy to stay outside. It was a mild, pleasant October night. I didn't drink, while a lot of my younger friends, like Tom Aherne's sons Ronan and Shane, and Tom and Claire and Edward Kenny, were too young to.

A few weeks later, it looked as if our dream year could get even better. We were five points up early in the second half of the Munster club championship semi-final against Kilmallock. And then I broke my collarbone. Kilmallock ended up forcing a replay, and they would win that replay, while I'd watch that game and attend my graduation out in the Regional Tech in a sling.

I was out of the sling by the time of the All Stars, though, and when I picked up the Texaco Hurler of the Year award the following January. The reports at the time said I was the youngest player to win that honour and only the third player to win it who wasn't from that year's All Ireland champions – two records that still hold today. That winter, there didn't seem to be a week that would go by when I wasn't picking up some kind of award. 'We're going to have to build an extension to house them all,' Mum said to one of the papers the morning we heard I'd be winning the Texaco.

As disappointing as those defeats to Kilkenny and Kilmallock had been, it had been some year.

I'd have to wait a long time to have a year like it again.

CHAPTER SEVEN
EVERY SINGLE BALL

'Gentlemen, we have our team now. We have the men we're going with, the men who have a chance to bring this club a third consecutive world championship. If you succeed, you will never forget this year for the rest of your lives. Gentlemen, this is the beginning of the big push'

VINCE LOMBARDI, FROM JERRY KRAMER'S *INSTANT REPLAY*

TUESDAY, 9 MAY 2006

Our big push started tonight. John Allen called a meeting for quarter past six and told us it's now seventeen weeks to the All Ireland final. Whatever we have to do between now and then to get there, we're to do it; Cork has to be first for Cork to come first. Seanie and Jerry reminded us just why we're to take our heart rates, why we do the warm-ups and warm-downs, why we eat and drink what we eat and drink before and during games, why there's no point in fellas dodging the ice baths or hopping in once for 20 seconds instead of carrying out the routine fully. There can be no excuses; if we're ever in doubt, we're to consult the 20-page booklet they gave us tonight on the science behind our training methods.

It was our first night back in Páirc Uí Rinn. So far this year, we haven't had training either there or at Páirc Uí Chaoimh, but for the rest of the year now we'll mostly be training there. Our summer gear also arrived tonight. Waiting for each of us as we walked into the dressing-room were a jersey, shorts and socks, all laid out. From now on, we will all wear the same gear in training. All we have to worry about are our own hurley, helmet and boots. Jimmy McEvoy has seen to it that even towels are now provided – another way of underlining that everything has to be that bit better this year.

After Seanie and Jerry spoke, John threw it open to the floor what tactics we might use for the year. We then all gathered our chairs around our Subbuteo board and fellas started moving casino chips around the place like Andy Gray on Sky Sports.

It's an exercise that has served us well. The week before last year's All Ireland final, we had a retreat down in Inchydoney, where we discussed what kind of ball we should play into the full-forward line. Up to then, everything had been directed down the channels. If John Gardiner got a ball, he was to play it down the wing instead of cross field, where there was a greater chance of it being intercepted. The problem was that this tactic became predictable: after the first two balls, opposing corner-backs could tell where Gardiner was looking to send it. For the final, we decided to go for variety. John had a free licence. If he noticed I was open, he could hit me instead of belting it down to Kieran 'Fraggy' Murphy every time.

We then talked about how we had kept getting caught in possession against Clare in the semi-final. John Allen has often reminded us that it's a support game, not a possession game, we play, but against Clare we had forgotten to make that distinction. The game plan had always been to get quality ball into the full-forward line quickly, just not hastily. If that meant making the odd pass back or solo run to avoid hitting it under pressure and having it land down on Joe's head, then taking that extra bit of time was fine. Somewhere along the line, though, lads had started to look to make that extra pass or solo run for the sake of it. Instead of getting the ball to someone, preferably a half-back, who could look up and place the ball in front of Joe, myself or Fraggy, fellas were trying to play it ten yards up to the half-forward line for the half-forward line then to play it up to us. That needless delay was leading to fellas being tied up.

Joe and myself suggested that maybe the best way to bring the half-forward line into the game was to get the ball into us first and we could then throw it back out to the half-forwards. I mentioned how in one drill the previous week I had found myself in the full-back spot with Timmy McCarthy running straight at me after taking a return pass from Sully, who was playing full-forward. The only way I could have stopped Timmy was to foul him. He had momentum; I was static. So, instead of Timmy and the other half-forwards always having to win their own ball and run with it head down, lads were now to hit the full-forward line which, in turn, could feed the incoming half-forwards.

And if you look back at that 2005 All Ireland final, that's how some of our first-half scores transpired. I came out and won a ball, gave it out to Niall, who was running through, and then broke past his man to point. Then I laid off another ball to Ben, who blitzed past his marker for another score. Those points were born on the Subbuteo board.

John is the key to all this. He's been an inspired replacement for O'Grady: he consults, dictates, manages, leads as the occasion demands. He realises that, at this point in the life cycle of the team, the players have the maturity to make contributions and decisions. But, as much as we can have our say, we all know that John has the final say. In one meeting last year, we were debating how to defend sideline balls and who should be the free man. Ronan Curran was arguing that if they had a midfielder taking the cut he should run back to the square because he was taller than Jerry and that Jerry could take up the centre-forward. Sully disagreed: Jerry should stay the free man and be the one to go back into the square, and Curran should stay on the centre-forward. Back and forth it went until John said, 'Look, we'll keep it simple. Ronan, you stick to your man. Jerry, you go back.'

This evening, John adopted a more facilitative style, especially when we were talking about puckouts. Last year, Donal Óg would give a signal and everyone knew where they were to go and where the ball was to go, or at least where it could go; each player still had the option to go down another channel if he saw something better on there. The thing is, we used the same signals for all five games, and, with us winning the All Ireland, teams will now be wise to our moves. Tonight, the question was whether to come up with a new signalling system or have none at all. We've decided to go with a new one and to try out two puckouts that we didn't use last year.

The meeting lasted about 45 minutes. When it was over, we ran downstairs and about 16 of us trained. The rest were either injured or had to rush off to meet up with their clubs. While we in Erins Own beat Sars at the weekend, Blackrock and Castlelyons and Na Piarsaigh still have club championship games to play this week. It wasn't exactly ideal, but then that's the way it has been for the last few years up until the end of May. By Thursday, there'll be no more club games this side of the Clare match. We had a good workout, the 16 of us who trained. And everyone made it to the meeting.

We all know now what we have to do. We all know the big push has started.

FRIDAY, 12 MAY

I felt sorry for John McIntyre tonight. We absolutely destroyed his Offaly team in a challenge game in Templemore, 3–20 to 0–8. Coming off, Ger Oakley shook hands with me and said, 'Sorry we didn't give ye a better game,' but McIntyre was even more embarrassed when he came into our dressing-room.

'Lads,' he said, 'first of all, I want to apologise for our display tonight. We thought we were going to come down and give ye a serious game . . . We told them at half-time they were a disgrace and sure the second half was even worse! I don't know, lads. We're just back from five days in Portugal, and maybe fellas were a bit tired, but . . . to be honest, lads, I'm shell-shocked. It's as if since the league game ye've gone from here to up here, and we've gone from here to down here. Ye won't have it that easy against Clare, lads, I can tell you that. Jesus, we won't beat Laois the way we played.'

Now, in a way, John's stream of consciousness didn't surprise us. He came in after the league game as well and must have spoken for nearly ten minutes. 'We knew the All Ireland champions were coming here for the last four months and we trained for it this past four months, lads. Ye're the benchmark, but fuck it, lads, we weren't going to let ye away easy today! Because hurling needs a strong Offaly, lads; you know that yourselves . . .' He's clearly a passionate hurling man. And a sincere man. Any man who visits us after the hiding his team got tonight deserves respect.

It's a hard thing to do, go into a losing dressing-room after a game, especially a championship. Ger Loughnane was very magnanimous in defeat when he visited our dressing-room after the '99 Munster final. So was Anthony Daly after we beat Clare in last year's All Ireland semi-final. They went up in my estimation after that. Brian Cody, a man I have great respect for, was also exceptionally gracious after we beat Kilkenny in 1999 and 2004.

Not all managers can face it, though. Justin McCarthy doesn't do it whether he wins or loses, which is fine. It's the guys who turn up after victory but remain absent after defeat who annoy me. In 1993, Páidí Ó Sé was over the Kerry Under-21s when they beat us down in the Park. Afterwards, a big crowd had gathered outside the dressing-rooms when Páidí strutted through with a towel around his waist, chest out, before giving us the usual spiel about Kerry's respect for Cork. The following year, he was still in charge when we went down to Tralee and beat them. This time, there was no towel, no chest out, no Páidí. In fairness to Páidí, though, I've heard he's changed and was very gracious after Kerry lost to Kildare in '98, and to Armagh in 2002.

The strange thing about tonight, it was actually a hard, dogged game in heavy conditions. In the first half, I got a goal and set up two others, but I still had my hands full with their young full-back Paul Cleary. By half-time, I was knackered. Walking off the field, I said to Seanie McGrath, 'I feel like getting sick.' I was at a conference in Kilkenny yesterday and again earlier today, and when I had a few hours to spare I decided to have lunch in one of my favourite spots in the world, Mount Juliet. Between the meal there and the sandwiches down in the Anner Hotel in Thurles listening to Sully talk about the Roy Keane testimonial he was at the other night, I possibly overdid it.

Thankfully, Mount Juliet's finest cuisine didn't come back up, but Cleary beat me out to nearly every ball in the second half. I've made serious progress since we last played Offaly, but I still have work to do. On my way home, I stopped off outside Thurles for a bottle of water. When I got back into the car, I had a text message from Tom Kenny. 'Spotted! What are the cones like?' I won't know, Tom, until 28 May. Then I can have ice cream in Thurles.

SUNDAY, 14 MAY

Only two weeks to the Clare match now, but as John Allen pretty much said to us before we started at nine this morning, it's not a matter of counting the days but making the days count. I'll be taking that advice. Two years ago, O'Grady gave us all notebooks and told us to write down after every session and every match three things we did well and three things we didn't do so well. Those weaknesses were then to form the basis of our goals for the following weeks and months. To this day, some lads still use the notebooks. I did it for about two weeks, then realised *an muinteóir* wasn't really going to follow up on his threat to check if we were doing our homework. I did it mentally, though, and still do, and right now I have targeted two goals.

The first is my striking off my left while running away from goal – something I worked on this morning. The second is my speed off the mark – something reinforced by how often Cleary beat me out to the ball the other night. This morning, Seanie broke us into pairs. A belt was tied around my waist and Conor Cusack was at the other end pulling the band until it was taut. Then Seanie would say 'Go!', Conor would pull and I'd start running towards him. Seanie had me using it a lot last year too. The spring effect trains my legs to move faster and gets me to run on my toes, as I'm more naturally flat-footed. I felt I was getting quicker as this morning's session went on, but I'll be seeing plenty of that band this summer as well, I'd say.

Session over, it's straight into the ice baths. I squat into the wheelie-bin, making sure I'm covered from my waist down. 'No,' says Seanie McGrath, 'sit in fully! Arms down!'

'Seanie, it's only my legs that need it. Sure, if I sit down fully, I won't be able to get up.'

'Yeah,' goes Kelly, watching on, 'he'll rust.'

TUESDAY, 16 MAY

I don't know if it's that we're flying or Wexford are in freefall, but we hammered them in Thurles tonight; the score was something like 6–20 to 0–16 in the end. I could sense from the moment I met up with the lads in the Anner after driving down from Cashel that everyone was up for it, knowing it would be our last game before Clare. Even at half-time, when we were cruising, Donal Óg told us we still had plenty to work on in the second half. We would now be playing with the wind into the town end. Had we forgotten how we had played with the wind into that end in the second half of the Munster final two years ago against Waterford? He'd be going more direct with his puckout, all right, but we weren't just to use the wind for the sake of it. This second half was a test to see how much we had progressed from that Waterford match, a test of our discipline and capacity to stick to our game plan. It was only in the closing minutes that we eased off. John took off four of the backs, and Wexford got five or six points on the trot.

I had come off myself by that stage. At half-time, Con told me the selectors wanted to take me off there and then, but I felt I needed the game, so John came over and said he'd give me another 15 minutes but that there'd be no point in risking me after that. Murphy's Law, of course, ten minutes later my legs were taken from under me. I could feel a slight strain in my knee, but even though I got up and seemed to run it off, John wasn't taking any more chances.

I'm happy enough with how I went tonight. I got a goal after about ten minutes, set up another and helped make a few others by dragging Doc O'Connor out the field and creating space for our half-forwards to come through. I have to work more on my shooting, though. Tonight, I got away from Doc, about 25 yards out on the right-hand side of the goal, turned onto my left and, running away from goal, shot.

I was falling back and trying to shorten the swing to avoid being hooked, and it curled outside the left post. I'm going to have to work on using my wrists a bit more and striking with greater conviction.

John must have been happy with the way guys were going tonight. In midfield, Tom and Jerry were on a pair of young fellas, yet left them for dead. The backs were amazing again, completely suffocating the Wexford attack. Curran especially is back to form. He is as good as any centre-back that has ever played the game. And upfront, Niall Mac looked very sharp; we need him going well on Seanie McMahon to win on Sunday week.

The talk of the dressing-room, though, is Cian O'Connor. Cathal Naughton scored four points when he came in against Offaly, but tonight he was suffering from an eye infection, so the selectors tried Cian on that wing, and he scored two goals and two points. With Ben doubtful, there's a real chance Cian might start against Clare. I thought the Erins Own selectors were mad trying him in the half-forwards earlier in the year, but maybe they were on to something after all.

Things are looking good. Well, at least they were until I ran into the dressing-room at the break looking to have a few Fruit Pastilles that Jimmy McEvoy said he would leave out for us. But there were none there, just two empty boxes. Next thing, Con strolls in, munching away. He's trying to tell me now that he didn't hear Jimmy say anything about Pastilles, that he never knew they were for the players. Yeah, right, Con.

THURSDAY, 18 MAY

The leg might have been OK on Tuesday, but it's not so fine now. Yesterday morning, before I headed to work, I ran down the driveway to open the gate and suddenly felt this sharp pain in my left knee. Declan O'Sullivan examined it tonight and told me that it's a strained medial ligament. 'You're lucky,' he said. 'You'll be grand for Sunday week, but you won't be able to train until Tuesday.' I was relieved to hear this, but I could have done with those three days of ballwork. Instead, tonight I was left doing these balancing exercises that Deccie designed for me to work on my leg.

We got our hydration results back tonight. The other week, before training, Seanie came in and, without warning, told us to do the necessary into a bottle and then do the same into another bottle after the session. It turns out I was actually more hydrated after training than I was before it, I had taken so much during that session, so I need to hydrate more during the day. That said, I'm still among the best in the group, judging by the group average he read out, and he was fairly satisfied with that group average. He's just trying to reinforce to us the importance of hydrating during the week, because it takes 72 hours really to hydrate properly. If you leave it to the weekend of a game and start drinking gallons, it'll just pass through, because the body isn't used to it.

My resting heart rate has come down too. In January, it was 64 beats a minute. This morning, it was 49. I'd say I'm fitter than I was going into the Waterford game this time last year. It's the ballwork I'm a bit worried about.

FRIDAY, 19 MAY

Deccie was missing tonight. He and Ben got marooned in Dublin after missing their flight back. They were up in the Mater Hospital about Ben's groin problem. The news was a bit better for Ben. He was feeling this pain, which was tolerable enough in itself, but his fear was that if he pushed it any more the pain would get worse. The surgeon has given him the all-clear, but he will more than likely need an operation in the off-season. It'll mean playing through the pain barrier in the meantime, but Ben's prepared to do that for Cork.

In fairness to Deccie, he hadn't forgotten about his other patients back home; he called Seanie with instructions on how to put me through some light straight-line running tonight. Seán Óg, Pat Mul and Niall Mac joined in for part of it. Seán Óg picked up a similar if less serious injury to me in the game against Wexford, and Pat took a knock against Offaly, while Niall was also nursing a leg complaint. There's no fear of any of us missing the Clare game, but under the regime we've had this past few years, if you have even the slightest niggle, Deccie won't let you train.

It wasn't the most strenuous workout. All I did was run up to the top, stop, turn around and run down again, time after time, barely breaking sweat. I can't say I enjoyed it; in fact, I was thinking during it, 'How does Sonia O'Sullivan do this for two or three hours a day? The boredom of it.' Thankfully, after about half an hour, Seanie told me to take an early shower.

In the dressing-room, Jimmy McEvoy, myself and Con were having a bit of *craic*. Last week, Jimmy asked each of us for a song for the team CD. Now we were looking through the track listing. There's some diversity there, from Dolores Keane's 'Caledonia', as chosen by Tom Kenny, to AC/DC's – and Sully's – 'Thunderstruck'. I'm glad there's a bit of Angus and the lads there; during the week, I was thinking I should have picked 'Heatseeker', but now that Sully picked what he did I'm happy enough with Nirvana's 'Smells Like Teen Spirit'. The one that we got the biggest kick out of, though, was Wayne Sherlock's 'Time to Say Goodbye', by Andrea Bocelli and Sarah Brightman. Says Con, 'Is Sherlock trying to tell us something?'

And, you know, you nearly wouldn't blame him for saying goodbye if he's not picked next week. He played wing-back against Offaly and was flying. The other night against Wexford, with Pat out, he came in at corner-back and was faultless again.

I said it to Cunningham that night: 'I don't know what you're going to do about the full-back line; how are you going to tell Sherlock he's not on the team?' He'd walk onto any other team in the country. Just think: the last championship game he started he won an All Ireland and an All Star for it, then he got injured and can't get back into the team. He's done absolutely everything that can be done to get back into that team and yet he still mightn't. That just shows you how good Brian Murphy and Pat Mul have been.

Sherlock won't walk, though. It's not in his nature. He just refuses to give in; he refuses to play the victim. Instead, he accepts it and comes in and trains even harder. He knows what we have is special. Everyone gets along. There was one time last year in training, all right, where Sully had a shouting match with Gardiner, but it was then forgotten about. The fact I can remember that just shows you how isolated a case it was. Here you encourage, not lambaste. Even when we're doing drills or playing a game in training and Sully hooks me, I'll say, 'Good hook, Sull,' and vice versa.

I don't know what you call that something special we have. Pat Riley, the NBA basketball coach, would call it innocence. He says it's the first quality any championship team must have. There's a huge difference between innocence and naivety, he says. Naivety means being gullible, a pushover, but the problem is that people get over that very quickly and go to the other extreme of the Disease of Me. Too many teams, he says, have too many players afflicted with the Disease of Me, constantly playing the victim, feeling the world is against them and owes them. The opposite of that, says Riley, is innocence. 'Innocence is about trust in a team. It's an attitude, a leap of faith, the sense that doing your most for the team will always bring something good for you, that everything you deserve will eventually come your way.'

Riley would say that Sherlock personifies innocence. He

doesn't calculate before he gives; he continues to give and give and give to the team, for the team. He gave a speech before last year's final, saying that, though it was killing him not to be starting, he was 100 per cent behind the cause. It'll be the same case next week, if it comes to it.

But, like I've said, I don't know how that can happen; I don't know how they can leave him out.

SUNDAY, 21 MAY

Deccie was back out on the pitch this morning, and he hates me for it; he says only for me he could have been enjoying the shelter of the dressing-room. Right enough, it's hard to believe it's May. Westmeath and Dublin were on the telly this evening, and it was more like water polo than hurling. How that game was allowed to be played, I don't know, let alone that Offaly and Laois played on the same pitch right after. Páirc Uí Rinn was practically waterlogged as well. I was jogging up and down the sideline, and there were puddles of water all around me. I've never seen the pitch in such a state before.

Thankfully, the knee is in better shape than the pitch. While the rest of the lads trained away, Deccie had me negotiating these cones. It meant a lot of twisting and turning and kicking off either foot, but the knee passed the test. Deccie has this thing of calling people 'Horse', and today I heard the magic words, 'You're good to go on Tuesday, Horse.'

TUESDAY, 23 MAY

John called a meeting for quarter past six this evening, but by the time I got down from work in Cashel it was six-twenty. The rest of the lads were togged off, watching footage of Clare. It was obvious from the conversation that followed what the footage was about: the Clare forwards favour their left side, most of the puckouts are aimed at Diarmuid McMahon and their wing-forwards like to make cross-field runs.

Seán Óg and Gardiner did a good deal of the talking, because they're the two that will be most affected by those runs. Seán Óg recalled how in the 2004 All Ireland semi-final Wexford's wing-forwards each sprinted across the full width of the pitch for every puckout and after 20 minutes were absolutely knackered. Seán Óg, though, was full of running, because he'd only go halfway across with his man, then leave him off and take up the other wing-forward coming across. He'll be doing the same on Sunday, if it arises; himself and Gardiner will swap at the centre-forward spot if the two wing-forwards both make cross-field runs. In other words, they'll be playing more of a zonal defence rather than marking them in the old, conventional man-to-man way.

Seán Óg did point out, though, that what Clare might try to do is get McMahon to go across but keep the other wing-forward over on his own wing, creating a possible two-on-one on that wing. The plan for Sunday is that if your man starts to cross over and the other wing-forward is coming against you, go to the middle, turn and take that other wing-forward up; otherwise keep following your own man.

John Allen then pointed out that he wanted our half-forward line to drop back for the Clare puckouts to minimise the space for the Clare half-forwards to run into. Last year, Curran had been exposed, and balls were landing right in front of the Clare half-forwards. This year, John wants to block those avenues and force Fitzy to play it high and long for the entire game, which should favour our half-backs. Everyone agreed. When John proposed that our full-forward line push out to the half-forward line, I suggested that I stay in, standing on the 20-metre line with my hurley up, so Fitzy has to at least get it over me, whereas if I stand back 40 yards from him he can drill a low ball out the field. John accepted my point, so we've decided that I'll stay in, but Fraggy and Joe will go out.

Once we got out on the field, John reiterated our motto for the year: *Gach Uile Liathróid* – Every Single Ball. He has this banner posted up on the dressing-room wall that the kids in his school drew up in big, colourful letters. *Gach Uile Liathróid*. It makes sense. He's often told us before, proper preparation equals performance, so we have to be tuned in for every single ball in training as well as in matches. We can't ever decide to take it handy, even in the warm-up.

And yet what do we immediately go and do? A few minutes into this four corners diagonal passing drill and Jerry Wallis is having to blow his whistle and call us in. 'Lads, not good enough! Too many fellas dropping balls; too many fellas not concentrating; too much talk; too sloppy. Now, we're going to start again. And we're going to keep starting again until fellas get it right.' And this time we do. Everyone is clued in to every single ball, and we go on to have a great session.

When we're finished, John calls us in to name the team. We are pretty sure of 13 or 14 of the team, so Cian's is the name I'm listening out for. When John comes to wing-forward, he names Ben. I look at Cian; he seems unmoved. John says, 'I'll come back to that,' and names the rest of the team. It turns out that team is just the one that will be going to the papers. He then names the actual team that will be going into battle. Ben won't be risked from the start; Cian will be on. John has already told both of them that. All the lads head straight for Cian to offer their congratulations. I do too and tell him he's earned the right to start, that it's probably best, given the spotlight that followed Garvan McCarthy when he was thrown in for the 2004 Munster final, that the papers don't know he's going to start. Next thing, Kelly is over too, and I joke that it's a bad sign when Cork have two Erins Own backs playing in the forwards.

We wouldn't get a game in the backs anyhow. Not even Wayne Sherlock can. I meant to go over to him after the team was picked, but between having the word with Cian and then going in to get my tickets from Jerry O'Sullivan, I didn't. Anyway, what could I have said? What could the selectors have said? But somehow they told him; somehow they left him out.

THURSDAY, 25 MAY

I hit the field half an hour early tonight. Neil Ronan notices. 'You're early,' he smiles.

'I need the practice.'

'Why do you think I was here at six?'

As if Neil needs the extra practice; his shooting is like radar.

He goes behind the goals and pucks balls out to me. Then Kelly and Seán Óg come out. They go behind the goal, with Kelly hitting balls out to Neil and Seán Óg cutting balls out to me. I hit every ball off my left, backing away, because nine times out of ten you shoot at this level, you're shooting off balance, over your shoulder. I'm getting the strike I want. It's come on a lot in the last two weeks.

After the session, John calls us together. He shows us our shorts for Sunday. Usually they have 'Corcaigh' printed on them, but this year he has decided to go with 'Corcaíoch'. It means 'Man of Cork'. We're proud to be men of Cork. Hopefully that's what we'll be on Sunday evening.

FRIDAY, 26 MAY

Tonight, we did what we do the Friday before every championship match: we had a dry run through our routine. It starts off in the dressing-room: 'Right, lads, we're going out on the field in a minute.' We go out in our training gear, run down towards our goal, hit a ball and then come back to the bench for the photograph to get it out of the way early. Tonight, Patsy Morrissey is the snapper. Then we go back towards the goal, with each forward paired with a back. I'm with Sully. He keeps feeding me balls, and I keep knocking them over.

Two minutes later, we break up into our warm-up grids. We have three of them: one for the backs, one for the forwards and one for the subs. I'm with Niall Mac in the red grid. We start off pucking along the ground to each other, then into each other's hand. Seanie calls us to come in closer and to start hitting the ball harder, then we go back out further again. Everything is timed to the last minute. Tonight, Seanie tells us that, as of now, there isn't a minute's silence scheduled for Sunday; it'll be straight into the anthem. We don't go as far as the parade or the anthem, though; instead, we stop at the warm-up and then go and get some more shooting practice in.

After a few minutes, John blows the whistle and says we've done enough. He says he wants us wanting more, and the more is Sunday.

It makes sense, John's decision to keep the session short. Then again, so did O'Grady's to have them longer. In 2004, after the photo and warm-up, he'd go through a series of scenarios. We'd even go through where we were to be positioned for a throw-in. He wanted us to establish a T-formation, with the ref forming the bottom spot, a Cork player either side of the pair in the clash and another Cork player behind the clash. On one occasion in that year's All Ireland, we had no one behind the clash. D.J. picked up the break uncontested. It drove O'Grady berserk. Even later in the week, amidst all the celebrations, he'd remind us of it.

We still follow many of O'Grady's pre-championship rituals, though. After the warm-down, we walk to the bottom corner of the field for our players' meeting. Again, there are two speakers:

first, the year's captain, then our resident speaker, Donal Óg. The theme is to be ready for anything Clare throw at us. Donal Óg says that if they want to drag us down into the gutter like they did in '98 we'll go down with them and fight our way out. Pat makes the same point, and we know he means it. When we were in Cape Town, Pat wandered into the wrong part of town, and some guy pulled a knife out at him. Pat pointed at his chest, saying, 'Come on!' The guy turned and ran. We're to have the same approach on Sunday. Bring it on.

At the same time, Pat stresses the importance of discipline. Clare are big men, a good team, a physical team, and it's going to be a right battle. But, whatever happens, we're to keep to our game plan, keep our discipline, uphold the motto we had last year: *Ceannairceach féin Smacht* – Rebels be Disciplined.

He then mentions this year's motto. Before we go out on Sunday, we're all going to get a stamp on our arms with the letters GUL, an idea John and the player reps – Gardiner, Tom, Donal Óg and Pat himself – came up with. 'If there's a moment on Sunday where you're knackered,' Pat says, 'have a look at it. Know there's 29 other fellas with that on their arm who are fighting for you and who you're fighting for. Fight for them, fight for yourself, fight for *Gach Uile Lliathróid.*'

Donal Óg has the last word. He reminds us of a point Seanie made earlier in the week. 'We've been listening to everyone say that Clare let us off the hook last year. Lads, we're the ones that let them off the hook, by not playing for 55 minutes and giving them false hope that they're as good as us. They're not. Let's show that on Sunday.'

He's right. Maybe we have given them false hope. After the semi-final last year, I was talking to Lohan up in the players' lounge, and he was thinking of retiring. Seanie McMahon was, too. They have given Clare incredible service, along with Colin Lynch, Frank Lohan, Davy Fitz and Anthony Daly. If we had beaten them by eight points, they might have all retired. But then they saw this hope. They started to think, 'We should have beaten Cork. We're not that far away. Let's give it one more shot.' And they've been right to. I'll be honest, I'm a bit apprehensive about Sunday; we've had our problems with Clare. But at the same time I'm more confident than worried. We feel we didn't perform last year. We want to show that Clare didn't let it slip last year, that we're the better team, that we're the champions.

SATURDAY, 27 MAY

I've spent a lot of today just chasing my tail – between work and organising and delivering tickets. I've been drinking a lot of water too. I drank about six litres yesterday and around the same again today. Unlike two months ago, my hydration will be right for this Clare game.

I've been told that the press are making a big deal out of Curran and myself being taken off last year, saying that Lohan destroyed me that day, and tomorrow I'll be all out to avenge that. Call it the Stuart Anderson in me, but I actually didn't feel I was beaten by Lohan last year. Before I damaged my shoulder midway through the first half, I felt we had broken even. He caught two balls, all right, causing the crowd to give this big roar, but he was inside the square for them, so I couldn't challenge him. If that kind of ball went into a Cork square, Donal Óg would claim it himself. Davy left them to Lohan. Then a ball broke, and I went down to pick it. I had damaged my AC (acromioclavicular) joint in the Munster final against Tipp, but it felt fine against Waterford in the All Ireland quarter-final, or so I thought. I didn't get any tackle on it that day, but I did against Clare. As I was holding Lohan off, he swung across me three times towards his own goal. The third swing blew my shoulder forward, and right away I knew I was in trouble.

I turned around to Dickie Murphy. 'Dickie, what do you have to do to get a fuckin' free around here?'

'He was playing the ball!' said Dickie.

'Dickie, he doesn't need three bloody swings to hit the ball.'

I should have gone off there and then. Every time I took a step, I got a piercing pain up through my neck. Con wanted to take me off at half-time, but, not for the first time in my life, I was too stubborn to listen. 'Don't take me off, Con! I'll be fine!'

John gave me another ten minutes or so, but it was no use. I was like a bear in that dugout, not because of how I played, but because I thought we were gone. Then Sherlock stepped into the heat of battle as if he had never been away from it. Gardiner moved to centre-back to dominate the rest of the game. Neil Ronan came on and tormented them. Tom and Jerry took over in midfield. They just refused to lose and ended up outscoring Clare nine points to two in that period to win by one.

I went into that dressing-room as if I had scored those nine points myself. Curran and myself were the first two in there. My confidence hadn't been dented one bit, but I could tell Ronan was subdued, so I hit him on the back.

'We've got another chance to put it right, Curran!'

Now we've another one tomorrow.

CHAPTER EIGHT
ICE CREAM IN THURLES

'You see, in a Munster championship or an All Ireland final, you must really put it up to your opponent. He is very mean, and you're very mean too. That's where the skills you've perfected come into play. There is very little he can do if you have the right equipment within yourself'

CHRISTY RING

SUNDAY, 28 MAY

We're here. I'm pucking a ball to John Gardiner on the practice putting area of Dundrum Golf and Country Club, a few miles away from all the main routes to Thurles. We're not long off the bus. Every man, woman and child seems to be coming up to this game. We were somewhere between Watergrasshill and Rathcormac, and it was like something from Exodus; traffic was at a standstill. With that, our two motorbike Gardaí started to pave a way by driving up the wrong side of the road and tearing around bends into oncoming traffic that didn't know how to react to their signals to push onto the hard shoulder. Even the card school at the back were bracing themselves: 'Jesus, we're goners!' Yet we breezed through Fermoy and Mitchelstown and all managed to get to the privacy and tranquillity of Dundrum.

We're here, and we're lucky, lucky to have a coach like John Allen. We're after that puckabout and lunch, and we're now listening to John in our team meeting. He's covering everything. First, he says we the players have covered everything. Our first touch? Check. Our hydration? Check. Our diet? Check. He keeps going down these points he has up on the flipchart and after every one makes an imaginary tick. He comes to 'speed'. He reminds us of something Seanie said the other week. Usually Seanie claims our sprint times aren't good enough, that we have to pick it up, but last Thursday week he was telling us that we were hitting the times he wanted. 'You all know that's unusual of Seanie,' says John. 'He's not easily pleased. This past fortnight, he's been pleased. So "speed", tick.' Every box is ticked.

He points to the wall and another poster the kids in his school have prepared for us: *Seasaigí An Fhoid* – Stand Your Ground. Today, we have to display aggression, but it's to be a controlled aggression. Some players never shut up; they're forever snarling, shouting or roaring at some opponent, official or teammate, and you can tell that they're rattled or unfocused. But the type who doesn't get involved and doesn't open his mouth, he's what John calls the Silent Pig. You don't know what he's thinking, and that can get you thinking – and distracted. Today, we'll project the impression that we're interested in one thing and one thing only: the ball. We'll stand our ground but play Silent Pig.

He points to another poster. It's of Davy Fitzgerald, livid and distraught after the final whistle last August. John says that we have the choice of either Davy being like that again or of him rubbing a Clare victory in our faces. Some paper during the week has described Davy as the one-man haka, but there's to be no Davy haka today. 'We stand here as Munster and All Ireland champions. At quarter to six, we still want to be standing as Munster and All Ireland champions. *Seasaigí An Fhoid.'*

This time, there's no need for anyone else to say anything. John has said it all, and, a few minutes later when I meet him in the toilets, I say, 'Well done there, John. Great speech.' He tells me how glad he is that I'm here, that in South Africa he thought I wouldn't be. Neither did I. Cape Town is a long time ago now.

The countdown is on now, but there's still half an hour to fill before we get back on the bus. I go back outside onto the practice putting green and puck around with Timmy Mac; we want to have tick after 'touch'. Then I pop into the team room. It's a familiar sight: Jimmy has the stereo blaring; our physios Dave and Chris are busy rubbing; Jerry Wallis is taking the spare hurleys and taping them up; Deccie is stretching Niall McCarthy; Neil Ronan and Curran are listening to their iPods; Jerry O'Connor has his eyes closed, relaxing, visualizing; Joe and Johnny G are pucking around; Tom is warming up. Other lads are getting changed, but I'll wait until we get to the dressing-room. Instead, I just relax, puck around and do as I always do around this stage before a game: keep visiting the loo. It's not a pleasant routine, but the alternative is worse: running out and, five minutes into the warm-up, be needing to go. And so, before any game, I spend a lot of time in the hotel and dressing-room loos, persuading myself to go. Today, the system doesn't need much sweet talk; I've drank so much water it's flowing through me.

We leave Dundrum, the 42 of us. Jimmy puts on our pre-match CD. First up is our old friend Al Pacino, with his 'inches' speech. Then it's Eminem, with 'Lose Yourself', Survivor, with 'Eye of the Tiger', U2, with 'Beautiful Day', the Dubliners, with 'Don't Give Up Till It's Over' and the Wolfe Tones' 'Celtic Symphony'.

As it ends, we're off the road again and set to enter hurling's paradise, Semple Stadium. Before we step off, John speaks. 'When we get out here, it's heads down, no talking to anybody. Everyone else is here to enjoy the game; we're here to win the game.' We do as we're told, but when we get to the dressing-room, the door is locked. Finally a groundsman opens the door, and we shut out the rest of the world.

The first thing I look for is the match programme. I don't know why; I hardly ever read it. It's just a habit, I guess. I get it and throw it into the bag. I tog off, then go into the shower area to puck the ball against the wall and get my eyes used to the helmet and bars. Boom, catch. Boom, catch. Gardiner is alongside me, doing the same. Soon, it's crowded. This isn't Croke Park, with its massive warm-up room; this is old-world Thurles, where you have only the dressing-room, a narrow corridor and this tiny shower area with Deccie and the masseurs, their three beds and everyone else walking in and out of the toilets, trying to keep out of Gardiner's and my way.

I see Cian coming out of one of the cubicles and ask how he's feeling. 'Not bad,' he says. I tell him what I tell every young player: keep it simple, stick to the basics and he'll be fine.

'Ten minutes to go!' says John.

'Right, lads, I have the stamp!' shouts Jimmy. One by one, we go up to Jimmy, roll up our sleeves and he stamps it on our arms: GUL. Everyone gets in on it. On match days, Tommy, our groundsman in Páirc Uí Chaoimh and Páirc Uí Rinn, has the job of handing out the jerseys and helping with the water. He's part of the group, and he loves the group, so he rolls up his sleeve and calls Jimmy over. 'Jimmy, throw that on there!' I smile. Doubtcha, Tommy boy!

Every player now goes round, shaking hands, bracing, wishing good luck. 'Right,' says John, 'we're going out in a minute.' He tells us all to sit down and mentions some key words: 'Discipline, hit the channels, quality ball, Silent Pig.' They're banging on the door outside. We get up to go, then Pat calls us all in. He follows the same theme: discipline, controlled aggression, *Seasaigí An Fhoid*, GUL. We're pumped yet relaxed, and, as we file out, the door isn't even banged, let alone unhinged.

'*Anois, a chairde, foireann Corcaí!*'

Suddenly we're out of the dark and into the light, off the concrete and onto the grass.

We go over to the new stand side for the warm-up. We start off in first gear, jogging. As Seanie always says, there's no point starting off in fifth right away, otherwise we'll be out of breath. Then he goes, 'Next level, faster!' so we move up another gear again. We just keep moving up gradually, focusing on our breathing, then our touch, so we're up to match pace before the game starts.

Next, we move back in towards the posts to do some more shooting. We've more time than usual today: Seanie's just learned that the game's to be delayed for five minutes. To keep us tuned in, Pat calls us into a huddle before the parade. Then he leads us around the parade. I look up and notice Davy Fitz bobbing up and down, slapping the bas of his hurley against his other hand. Then he glares over at our lads and spits down on the grass, halfway between their line and ours.

Clare break from the parade first, but we stay our course. Then we run to our respective lines. The six of us forwards stand together to face the flag. I've Niall to my right and Cian to my left and put my arms around them. For a second, Thurles is silent. Then the band starts up 'Amhrán na bhFiann'.

I run in towards the square. Lohan turns round and puts his hand out at the same time I extend mine. We say nothing; like me, he doesn't see the sense in fellas wishing each other good luck. Some guys don't even like shaking hands. No one has ever refused mine, but some will take a step back as you come in to discreetly avoid any interaction. Lohan isn't one of them, and we shake hands.

And then, seconds later, we're exchanging shoulders. I get out in front of him to win a ball played along the ground, pick it up, and, for a second, I look to take him on. I'm in danger of over-carrying, though, so I throw it up to tap it on the hurley, only for Lohan to flick it away over the sideline. A big cheer goes up from the Clare crowd, but immediately I spot Niall's open, so I quickly take the sideline ball and hit it along the ground to Niall, who spins past McMahon to point off his right. 'OK, that worked out all right,' I say to myself, 'but you showed too much of that ball to Lohan. Next time, keep it in close and tight.'

And, next time, that's exactly what I do. Jerry hand-passes it out to me, and straight away I take Lohan on. He swipes across, but I hardly feel it and start soloing in. He swipes a second time and this time knocks the ball off my hurley, but I pick it up, turn back inside and hook it over off my left. Against Offaly and Wexford, that ball was going wide. It's true what they say: practice makes perfect.

Other things from the training ground and challenge matches aren't translating, though. The three previous scores have all been for Clare, and so will the next three. I turn around after my point and, from the puckout, Tony Carmody is pointing off his left. A minute later and Barry Nugent is belting over his second point of the day. We're too loose, and they're wired.

Davy Fitz is coming out, roaring to no one in particular, 'Think of the hardship, lads! Think of the hardship!' Next thing, he's pumping his fist again after making a brilliant diving save from Joe and swiping it away before I can latch onto the rebound. Tom puts the 65 wide, and again Davy's jumping around the place.

But then things start to turn for us. Davy opts for a short puckout that doesn't come off, and I'm in to win a free off

McMahon that Joe taps over. Tom cuts through the heart of the Clare defence with this amazing run from midfield to the 21 to make it 0–6 to 0–4. And, after that, everything clicks into place. Tom and Jerry link up beautifully, Curran roars into the game with a monstrous point, Brian Murphy doesn't give Nugent another puck. All of a sudden, the Clare forwards are just like their unfortunate counterparts from Wexford and Offaly a few weeks back: hooked, blocked, smothered, dominated by the best back line in hurling.

Upfront we're doing our bit too. Niall is dragging McMahon out of the middle. Cian and Timmy are creating a lot of space for Joe with their movement. Fraggy gets a partial block in on Gerry Quinn, meaning instead of flying 70 yards down the field it only goes as far as Joe, who kills it dead and drives it over the bar to put us a point up. It's a lovely bit of skill from Joe, but I run out to Kieran to shout, 'That's your score!' Clare stay in it with a soft free or two, but we're on top, and, just before half-time, we win a free ourselves when Lohan pulls across me. They're rattled; we can tell. Davy comes running out to roar at the ref; in fact, they're nearly all converging on Barry Kelly. Barry's having none of it and moves the ball across right in front of the posts. Tony Griffin pushes Fraggy as Joe's lining up the free, so I go over and steer Tony away. 'Relax!'

He looks at me. 'You relax!'

'Tony,' I smile, putting my arm around him, 'I am relaxed!'

Moments later, we're both in our dressing-rooms, Joe having popped over that free to put Cork two up.

Inside, we have a few minutes to ourselves; outside, the selectors form a conclave. Sully is sitting just over from me. 'Well done,' I say to him. 'Ye've them tied up.'

He nods. 'Yeah. We had a shaky start, but we're all right now.'

Jimmy comes round with wet towels, and then a fresh jersey

for each of us for the second half. I take in some liquid and, since Con's left a few this time, some Pastilles too.

John comes in. There's no change in personnel and no real change in tactics. Donal Óg will be going a bit longer with the puckout now that we've the breeze, but we're not to play stupid high balls just for the sake of it. I reiterate the same point: the breeze isn't going to win the game for us; we've got to keep doing the right thing.

'That's it,' says Sully. 'No let-up. Let's beat these fellas by ten if we can.'

And that's the mentality we go back out with for the second half. A minute after the restart, Gardiner makes a block, and Curran drives it over Lohan and myself into the right corner. Lohan gets out in front but, instead of opting to pick it, tries to flick it away. I anticipate that and put the hurley out to block his, lift and again cut it over the bar off my left.

Lohan's not playing Silent Pig. From the puckout, they win a free around our 65, which Seanie McMahon takes. 'Get over, get over, get over! Ah, fuck it!' Lohan grimaces.

Davy's still optimistic. He comes out again. 'Remember the hardship, lads! Remember the hardship!'

Joe pops over a few more frees. Again, Lohan and myself battle for a ball, and he ends up catching me on my right knee. Play continues, but my leg's dead, and when the ball finally goes out I go down, and Con and Deccie come in to treat me. It turns out I've a cut as well.

'Come off as a blood sub; we'll give you a rest,' says Con.

'I don't want to go off. Throw a bit of Vaseline on it there.'

Barry Kelly is standing over us. 'Con, you're going to have to take him off if you don't get him up fast.'

I look up. 'Two seconds and we'll be with you now, Barr.'

He looks at me, slightly surprised, disappointed even. 'You'd think you'd get my name right, anyway!'

I look up again. 'I know your name's Barry! I called you Barr! Barr for Barry!'

Barr smiles and helps me back up. As we've been having our little chat on the nuances of salutations, Cork-style, Con's applied the Vaseline to stop the bleeding and Deccie's been rubbing and moving the leg. I try to run the knock off. It doesn't feel right, but it doesn't matter; the rest of the lads are completely on top and our lead is now out to eight. Even Davy seems resigned to a Cork win. Instead of asking fellas to think of the hardship, he's thinking of a clean sheet and urging them to bring us down if we're going through.

I'm not going to put one past him anyway. I can't drive off that leg, and Lohan's cleared the last two balls. There's no point in letting him clear another few uncontested and being the cause of a Clare goal when Neil is raring to go. With ten minutes left, I hobble off and lay down by the sideline.

Deccie comes over and starts icing the leg as I sit back watching the game. Joe points another beauty; we have it for sure now. Deccie starts moving the leg to see where the pain is. He tells me I'll need it X-rayed; a bone might be broken. Great. That could be the Munster final gone. I try to stay positive. The fact there's a cut means maybe it's just a bad belt; maybe there's no tear or break. Better still, we've won. The final whistle's just gone, and the scoreboard reads: Corcaigh 0–20 An Chlár 0–14.

Ollie Baker comes over. 'Well done. We'll see you again later in the year, hopefully.'

As I limp along towards the tunnel, Lohan comes over, and we shake hands.

Back in the dressing-room, there's a lot of shaking hands and pats on the back. There's no yelping, no cheering, just a nice inner glow that we're back, we still have it. I know how I want to celebrate. A little while after my shower, I'm throwing the crutches Deccie gave me into Jimmy's van parked right outside the stadium. Jerry comes over to us. 'I'm going for my ice cream now, Jerry!'

'I'm going to have one too,' he says, rubbing his hands. 'To be honest, I sneaked in for one after the Wexford match the other night as well!'

And there he was, telling us all along to resist desserts, that if it was good enough for him, it was good enough for us. That's it; when we get to that Centra across from the Anner Hotel, I'm having a few Moros to go with the '99.

When Jimmy and myself get back to the hotel, it's obvious most of the lads have stopped off for refreshments themselves. Tom and Seán Óg are the only ones there, while the rest of the lads are having a beer with the supporters somewhere down the town. The intermediates are here, though.

'Heading out tonight, Brian?' one of them asks.

'Hardly,' I say, looking down at the crutches.

He looks around. 'Come here, you don't mind if I borrow that top off you there? The girls might think I'm one of the seniors.'

Fair dues to him for trying, anyway.

Back on the bus, there's more laughing and wisecracks. The team CD is a major source of material. Everyone's in on the Sherlock joke now. Poor Kelly's choice is coming under a lot of scrutiny as well. I'm sitting just behind Tom Kenny and Killian Cronin and across from Cathal Naughton and Shane O'Neill, and they can't understand why he's gone for 'One Moment in Time'.

'Is Kelly off his game or what? Whitney feckin' Houston?'

I have to defend my clubman. 'Ah, lads, I remember that coming out around the time of the '88 Olympics, and they had action clips from it going along to that song, and I remember thinking it was brilliant. Did you never see that?'

Shane O'Neill looks at me as if I have two heads. 'I was two!'

Cathal Naughton also shoots me an incredulous look. 'I was one!'

Pat Mulcahy comes to my rescue. 'I remember it! And I remember the '84 Olympics too!'

'Pat, I can remember the Moscow '80 Olympics!'

And, for the rest of the trip, I forget there's anything wrong with my leg.

And maybe there isn't that much wrong with it. I'll know in the morning. Right now, all seems well in the world.

MONDAY, 29 MAY

The leg's fine, thank God. I called into Con's office at quarter to ten this morning for my referral letter for the Bons Hospital and then went for what seems to be the routine the morning after every Munster championship match for me now: the X-ray. There isn't any break, just a bruise on the bone. I called Deccie and Con to relay the news. They already knew; they had already been on to the hospital. I should have guessed. My Big Brothers are always watching.

I read a good few of the papers while I was waiting around today. Some pundits are saying Lohan and Seanie McMahon are finished. I don't know if that's right, and I don't think it's fair, and a bit of me feels for them today. Because, as much as Lohan and myself might knock lumps out of each other, and as much as Davy might talk and throw shapes all about the place, I have massive respect for the likes of them and McMahon and Frank Lohan and Colin Lynch. They brought a county with no winning tradition two All Irelands in three years, and yet here they are, nearly ten years later, trying to bring it a third, still going strong, still playing in the same positions. It's been easier for me; I've played corner-back, wing-back, centre-back, full-forward. Lohan's played virtually nowhere else than full-back. Seanie's played virtually nowhere else than centre-back. Yet, year in, year out, the likes of them and Davy keep coming back for more. I'm actually glad for them that they can come back for more this year, even though we might meet them again and they'll be much tougher to beat in Croke Park.

Because, believe me, I know what it's like to lose a Cork–Clare match early in the summer.

CHAPTER NINE
THE WILDERNESS YEARS

'And then in one game it could be all over for another year. All the tactical talks, the 'listen hard, lads' sessions in freezing dressing-rooms, the warnings about keeping the head from the throw-in, staying cool as the roar rocks the stadium in the first ten minutes count for nothing, as nobody remembers a first-round loser'

DECLAN HASSETT, *THE WAY WE WERE*

THERE WAS ONE DOWNSIDE TO ERINS OWN WINNING the county in '92. I had to captain Cork. That might sound daft, but what would have been an honour at 25 was a hindrance at 20. It wasn't that it affected my game, it's just that it enhanced no one else's.

My first day in the role was a league game up in Parnell Park. Before the match, Frank Murphy, a selector that season, called on 'our new captain to say a few words'. It was obviously an inspired speech – Dublin beat us. At the time, I consoled myself with the thought that our veterans could hardly have been up for Dublin in October, but after a few more games I got the sense they weren't up for listening to me either.

Who could blame them? Tomás Mul, Cunningham, Hennessy, Hartnett, Seanie O'Gorman, Seanie and Teddy Mac: what was I going to tell them? They had won and seen and heard it all. They may have respected me as a player, but not, it seemed, as their leader.

We've been lucky with captains in Cork these past few years. Personally, though, I think we should do away with the system of county champions selecting the Cork captain. The clubs will hardly allow that, but the status quo can compromise Cork's chances of winning All Irelands. In the '90s, we had captains in hurling and football who were struggling to get on or stay on the team. They didn't need to be worrying about the toss or how to gee up the lads. I know in '93 I'd rather have left all that to someone else.

I was fine with lifting cups, though, and that May I got to raise the National League trophy after we broke Wexford hearts and gripped a nation. I don't recall those three games in Thurles in any great detail – how one was distinct from the other. They just all seemed to blend into this one sweeping match. Wexford were desperate to win; we were too stubborn to lose.

Three weeks later, though, we did lose. On a dour, drizzly day in Limerick, Clare dumped us out of the Munster championship.

I wouldn't go along with the popular theory that we were tired or tipsy from the Wexford games; I think we just totally underestimated Clare. We'd played them a few months earlier in a play-off to make the league quarter-finals, and they'd been a shambles. If our league run cost us that year, it was that game in Thurles, not the trilogy with Wexford. We thought we'd just have to turn up and hammer them again. And when it dawned on us that it wasn't going to happen, we began to flounder.

I was moved all over the place that day. During that league,

I'd played in seven different positions – all six spots in the back and centre-forward. Hardly a week would go by without there being an article saying Corcoran for centre-back or Corcoran for midfield or Corcoran for centre-forward. Privately, I was praying for some stability, but it didn't come against Clare. I ended up playing in four positions. I started at wing-back on Jamesie O'Connor. Then, after Jim McInerney scored a goal, I was switched into the corner to mark him. Then, when Sparrow O'Loughlin got hot, I was moved onto him and then, near the end, went to centre-back while Jim Cashman was pushed out to the wing. I felt like a one-man fire brigade, asked to put out fires all over the place.

I was in a state of shock afterwards. In 70 minutes, our dream, our season, was suddenly gone.

So were the Canon and Hennessy. I was sad about that. The Canon might have put up this front of being dour and abrupt, but behind it all he cared. He was the first man for a song or to share a joke, more often than not with our resident comedian Hennessy. The two of them were like a duo on a sitcom. Often, the Canon could keep with Hennessy as well as anyone, but there were times when Hennessy would leave even him stumped.

After the first two days against Wexford, the Canon wasn't happy. Hennessy wasn't going well. A lot of fellas weren't going well. So he called a team meeting. 'Gentlemen,' the Canon declared, 'there are only three players in here performing to the required level!' He continued, until Hennessy's hand went up. 'What is it?' the Canon barked.

'Sorry, Canon,' says Hennessy, taking a quick glance around the dressing-room. 'I'm struggling here. Who are the other two?'

Other nights, we'd be training, doing laps of the tunnel in the Park. Next thing, as we'd be over on the open stand side, Hennessy would hop up onto the steps, take a seat in the stand, stretch back and wait for us to go around another few times before joining back in.

The Canon was a gas man too. We all knew he loved coaching and being around players, but sometimes he'd let on that he didn't. Sometimes he'd let on he couldn't stand us. We might be training and, halfway through, he'd pronounce, 'I'm not happy with this application, this attitude! You're wasting my time!' and storm off the field and out the door. We'd find out later that he had a funeral or something to go to all along.

He was a proud man. It wasn't just a showdown between Cork and Tipp; in his mind, it was O'Brien versus Babs. We were his players. One time, Tom Aherne in the *Examiner* asked me to stand in for a few photographs with Justin McCarthy, who was doing a column for the paper. Justin's article was to be on skills, so the plan was I'd maybe swing on the ball and Justin would come in and demonstrate how to execute a block or hook. Being friendly with Tom, I agreed. So I made my way down to the Mardyke to team up with Justin and the photographer. When we got there, the Canon was just finishing training UCC. I could tell he wasn't happy, that there was obviously some history between him and Justin.

'Will you be at training tonight?' he barked.

I nodded, he went off, and Justin and myself went on with the session for the paper.

That evening, I was one of the first out at training. The Canon came over. 'What were you doing today with *that man*?'

I tried to explain I was just trying to do Tom a favour. The Canon wasn't having it.

'People will be looking at the paper now, and they'll think you're getting special coaching from him! *He's* not your coach! *I'm* your coach!'

He became so animated that our trainer Gerald McCarthy came over to see if everything was OK. You can understand why: seeing the Canon shouting at me must have seemed rather odd. And it was. We never had anything like it before or after. I was happy to have the Canon as my coach. He and Gerald complemented each other well in the early '90s. It was the classic good cop/bad cop routine – and even then the Canon could only play the baddie for so long.

AFTER THE CANON AND GERALD, JOHNNY CLIFFORD stepped in. He was like an older Gerald – a real gent and a real hurling man – but his two years ended like the Canon's last: in Limerick, in the first round, beaten by a puck of a ball.

In '94, we started like a train in the rain against Limerick, but a couple of Gary Kirby goals followed by a couple more from Pat Heffernan denied us.

The following year's Munster semi-final against Clare was incredible. As the game was about to enter injury-time, Kevin Murray belted in a goal to put us two points up. Our supporters were sure we were back in a Munster final. When a ball went out over by the sideline opposite the Mackey Stand, I'm told a couple of them sprinted across the field so they could join our mentors and subs in their moment of victory. Two minutes later, the final whistle went. Our two friends came sprinting out, smiling and jumping and waving their Cork flags. All of a sudden, they stopped in their tracks, stupefied. Why were there so many Clare men on the field? Why were our lads looking as if they'd lost?

What the two boys had missed while running across the field was a sequence of play that changed hurling history.

That sideline ball Clare had won: it had been won by their centre-back Seanie McMahon, playing as a corner-forward. Ten minutes earlier, he'd broken his collarbone. Anyone else would have gone off, but that day we learned that McMahon wasn't anyone else. Clare had used their three subs. He felt he could still do something. And he did. Swinging with one arm, he broke a ball off Timmy Kelleher that went out for that sideline ball. Fergie Tuohy took it, floated it in to the edge of the square and then Ollie Baker, one of those subs, batted it to the net, unknown to our two amigos. Yet, if it wasn't for that, most of Ireland probably would never have heard of Ger Loughnane.

Instead, they wouldn't hear of us for the rest of the year and of some of our lads ever again. Yet who knows how we'd have done had we got over Clare that day? On the day itself, neither side had looked hectic, but Clare went on to win the All Ireland. The previous year, Limerick had gone on to reach it. In June, you'd be depressed, but by September you'd be dreaming again. 'We're not that far away,' you'd say to yourself. 'We're really not that far away.'

That September, I felt particularly optimistic. The same day that Clare won their first senior All Ireland in 81 years, our minors drilled Kilkenny, and on the Monday I went down to their homecoming in Daunt Square. I looked up at that stage, and I saw the future: Donal Óg, Seán Óg, Joe and Mickey. I listened to their manager, Jimmy Barry-Murphy, and began picturing him as our manager. Was this the man to save Cork hurling?

The following month, the county board gave him that job.

He knew it was going to be tough.

But none of us had an idea of just how tough.

FROM THE MOMENT JIMMY, TOM CASHMAN AND TONY O'Sullivan took over, expectations and optimism soared. The back page of the *Evening Echo* dubbed them 'The Dream Team', and at the start they did just what the label said. One of their first calls was to play me at centre-forward, and, at the start, it seemed an inspired decision as well as a popular one. We won our last three league games before the Christmas break, and I'd managed to score 1–22, of which 1–11 was from play. The hype machine went into overdrive. 'In the space of just over a month,' wrote one tabloid journalist, 'Corcoran and Barry-Murphy have done for Cork what Cantona and Ferguson managed at Old Trafford. They have resurrected a corpse-like giant from a shallow grave of despair.'

The optimism was short-lived. By March, Tipp and Clare had hammered us – in Cork – and we'd been relegated. Wexford also trimmed us in a challenge game before the championship. Jimmy, Tom and Tony kept changing the team and positions, but in trying to find the solution only added to the confusion. My stint at centre-forward seemed one of the few successes from the league, yet ten days before the championship I was thrown in at midfield towards the end of a trial game against the intermediates. Before I knew it, I'd run onto four balls, put the four of them over and was starting in midfield for the championship.

And yet, for all the instability, Stuart Anderson here still fancied our chances against Limerick. For one, it was in the Park. Cork had never lost a championship game in the Park. In the weeks leading up to the game, as I drove to training, I'd look across the marina and see the stadium and think of how this was surely the year we'd start winning championship games again.

On 26 May 1996, I drove past the Silver Springs again, too depressed to go into town and too depressed to look over at where one of the biggest humiliations in Cork hurling history had taken place. The lads who did venture into town were just as embarrassed. The scoreline said it all: Limerick 3–18, Cork 1–8.

My own contribution to the cause had been severely limited when, in the opening minutes, I took a knock on the knee that forced me to hobble into the full-forward spot. In hindsight, though, we were doomed from the start. Most of our team had played or would play in an All Ireland final, but at that point most of them were either too young or too old. Limerick were too fast and too strong. We didn't know it at the time, but Baker's goal the previous year had changed hurling. Clare's power game and commando training were the new template, the new law, and if you didn't subscribe you didn't survive. Limerick had signed up. We hadn't.

Of all the defeats I've suffered in my career, Limerick '96 is among the worst. It was certainly the worst up to that point – because we hadn't competed. In '94 and '95, I'd never doubted that some day I'd still win my senior All Ireland. But, after '96, I did. I even began to wonder if we'd ever again win a first-round game. If someone had said to me the morning after the '92 All Ireland that four years later my only championship win in hurling would be over Kerry, I wouldn't have believed them. But if someone had said to me on 27 May 1996 that Cork would win an All Ireland within three years, I wouldn't have believed them either.

If it was a chastening experience for the players, it was absolutely devastating for Jimmy. The *Examiner* printed stinging columns and vicious letters. The criticism wounded Jimmy, but he refused to let it break him. In a perverse kind of way, it was actually good for him and for us. If it had been any milder, Jimmy might have cut his losses and walked away. But it was so severe, so damning, that it brought out the stubborn streak in him. No way was he leaving it like this. Seeing him find that strength gave us strength. Someone still believed in us, and so we still believed in him.

We made progress in '97. We didn't have a trophy to show for it – we didn't even win a championship match – but we rattled Clare at the peak of their powers. Jimmy had yet to subscribe to commando training, but he had gone with youth and stuck with me at centre-back, and we ended up pushing Clare in what was, in hindsight, probably a classic. Seanie McGrath from Glen Rovers made his debut and ended up with five points. He would have scored even more if we'd played better ball into him, but, in the second half, our half-backs, including me, got sucked into a virtual game of tennis with their half-backs by pumping high ball after high ball on top of them. The pitch in Limerick might have been tight, but we should still have been cuter and more varied in our play.

At the end of that year, Loughnane would say that, 'as a hurling man', he couldn't understand why I hadn't won an All Star nomination for 'the best performance [he'd] seen' that year, but on the day itself it wasn't compliments we exchanged. In the closing minutes, we were only two points down when we won a sideline ball inside their forty-metre line. Just as we were lining up the ball, Loughnane kicked it away. It gave Clare more time to regroup, and within a minute they'd swept downfield, Sparrow O'Loughlin had won a ball and, just as our full-back John O'Driscoll came in on him, he laid off to Stephen McNamara, who blasted past Ger Cunningham to seal the win. As Sparrow was being treated on the ground, Loughnane rushed in complaining to the ref. I roared at Ger to get off the fucking field. I was fuming.

An hour later, at the shop across the road from the Gaelic Grounds, I was still seething at how the game had turned out. We might have restored some pride, but for the fourth time in five years our summer had ended in Limerick.

Were we ever going to win in this bloody town? Was I ever going to walk down the Ennis Road to this place with a smile on my face? Was I ever going to play more than one game each summer?

I suppose in a way, though, I did have a backdoor.

It was called football.

CHAPTER TEN

THE BIG BALL

'Football is a game for madmen'

VINCE LOMBARDI

DOWN THROUGH THE YEARS, I'VE HEARD A LOT ABOUT
Vince Lombardi: how driven he was, how obsessed he was,
how he'd do anything to win. I obviously never got to meet
or work with Lombardi, but I think I worked with a man just
like him. For four years, I played football for Billy Morgan, and
not once in that time did his intensity waver or wane. It was
as if he'd never contested or won all those All Irelands from
'87 to '90. All he craved was the next, as if it was his first. I've
met some extraordinary people in my life, but, of them all,
Morgan is the most intense.

In 1992, I resisted his overtures to join the football panel,
because I wanted to establish myself on the hurling one first,
but a year later he asked me to meet him in the old De Lacey
House on Oliver Plunkett Street. When I walked in, he had
Ray Cummins and Jimmy Barry-Murphy either side of him.
Billy hardly had to say a word. The two boys said it all for
him. It was possible to play both the hurling and football,
especially when you were young. Some day, you might have

to focus on one, but you'd regret not trying both. And so, the Tuesday after my last game for Canon Michael O'Brien, I walked straight into the dressing-room of another coaching giant.

It wasn't as if I could walk right onto the team, though. The lads were playing Kerry in Killarney the following Sunday and had just beaten Clare, the reigning Munster champions. But, after the lads negotiated Kerry, Morgan went straight to work on his new project.

He knew I had promise, but he knew I was raw – senior inter-county football was a different ball game to junior with Erins Own – so Billy started bringing me into the Park for some one-on-one coaching outside of training. He'd run at me and sidestep me. We'd shadow and we'd tackle. Any football coaching I had missed out on, playing so much hurling, I was going to get it now.

A few weeks later, in the Anner Hotel, he came over to tell me I'd be starting in that afternoon's Munster final. Niall Cahalane had failed a fitness test, so I'd be marking Peter Lambert in his place. Lambert was about the only Tipperary footballer I knew, because he played his club football in Cork with Nemo. And that meant Morgan knew him inside out.

'He has this left-legged dummy,' Morgan said. 'He'll try it all day.'

So I didn't fall for it. Instead, I stayed standing up, or I'd flick the ball away; I just knew Lambert was going to solo instead of shoot. By the end of the game, he hadn't scored from play and I'd a Munster medal.

The next day out, in Croke Park, I held my man scoreless again, and we blew Mayo out of it by 20 points. Two years after the infamous heave against him, Morgan was back in an All Ireland final, and, just a year after losing to Kilkenny, I was too.

When I look back on it now, we had some collection of players. The core was still made up of the winning side of '89 and '90 – John Kerins, Steven O'Brien, Tony Davis, Shay Fahy, Barry Coffey, Danny Culloty, John O'Driscoll, Michael McCarthy, Teddy Mac and Cahalane – but it had been infused with hungry, young players like Ciaran O'Sullivan, Colin Corkery, Joe Kavanagh, Mark O'Connor and Don Davis. Derry were going to be by far the best team we'd played all year, but, as far as we were concerned, we were the best they'd meet too.

The first half was frantic. Their captain and centre-back Henry Downey was having an incredible year, yet, within five minutes, Joe had blown past him to blast to the net. Tony Davis was bombing forward for us; then their wing-backs Gary Coleman and Johnny McGurk began bombing forward for them. In midfield, McGilligan and Tohill were having a titanic battle with Fahy and Teddy. A few minutes before half-time, we were only a point down, playing against the breeze, when the game turned.

Niall Cahalane and Enda Gormley had a spat off the ball. Tommy Howard went over and booked Cahalane, but that wasn't the end of it. Gormley would later claim that he roared at Howard furiously and pointed to his jaw. 'His [Howard's] expression changed after that,' said Gormley in the book *Sons of Sam*. 'I think he realised he had goofed by not sending Cahalane off.'

Then Eamon Coleman came tearing onto the field. 'Ya chickened out!' he roared at Howard. 'Ya chickened out!'

A minute later, Tony Davis, who was having a blinder, mistimed a shoulder tackle on Dermot Heaney out by the touchline. In today's game, it would have been, at worst, a tick. Howard sent him off. Even the Derry boys knew it wasn't right. 'It wasn't a sending off,' admitted Gormley. 'I think it was balancing the books a bit.'

If it balanced the books, it imbalanced the game. Shortly after half-time, a John O'Driscoll goal put us in front again, but Derry made full use of the extra man, with those half-backs pushing up at every chance. A few points from McGurk and a few frees from Gormley later, and for the second year straight I'd lost an All Ireland final.

Again, I was distraught, yet, in a strange way, it was some consolation that Joe Brolly had outplayed me. I hadn't deserved to win. In '92, I'd played better than my man, and yet Eamonn Morrissey had his medal and I didn't. I was still in a dark mood, though. Our post-match meal was out in Dun Laoghaire, and for all the good company that our selector Teddy Holland and his family were, I'd rather have been somewhere else. Other lads tried to drown their sorrows, but I couldn't. I just wanted to be alone, anywhere but at another losers' All Ireland function.

It was only a game we lost that day, though. In the days and years to come, we'd lose friends who'd played on that day. Two of the four men who marched ahead of me in the parade would die tragically: the late, great John Kerins and the late, great Mick McCarthy. I didn't know Mick that well, him being a forward, me being a back, but what I knew of him I liked, and I was horrified to hear about his car accident. I knew John better. He was a sort of father figure to me in '93, just as his fellow Barrs man Cunningham had been in '92, and was nearly a brother to the other lads. I met them at the removal when John was taken from us in 2001, and we reminisced about the brilliant shot-stopper he was and the way he could land a kickout to you on a plate from 50 yards.

We couldn't have known what would happen to John and Mick back in '93, but on the Tuesday morning after that football final we learned that our old masseur, John 'Kid' Cronin, had passed away. Everyone loved Kid. He was our comic, our confidant, our friend. After a match, he'd always sit next to the player who hadn't played that well, never the star. At half-time against Derry, he noticed Tony Davis moving slowly across the field on his own, fell back from the main party and escorted Tony to the dressing-room. When the hurlers had been on holiday in Morocco earlier that year, a line of us would be outside his door every morning, waiting for the Kid to put on our suntan lotion. He always had a joke, and, even if it wasn't that funny, you'd laugh anyway, because Kid's laugh would make you laugh. He'd tell the one about Napoleon summoning his aide before the Battle of Waterloo, asking him to bring a red jacket.

'And why do you want a red jacket?' the aide asks. 'Our uniform is blue, sure!'

'Well,' says Napoleon, 'if I get wounded, my soldiers won't see the blood. They won't get demoralised.'

'Excellent idea! No problem!'

The aide starts to head off, when Napoleon calls him back. 'By the way, get some brown pants too.'

And with that Kid's bushy eyebrows would rise, and he'd giggle and cough and giggle and laugh.

I couldn't believe it when I heard Kid had died hours after our homecoming. Just that day, at the function in the Burlington, I had been sitting at the same table. On the train up on the Saturday, we had a good chat as well. We were just after pulling out of Kent Station, and, though it was the eve of a football final, we talked about hurling. The train came out of the tunnel in Blackpool and into the countryside, and, just as we were passing Kilcully graveyard, Kid said, 'Some day, I'll be in there when you're coming back with the Liam McCarthy. Hold the cup out the window to me and I'll wave back at you.'

Little did we know that the following week he'd be resting in that graveyard.

For the next six years, I would do everything I could to get my hands on Liam to hold out to him.

And, as he liked his football, I tried my best to show him Sam, too.

IN 1994, I MANAGED TO GET MY HANDS ON AN ALL Ireland. I was full-back on the Under-21 side that had eased through Munster, hammered a fancied Laois team and then beat Mayo in the final in Ennis. Most of the minor team of '91 and its spirit were still intact. Talents like Martin Cronin and Damien O'Neill were on board, while the passion of our manager, John Fintan Daly, bordered on Morgan's.

Mayo also had some gifted footballers – by now, they had a new full-forward called Ciaran McDonald – but there was just something about playing them in All Ireland finals that brought out the best in me, and I ended up having one of my best games ever with Cork. It was just like '91 – my seventh and last shot to win an All Ireland in the grade – and nothing, not even McDonald, was going to stop me getting it.

Once I did, I was sure I was going to complete the set. Earlier that month, I had been on the senior team that had lost an All Ireland semi-final to Down, but Ulster's dominance was going to have to end sometime. We'd won Munster. Now our Under-21s had won an All Ireland. When I walked into all the hollers and hugs in the dressing-room that day, I saw an exuberant Frank Murphy and winked, 'We've just the senior left now, Frank.'

Twenty minutes into the following year's All Ireland semi-final, the prospects of completing the full set were looking good. We were outrunning, outplaying and outscoring Dublin. Then Dublin won a questionable free. Keith Barr picked out Jason Sherlock with a ball. Jason shimmied, poor Mark O'Connor slipped, and next thing the Hill was going 'Boom,

boom, boom, let me hear you say Jayo!' After that, everything seemed to go wrong. Podsie was taken off, harshly, as it seemed to us. Fahy was brought on – at wing-forward, when Dublin had taken over in midfield. And, to compound matters, I was moved out of the half-back line and into the corner to take up Mick Galvin.

I hated playing in the full-back line, absolutely hated it. I know I'd played full-back at minor and Under-21, but, at senior, opponents were no longer thumping the ball in any old way. I was never a stopper, I was a ball player, and I'd been flying in the half-back line that year. Feck it, I'd been flying that day against Dublin. All that changed in the corner. Galvin took me for a few points, and the Dubs beat us by a few points. As I trooped off, beaten in Croke Park for the fourth time in four years, I was baffled as to why Billy and the selectors still felt that I could play corner or full-back.

They wouldn't be the only ones to get that call wrong. Larry Tompkins would too and so would the club. In 2001, the club went on a run in the East Cork football championship. I was playing midfield and loving it. I didn't have to worry about stopping anyone; I was just able to play and go up and kick my three or four points a game. Then we got to the final. Our opponents were Cloyne, and at full-forward they had a certain Diarmuid O'Sullivan, owner of one of the most lethal left boots in Cork. When the team was announced, I was full-back on Sully. We were going to sacrifice our top scorer to mark theirs.

A few minutes in, a ball came in. We both juggled with it before it fell to the ground, and Sully tipped it over the line. Then he got a ball out on the wing. I shepherded him out towards the touchline, forcing him to launch a Hail Mary 50 yards out from our posts. Straight over the bar. By half-time, we were being destroyed, so I was pushed out to midfield. I kicked four points from play, but we ran out of time; Cloyne won by two points. And again I came off a field privately berating the fact I had again been asked to forsake my own game to mark a danger man. I didn't say anything, though, and in '95 I was hardly going to complain to Billy either.

If Billy had a fault, it was his short fuse. He'll admit that himself. One night, we were having a game in training, and Morgan, being the liveliest 40-something ever known, was playing too. A ball broke, and Billy and Gary McPolin both went after it. McPolin was a lot like Billy. He was hardy, and his attitude was 'Well, if you're playing the game, you're playing the game'. Next thing, McPolin had flattened Billy with a shoulder, and Billy was on the ground. And the moment after that Billy was back up and McPolin was on the ground.

We were shocked. This once, Billy's passion had brought him too far. In fairness to Billy, he knew it too. The next night at training, when he was picking the teams, he quipped, 'Well, Gary, I better go with you tonight!' We all laughed. If at times Billy's passion got the better of him, though, it was that same passion that served him and Cork so well. Long before today's video analysis and stats became the norm, Morgan was showing us clips from our games and clips of upcoming opponents. Long before Andy Gray and Sky, long before O'Grady and John, Morgan was out with the Subbuteo board, showing us how to play and how we'd win. Long before teams were doing systematic weights, he brought a bodybuilder into the set-up to show us how to lift weights. The man was simply way ahead of his time.

And he knew footballers even more than he knew about football. He was the first guy to the bar after games and the first to crack a joke in the dressing-room, but we always knew there was a line; we always knew he was the boss. When he talked to you, it was just like Jimmy with the hurling: the fact it was him who was saying it made you take to that field feeling like Superman.

When Kerry beat us in the Munster final in 1996 and Billy decided to walk away, the board had a dilemma.

Who had anything like his drive, his leadership, his passion?

Billy told them it could only be one man.

Larry Tompkins.

IN LANCE ARMSTRONG'S BOOK *EVERY SECOND COUNTS*, Armstrong talks about a climb in the Alps called Hautacam. Months before the Tour de France proper, Armstrong went out in the snow and the sleet and climbed it. When he got to the top, his assistant stuck his head out of the car window and told Armstrong to hop in and have a cup of tea. Armstrong declined. He didn't feel as if he knew the climb; Hautacam wasn't his 'friend'. So he cycled back down and, after taking 30 minutes to do that, took another hour to ride back up. That night, he sent his physiological data to his coach, and when the coach studied the readout, he called Armstrong back. His file must have been corrupted. The numbers were strange. There were two sets of them.

'That's right,' said Armstrong.

'You did the climb twice?'

'Yeah.'

The coach went quiet for a moment. 'You sick bastard.'

Larry Tompkins wouldn't consider Lance Armstrong a sick bastard. He'd consider him a kindred spirit, someone who has what it takes to win an All Ireland. And if Lance ever needed someone to go up Hautacam a third time with him, I have no doubt Larry would gladly have grabbed a bike and joined him.

✻   ✻   ✻

THE NIGHT AFTER THE DRAWN 1996 ALL IRELAND FINAL
between Mayo and Meath, the Cork footballers had their first
training session under Larry Tompkins. The message was clear.
We were going to be playing in that fixture in a year's time.
However tough it might be, whatever it would take, we were
going to get there.

The following Sunday morning, we were in Inchydoney for
half-eight. And for the following nine months we would go
there constantly. We had this circuit, in the middle of which
there was this huge lump of sand. When you stood in it, the
sand would be up to your knees, and you'd have to crawl to
get to the top of it. Then you'd have to run down and around
and then up again. Then we'd have to run around this foot-
worn track. In all, it would take about ten minutes to do one
round of it, and most nights we'd have to do three rounds,
the third as fast as the first. Your lungs would be coming out
of your ears, your heart bursting out of your chest. Then you'd
have to walk chest high into the freezing water and back again,
out into the breeze and the rain.

Then there was the hill in Macroom. It was our Hautacam,
but it never became our friend. First, we'd warm up on the
club pitch below. And by 'warm up' I mean we'd do about
forty minutes of running around the field in pairs, with the
two at the back sprinting to the front every few seconds. Then
we'd have to face the hill. And the hill was a bloody long hill,
at least a hundred steep yards.

It always seemed to be pitch dark there. There was a
makeshift light at the top, but even there you'd barely be
able to make out who everyone was. You could spot Corkery,
all right, hiding behind one of the trees, probably wondering
where the nearest football or asylum was. But when Larry was
up there, there was no rest for the good, the bad or the wicked.
One night, as I dragged myself up it for the umpteenth time,
I could feel the vomit in my throat. I stopped, but, just as I

leaned over to puke, Larry grabbed me and threw me down the hill. My legs went into freefall and then my stomach into overdrive. I puked all the way down to the end.

Waiting there was Frank Cogan, ready to push me back up.

On nights like that, as you could hear the pounding and panting and puking all around you in the dark, I seriously questioned our sanity. But this was Larry Tompkins driving us on. He wasn't asking us to do anything he hadn't done himself, and he'd been the outstanding player of his generation. He could rightly say that he wasn't asking us to do anything that different to what Loughnane and Maughan had their players doing in Clare and Mayo. Hurling and football had changed, and if we wanted to win we'd have to change. 'You don't want to be SOFT!' he'd snarl. And we didn't want to be soft. We wanted to win. And, during our first league with Larry, we'd win and we'd win and we'd win. By the start of May, we were in the league final.

Larry had tried me at centre-forward for that entire campaign, and I'd enjoyed it there. I was winning ball, laying it off, taking the odd score. On average, I was chipping in nearly two points a game. I'd even scored a goal there for Munster in the Railway Cup final. My attitude was that if I got a score, great, but the important thing was to set up a score for someone else. And for the most part I was doing that. I was hitting fellas coming past on the overlap, spraying it into the corners, looking for the return.

Then, the Thursday before we played Kerry in that league final down in the Park, Larry told me to run at Liam O'Flaherty every time I got the ball. It hadn't been my game up till then; instead, it had been to move it on quickly. But I tried to carry Larry's instruction out and for the first half played well, scoring a point and setting up another one or two. But then I was moved to the wing. And then Corkery, who had cut his honeymoon short to play, was called ashore, and I was pushed into the corner. And whatever I might say about being a corner-back, I was never a corner-forward. With eight minutes to go, and Kerry beginning to pull away, I was taken off. Larry was standing on the line as I walked over, but I couldn't even look at him. Another league medal was gone, and with it, I just knew, so was my stint in the forwards.

The championship was what all the hard work had been for, though. That's why the panel had assembled 185 times in 270 days, and at half-time in our first-round game against Clare in Ennis it all appeared to make perfect sense.

Damien O'Neill had broken his leg shortly after the Kerry game, but now Fachtna Collins and Pat Hegarty had come in to dominate midfield just like they used to do in the minor days. Upfront, the Nemo trio of O'Brien, Corkery and Kavanagh were combining beautifully. At corner-back, Eoin Sexton was having a dream debut. And at centre-back I was going very well myself. Shortly before half-time, I broke forward again and kicked a point on the run to put us five points up. Would I have got that point if I hadn't played upfront in the league? Would I have broken those tackles if it hadn't been for those nights on the hill in Macroom? It was as if all along Larry had this grand vision, and now that vision was being realised, premiered, unleashed.

But then things began to unravel. Dorgan and Martin Cronin, probably our two best players in the league, couldn't get into the game. Neither could Ciaran. Our wides tally started mounting. Even Joe's radar was off. And Clare were gritty. The previous year, it had taken a massive Corkery 45 to get us out of Ennis with a draw, and then, in the replay down in the Park, Ciaran had to play the game of his life to see them off after extra-time. Now they were starting to claw into our lead again, with Ger Keane causing havoc on the wing and Francis McInerney picking up a few breaks after moving to midfield. Just as the game was entering injury-time, though, Fachtna kicked his third point of the game, and our lead was back out to three.

Then a ball was played down the left wing. Michael Curley somehow adjudged Ciaran had fouled Odran O'Dwyer. It was still a difficult angle to score from, but Ger Keane managed to put it over. Now the gap was down to two.

Then, deep into injury-time, they won another free, this time in front of the posts. A point was no good; a goal simply impossible. But Keane played a short free to Martin Daly, and somehow Daly got a shot off that went under three sets of legs and slid into the net. The second Kevin O'Dwyer kicked the ball out, Curley's whistle went and 15 Cork footballers dropped to their knees. A season that was meant to end in front of 70,000 in September had ended in front of 14,000 in June. A fortnight after losing to Clare in the hurling, here I was after losing to them again. A supporter came over to me, taunting and waving his Clare flag. 'Ye can't beat us in nothin'! Nothin'!' And nothing was said in our dressing-room. Outside, you could make out the sound of the whole of Clare going mad; inside, there was just the sound of dripping water and of shattered dreams.

If I had to pick the moment I started to get seriously disillusioned with Gaelic games, the day the countdown to my retirement began in earnest, it was that one in Ennis. I was sick for months after it. What had those last nine months been about? What was my life about? Was I wasting it away? Everyone else my age was out enjoying themselves, going to Australia, seeing the world; here I was, killing myself for two games all year. You'd actually wake up in the morning and say to yourself, 'God, it's not morning already, is it? Shit, we've training now in 12 hours!' You'd mind what you'd have for breakfast because it could come up that night on the hill in Macroom.

Then there were mornings where you'd wake up and think, 'Oh, God, we've training tonight. Wait a minute! No! We don't! It's Tuesday! We don't! Thank you, God!'

There was never a morning you'd look forward to training. It was dread. Pure dread.

One story sums up the madness of it all. One morning that October of '96, we were training down in Inchydoney, and, after three runs of the circuit, half of us were keeled over, the other half flat on our backs. An English couple were walking by on the beach, and they asked were we some kind of football team. The lads told them we were.

'And when's your game?'

Kevin O'Dwyer found the strength to lift his head. 'Next June!'

And yet, I know, Larry's way might have worked. No team for the rest of that championship played better football than we did in the first half of that game in Ennis. I never played better football than I did in '97, and I hadn't played as well for years in the hurling championship as I did in '97 either. Larry had me unbelievably fit, and if we had gone on and won the All Ireland I'd have been the first man up to say, 'Put it there, Larry, boy!' That day against Clare, I felt I could go up and down that field all day. But other fellas couldn't. Players who had been flying it up the hill in Macroom back in November were either carrying injuries or burned out by June.

I'm sure Larry has some regrets about that day and that year. He's on record as saying he should have had Niall Cahalane on for the closing minutes of that game. I can see why. Cahalane was of the same breed, as well as the same club, as Tompkins – the ultimate competitor, the ultimate warrior.

Even in sprints in training, Niall had to win. You'd be lining up beside him, waiting for the whistle, when, next second, your shorts would be down to your knees. Another night, he might even give you a flick in the balls. He had to win, win, win.

And he had to play, play, play. Even now, thinking of what he went through to play for Cork makes me wince. The day of the Down game in '94, he got off the bus in Croke Park using crutches. He then went into the dressing-room, lay down on the bench, put his arms around Conor Counihan and then braced himself for Con's injection. The needle plunged into the ankle, onto the bone, and Cahalane took it. He might have squeezed the life out of poor Counihan, but he took it, and he went out and marked Mickey Linden before getting onto the bus with those crutches again.

In those days, I feared Niall would push himself so hard he'd be crocked later, yet up to 2003 he was still the best club midfielder in Cork and putting it up to Darragh Ó Sé in the Munster club championship at 40 years of age. He was an exceptional player and an exceptional man.

Tompkins was cut from the same cloth. In 1998, at 36, he was still probably the best forward in the county, and for that year's first-round match down in Killarney, decided to start himself. Looking back, it was asking too much. He put a lot of energy into geeing us up in the dressing-room that day, energy he needed on the field. How could he concentrate on his own game and at the same time judge how his full-back line were going and what switches were needed? It was impossible, and I felt sorry for him. Because if Larry had entered and watched that game solely as a coach, he'd have seen I shouldn't have started or lasted.

I'd hardly any football done going into that game. I'd played all through the winter and spring, but then, for the league quarter-final against Donegal, I was moved back to full-back. It would be another two months before I would touch another football. In the meantime, the hurlers had gone on a good league run, beating Clare in the semi-final and Waterford in the final in front of full houses in Thurles. We had a new trainer, Teddy Owens, whose enthusiasm was infectious. The

Under-21s were oozing confidence, having won an All Ireland the previous year. We were playing games every second week and winning every second week. We even won a championship game – in Limerick, beating the home side in the first round. There was a buzz about the camp, and I didn't want to be anywhere else.

But then we ran into Clare in Thurles. Once again, my hurling summer was over in June, and once again football tapped me on the shoulder, asking me to give it a shot. And so, the Thursday after Thurles, I was flown down from a work course in Dublin to play in an A versus B game, won a few balls that broke my way at corner-back and, the following Tuesday, was picked at full-back to play the All Ireland champions in Killarney.

I have never regretted playing football. But I regret playing that day in Killarney. I was only kidding myself, thinking I could get away with ten days' preparation ahead of facing Mike Frank Russell and Johnny Crowley. To have any prayer of marking two players like that, your reading, your anticipation, has to be spot on. Mine was completely askew. I felt as if I had been parachuted into the middle of a rugby game. It was like being asked to play golf left-handed.

Early in the second half, I ran out the field when Paddy Russell suddenly blew his whistle and pointed for a free in.

'What? What was that for?'

'You bounced it twice.'

'I couldn't have bounced it twice!'

'You bounced it twice.'

It was that bad.

In the end, Kerry beat us by three points. And, as I walked off the field and towards the dressing-room, I said to myself, 'Never again, Brian. You've just played your last game of football for Cork.'

Then, on the way out of that dressing-room, after I'd showered and changed, I overheard two old Kerry fellas standing by the side as I drooped past. 'That's Corcoran there,' one said to the other. 'He's a better hurla' than a footballa'.'

And it hurt and it stuck, for the whole journey home and for the whole of that night. *He's a better hurla' than a footballa'*.

Four years earlier, we had played Kerry too, and I'd held Maurice Fitzgerald scoreless. I had played a lot of football that year, and probably played as well that day as I ever did in hurling. I cut out every ball into Maurice, I covered acres of ground and my distribution off both left and right boot was pinpoint. I played some great games in the half-back line, and I firmly believe that if I had been picked there more often I would be remembered as a much better footballer. I'd play there like I'd play there in hurling: just read the game and play the ball. I'd play centre-back for the league but, come championship, Steven O'Brien would invariably come in there, and I'd be moved. And that was fine by me. Steven was the best centre-back in the country and a man, if ever I was in a war, I'd want in that trench with me. But, instead of being just moved out to the wing, I always seemed to be stuck in that blasted full-back line for every big game we had. I'd have nearly preferred to be on the bench than in there.

Steven could empathise with me. He had come onto the team and won his All Irelands as a corner-back and full-back, but he had too much football to be kept in there. One year, we went up to Newry. I was centre-back, and Steven was full-back. Mickey Linden absolutely skinned him. I could tell by the glint in his eye Steven wasn't that bothered. The next day, Steven was centre-back and I was full-back.

But I was never a senior full-back or corner-back. And in Killarney that day it really showed and it really hurt. The likes of the two boys in Killarney weren't going to remember me for the game I had on Maurice down in the Park in '94 or on Billy O'Shea in Killarney in the Munster final of '95. Instead,

I'd be remembered as a footballer for chasing after Joe Brolly around Croke Park and Johnny Crowley around Fitzgerald Stadium.

I had to let it go, though. As much as a part of me felt like showing the two boys how wrong they were, another voice drowned theirs out. It was that of Mark Landers, who had been called into the hurling panel that year. 'Brian, until you pack in the football, we won't win an All Ireland.'

For years, people had been advising me to pack up 'that old football'. I'd pay no heed to them. What was I supposed to do every May or June after the hurlers were knocked out? Just watch Cork football teams beat – or lose to – Kerry, when I maybe had something to contribute? Brian Corcoran's commitment to football hadn't been the difference between the Cork hurlers winning or losing Munster or All Ireland titles, at least not up till then. I hadn't played hectic in Limerick in '94 and '95, but that was more to do with my exams than with my football. Every year, the footballers had a chance to win an All Ireland – often, a better chance than the hurlers. After the 1992 All Ireland hurling final, I would play only one hurling match in Croke Park over the following six years, a league-relegation play-off game against Antrim. I would play at least one football game there every year in that time. Why forsake that opportunity, that experience, for a distant hurling All Ireland that might never come?

In '98, though, things changed. The hurlers were edging closer to winning Munster and All Ireland titles. And maybe if I concentrated just on hurling it would help us get over that line. That autumn, I called into Larry's pub to tell him how I was thinking. He told me to think about it some more and come back to him in January. And so I did. I hadn't changed my mind. Larry understood. And, in fairness, he always did. Hurling was my first love.

I don't know if I ever loved football. At times, I even wonder how I stuck at it so long. Most sessions were at least two hours, often two and a half. In hurling, the sessions were shorter, snappier. In hurling, you'd come off the field with an appetite for the next night. In football, you often couldn't wait to get off that field.

So why did I play? I suppose I loved the challenge that went with it, the thought of playing in the half-back line and running with ball and picking a man out with a 30-yard foot-pass, the buzz and the camaraderie from the minor and Under-21 days, the honour of being the only Erins Own man to ever play senior football for Cork, and, ultimately, the respect I had for footballers and the dream of winning a senior All Ireland medal with them. Men like Tompkins, Morgan, Counihan, Cahalane, Ciaran, Kavanagh, O'Brien, O'Connor, O'Dwyer. I could name them all. It's a wonder and a shame I didn't win an All Ireland with those men, and that some of them never won a senior All Ireland at all.

They went very close in 1999. That September, they played Meath in the final. I watched it from a corporate box, because I had received a gift of two tickets for there. It was a different world. When Benny Coulter and Down beat Mayo in the minor final, Elaine and myself were the only two in the box watching the game; the others were inside, watching the Formula One. The main course was only served at three-twenty. Elaine and myself and four or five others gulped it down, forsook dessert and rushed back in for the throw-in of the match, but the others stayed in there, eating and drinking away, watching their Formula One on the box. It was surreal, knowing so many people back home who were searching everywhere for a ticket, and here we were, surrounded by empty seats and indifference to the plight of Joe and Ciaran and the other lads.

I was convinced that Cork were going to win, especially after Joe got another wonder goal after half-time. But then Trevor Giles started to pull the strings, Seán Óg – probably Cork's best player that day – could only contain Graham Geraghty for so long, and in the end Meath won out by three points. I was gutted for the lads, especially Joe and Ciaran, who had been so near and yet so far in '93 as well. But as much as I felt for them, I wasn't sad that I wasn't out there this time with them. Cork football had done well that year without Brian Corcoran. And, as it had turned out, Brian Corcoran had done well that year without Cork football.

That prize of corporate tickets hadn't been just any present. It was for how I'd played in a certain game two weeks earlier.

CHAPTER ELEVEN

LOVE AND GLORY

'We realised that just to do as much as everyone else wasn't going to be good enough. We needed extra training, extra fitness, extra speed, extra strength – the lot. If there was one thing I would say to the lads thousands of times, it was, "Every year, a bunch of men win Munster. If you can hurl well, that's wonderful, but you must be a man first. Men win Munster."'

FORMER CLARE TRAINER MIKE MCNAMARA,

TO HELL AND BACK

ON THE MORNING OF 26 DECEMBER 1998, A DOZEN CARS assembled outside the Glen Rovers Hurling Club. Donal Óg Cusack glanced around the car park. In two or three cars, he could see lads yawning and stretching their arms; in two or three others, fellas shaking and holding their heads, heavy from the excesses of the previous day and night. Then he looked into mine, and there I was, polishing off a box of Cadbury's Roses. Obviously Jimmy and Tom and Teddy were trying to send out some signal by calling training for St Stephen's Day, but it was probably only going to be a light puckaround. Another Dairy

Milk and a few more of those Hazel Whirls and Chocolate Bites weren't going to do any harm.

About half an hour later, those same chocolates had come up and been spewed out. We hadn't gone for a puckaround up on the Glen Field; instead, we'd gone for a six-mile run through the valley by the Glen. Christmas was over. The old way was over. To beat Clare, we would have to outwork Clare.

We would have to work smarter, too, which is how the hurlers met the other Seanie McGrath, the PE guru from Bantry, for the first time. Teddy Owens had been a revelation to us the previous season, ever since the first time he entered our dressing-room before a south-east league game in Midleton and boldly told us how Waterford played and how we'd beat them that day. But, as much as Teddy knew, he also had the sense and humility to consult others, such as fellow PE trainers like Seanie and Donal O'Gorman. And together they decided there was no sense in a chocolate lover like Brian Corcoran doing the same training in January as a thoroughbred like Seán Óg Ó hAilpín.

So we were divided into three groups: the very fit, the so-so fit and the not-so fit, or the Fat Club or the Teletubbies, as we were also known. We were at point A, and by spring we'd be at point B, and then for the summer at C. Sprinting right away wasn't going to work off our excess body fat. It was better for us to run slower and for longer.

One night that January, we ran 26 laps of the tunnels of Páirc Uí Chaoimh. Most nights, we'd do eight. At the start, the eight laps would take us nearly twenty minutes to complete, but over the weeks it became a race, and the times kept coming down, eventually to around the fourteen-minute mark. Then we moved on to sprint and strength work, while the middle group joined Seán Óg's plyometric sessions.

I'd done weights before with the footballers, but '99 was the first year the hurlers really got into them. Derek Barrett, Sully and myself were the strongest on the panel, and, by the end of March, we were squatting 32 st. Lifting a weight like that requires technique as much as strength. You have to shuffle under the bar, step in under the holder, rest it, and then, using the strength of your legs, start to raise and stand up. One night, though, when we were lifting, I moved my head too far forward, and the whole thing collapsed, hitting the two safety bars. Everyone looked around to find me lying on the ground and the weights bouncing up and down on the safety bars above me. It had been a close one.

But I suppose I had an excuse. My technique was a bit rusty because I had been away for three weeks. I had been on my honeymoon.

IN AUGUST 1996, I RECEIVED A PHONE CALL THAT changed my life. Dr Con Murphy, in a moment of genius, recommended me as a date to this girl named Elaine. Now Elaine was on the other end of the phone, wondering if I was interested in meeting up. The Friday after Kerry ended Cork's involvement in that year's championship, I was sprinting up McCurtain Street to meet my blind date for eight o'clock in the Corner House for a drink before heading across the road to City Limits Comedy Club.

Before that, I hadn't liked nightclubs and pubs and the pressure of having to chat up women. It just seemed so forced. Most girls, I didn't have a lot in common with. Those who were interested in hurling and football didn't really appeal either, because the games were the last thing I wanted to talk about on a night out. But with Elaine, nothing was forced. There was no bull, no pretence, no mention of the Gah. She didn't know who I was, so the pressure was off. After the club, we went for coffee in Tribes coffee shop off Grand Parade, and we wondered what Dr Con had been thinking. We had very different lifestyles, different interests, different ambitions, and yet, by the end of the night, I knew he had been spot on. I knew I wanted to know much more about this beautiful, confident woman who would show me that there was far more to life than hurling and football.

Elaine would introduce me to a whole new world of alternatives: alternative schools of thought and therapies, alternative foods that I wouldn't have tried by myself, Lyric FM, walking boots and, most importantly, fun, which at the time was a big alternative for me.

The Comedy Club became a favourite haunt of ours, but I felt particularly at home in Sir Henry's. The clientele there was hardly GAA hard core, and I loved the anonymity you had in there. One night, though, I was going up the stairs when this fella coming down looked at me. I looked at him. Did I recognise him? Did he recognise me? Then his face brightened. Either he knew me as a) the GAA player, b) someone from work or college, or c) Marco Pantani, the cyclist.

Next thing, he greets me like a long-lost friend. 'How's it going, boyyy!'

'Not too bad!' I smile, trying to figure where I know him from.

'Jesus, I haven't seen you in years!' he says, hitting me on the arm.

Right, I think. He knows I'm not Marco Pantani. But do I know him? Is it from college? Is it from the hurling? I'll play along till I figure it out.

'Yeah, I know,' I say, hitting him back. 'How are you keeping yourself?'

'Flying it, boy! Flying it! Come here, you seen Mary at all lately?'

'God, no, I haven't,' I say, while thinking, did I hang out with a Mary in college?

'What about Paul?' he says.

Paul. Hmmm.

'No, I haven't seen him in ages either.'

'Right, right. So tell us! What are you doing these days?'

'Well, I'm working down there in Janssen Pharmaceutical.'

His eyebrows crease. 'What are you doing there?'

'IT.'

He looks at me again, stands back, then leans forward again.

'You weren't a bouncer in here a few years ago?'

'No, eh, I wasn't.'

And then it was one of those 'that didn't happen' awkward moments before we went our separate ways.

And for ages that was the nearest anyone came to recognising me in there. I was free to dance how I liked, act how I liked and, one night, dress how I liked. There was a fancy-dress party, and I went as a transvestite with a wig and a D-cup and some face paint that made me look like a cross between the Ultimate Warrior and Danny La Rue. There was no other place in the whole wide world I'd have gone dressed up like that, only Henry's.

We walked in the door.

'Corcoran! Come here, is that you? Christ, it is! What's the story, boyyy?'

It was an old teammate from Erins Own. Soon, word was out all around the club. And, even on my wedding day, John couldn't resist bringing it up in his best man's speech.

✻ ✻ ✻

'The crisis of today is often the joke of tomorrow'

H.G. WELLS

SHORTLY AFTER I RETURNED FROM OUR HONEYMOON in Orlando, a last-minute Liam Cahill goal in Thurles ended whatever chance Cork had of making the league play-offs and retaining our title. Losing that day to Tipp was tolerable, as was losing to them there again in a challenge game a few weeks before our Munster semi-final against Waterford. But then we lost to Tipp in another challenge game in the Park. It wasn't tolerable. It was a catastrophe. In the first half, we'd been playing with the breeze, and yet Tipp destroyed us. Then they turned round and continued to drill us until, with 15 minutes to go, Jimmy and Nicky English agreed to call a halt to the game.

We went back into the dressing-room, and Landers, our team captain, came over to me. Teddy had just spoken to him. Jimmy wanted a word next door with the two of us and Fergal Ryan.

We went in. It was just the four of us: Jimmy and his three most senior players.

'Lads,' said Jimmy, 'I'll be straight up. I mightn't be the right man for this job. If I'm the problem, say so, and I'll walk away.'

We reassured Jimmy that he wasn't the problem, that we wanted him to stay, that he had to stay. The intensity in training and the hurling drills would have to go up a few notches, but he would have to stay.

That Thursday night, we had our best, sharpest, most intense training session of the year.

The following week, Jimmy decided to give six players their championship debut: Donal Óg Cusack, Wayne Sherlock, Mickey O'Connell, Timmy McCarthy, Ben O'Connor and Neil Ronan. The six of them were all twenty-two or younger. A few weeks earlier, we had been favourites to beat Waterford. Once people heard the team selection, the pendulum swung. Jimmy was convinced, though, it was the way to go. 'I had faith in the players,' he would later say. 'I picked a team of hurlers.'

It was a huge call. Lose and we were gone for the year and Jimmy was gone, full stop. Win and we were back in a Munster final – and Croke Park. The Tuesday night in training before that Waterford game, I told the lads in a huddle about the day I was up in Croke Park a few weeks earlier for the launch of the Guinness Championship. 'Lads, it's a long time since Cork have been up there, but it's a beautiful pitch, and, I tell you, when I looked around it, I said, "I can't see us being beaten if we get up here." It's where we belong.'

The day of the game, Landers reiterated that theme. It was our first time going to the more secluded environs of Dundrum House rather than the Anner Hotel, and before we left for Thurles, Landers called us all in. He showed us his clenched fist, then opened it, and in his palm was a Celtic Cross, a senior All Ireland medal.

'Lads, not one of us here has one of those. The selectors – Jimmy, Tom, Seanie [O'Leary], Johnny [Crowley] – God knows how many they have [18], but they can't win it for us. We have to go out and win it for ourselves. Days like this, they're precious. Because we don't want to end our careers not having one of these in our hands.'

You could see lads staring at the medal as if it was the Holy Grail. The tone was set. Nothing, not even the best Waterford team in over 30 years, was going to stop us getting to Croke Park and getting our hands on that medal.

That game in Thurles would turn out a lot like the previous year's league final and the other epic games we'd have with Waterford in the years to come. It was frenetic, it was tight and the momentum changed again and again. It was three points each after quarter of an hour. Then I soloed upfield and, from about 70 yards, struck it over the bar, and suddenly Mickey O'Connell started scoring for fun from that range. By half-time, we were three up, and, entering the last quarter, we'd stretched the lead to five, but then Paul Flynn buried a free to the net and Dan Shanahan followed it up with a point to cut the deficit to one. Would the kids survive their onslaught? Would all those runs around the tunnel and through the Glen tell?

Twelve minutes later, Aodán Mac Suibhne would blow his whistle, the trigger for an iconic GAA moment: Jimmy running onto the field, arms raised, mouth open. In those last twelve minutes, we had outscored Waterford by eight points to three. Landers belted over a point just after Shanahan's, Mickey would bang over his seventh and eighth points of the day, another debutant, Timmy, would scorch through the centre to flip over his third and Ben would score the first of many points he'd fire over for Cork out on that wing. Meanwhile, Sully, playing his first championship game at full-back, had hardly given Flynn a puck.

Seven long years after '92, we were finally back in a Munster final.

* * *

'Tipperary will win the league but Clare are the team everyone wants to beat. We may have lost to them in three of the last four years, but if we're to win a Munster title I hope we play Clare. They are to us what Dublin were to the Kerry footballers in the '70s. Dublin had the upper hand for the first few years, and Kerry had to beat them to prove themselves. We'd love a crack at Clare this year. It wouldn't be the same without them'

BRIAN CORCORAN, 16 FEBRUARY 1999

A FEW MONTHS BEFORE THE SUMMER OF '98 AND Colin Lynch, Jimmy Cooney, and Loughnane's 'state of the nation' Clare FM address, we beat Clare by 11 points in the national league semi-final. Afterwards, all kinds of stories did the rounds, including one that they had trained in nearby Templemore the morning of the match. It wasn't true, and neither was the notion that they hadn't cared about that match. Towards the end of the game, a few of their backs started to give a few of our forwards a few raps of the hurley. They wouldn't have resorted to that if they weren't cranky, if they hadn't wanted to win. We drew confidence from that. That game mightn't have been championship, but it had been played in championship conditions in front of a championship crowd. Our time was soon.

The apprenticeship was not yet complete, though. When we met Clare again two months later in the Munster semi-final, they were breathing fire. Afterwards, Liam Griffin would call it The Last Game Ever, because that's how Clare approached it. They tricked us with their dummy team, they bullied us with their sneers and shoves and stares, but, above all, they outworked and out-hurled us.

In the league semi-final, I had been allowed to dominate the game from centre-back. Clare made a decision that I wasn't going to be allowed to do that again. They put Jamesie O'Connor at centre-forward, and he tried – with success – to drag me out to the wings. When I did get on the ball, I'd be immediately swarmed by Clare men. It was as if there were two of them for every one of us. At one stage, I got a ball and turned, only to find P.J. O'Connell. I turned again, and there was Jamesie. I couldn't turn again, so I had to hit it, but when I did it was half-blocked, and it went over the line. And as it trickled past Loughnane, he jumped up, punching his fist into the air, as if Clare had scored a goal.

They would continue to make statements throughout their 0–21 to 0–13 win, but 12 months later those statements had not been forgotten. The day of the 1999 Munster final, Landers had another motivational trick up his sleeve. This time, he put a tape into a VCR and pressed play. It was a clip from The

Last Game Ever. Joe Deane had won a free out around the 40-metre line when suddenly Ollie Baker came in and kneed him in the back. Seanie McGrath from the Glen came in to offer Joe some support, but then Anthony Daly came rushing in, to sneer in Seanie's ear and dig him in the back.

'Lads,' said Landers, 'last year we allowed two of our smallest players to be pushed around, intimidated, by two of their biggest players! Where were the rest of us, lads?'

He then pointed to the screen, where the frame of Seanie and Joe and Baker and Daly was frozen.

'That will not happen today.'

It didn't. It wasn't that we went toe-to-toe with Clare or tried to push or bully them – that wasn't the way we wanted to play; that wasn't the way we were set up – but this time we were the ones playing with our chests out. This time, we were the ones chasing them down.

Clare would come thundering back and, with a few minutes to go, had a 13-metre free to level the game. But somehow David Forde blazed wide, and after that we sprinted towards victory. We won a couple of balls around the half-back line, Joe pointed a few frees and then I caught a high ball and came bursting out with it. The Cork crowd went wild and, seconds later, even wilder, as Mickey picked out Ben, who sped past Frank Lohan to point from the wing. At last, we had beaten Clare.

'It was a huge occasion for us,' I'd tell reporters in the dressing-room afterwards. 'If they had beaten us today, then it would have put us back again, and, while we had the option of the backdoor, we didn't want that.'

All these years later, I'd say the same of that day. History shows that game was to us what '78 was to Kerry, that it was the day the torch was handed over in Munster.

But we wanted more than to be top dogs in Munster.

✳   ✳   ✳

'Cork–Offaly was a wonderful game and a credit to both teams. I have seen a lot of hurling in my time, but the performance of Brian Corcoran yesterday will live in the memory forever'

JOHNNY CLIFFORD, *EVENING ECHO*,
MONDAY, 9 AUGUST 1999

TO WIN, A TEAM MUST FIRST BE UNITED, BUT NOTHING makes a team more united than to win. Now that we were out of Munster, we were up in Dublin for the semi-final, staying overnight, getting the train up and down, killing time, all together. It was rarely boring, especially with someone like Seanie McGrath of the Glen around. If you put Seanie in any company, he'd be the life and soul of the party, while Mickey O'Connell and John Browne were good for a laugh, especially with their routine of sucking in a helium balloon and then mimicking Ger Loughnane with a high-pitched voice.

On the field, the team was gelling too. Taking over from Ger Cunningham would have daunted many a keeper but not Donal Óg; even then, he was devising a puckout strategy with our centre-forward Fergal McCormack and wing-forward Neil Ronan and checking out the stats that Teddy used to compile.

Sully and John Browne had swapped spots from the year before, with John now in the corner, and, along with Fergal Ryan, they made up probably the best full-back line in the game. Wayne Sherlock was playing like a veteran instead of a newcomer, Seán Óg was steadiness personified while covering acres of ground, while Landers and Mickey, neither of whom had played in midfield during the league, had just got the better of the two best midfield pairings of '98.

Centre-forward had been a problem spot for Cork for years, but McCormack's hand, strength and vision had solved it.

Outside him, Timmy and Ben were full of running, constantly providing him with an outlet, while inside Seanie and Joe were linking up like they used to for UCC in the Fitzgibbon days, with plenty of help from Neil. On the bench, then, we had plenty of options, especially with the craft and strength of Kevin Murray and Alan Browne.

The backroom team complemented each other too. Jimmy had a deep passion for the game, but it wasn't something he proclaimed. He was measured, understated, even tempered. So was Tom Cashman; Teddy could do the shouting and geeing up for them.

They were also smart. The night before our All Ireland semi-final with the defending champions Offaly, they brought us to Croke Park for a look around and puckaround. I had been the only player to play a senior championship match there. Ben O'Connor had never even been there before as a spectator; it wasn't as if Cork had given him a reason to go up there during his teenage years. But, because of the visit, Ben now felt at home in Croker.

That game against Offaly is considered a classic. When you're playing, though, you're not really aware how good a game is; all you're focusing on is the ball and the score. What I do know is that we won, 0–19 to 0–16, and that I felt in the zone that day. Physically, I have never felt better during a match. I came off the field feeling I could have gone back on and played another game.

'I don't know what you've done to us,' I said to Teddy on the train down afterwards, 'but it's worked. I feel as fresh as a daisy.'

Neither of us was getting carried away, though. As I again said to reporters after the game, 'This victory is only a stepping stone. Now we face the biggest day of our sporting lives.'

✻   ✻   ✻

'D.J. emphasised goals. "There's goals there," he'd say. "We'll bury them." He'd put goals into their mind'
FORMER KILKENNY SELECTOR JOHNNY WALSH

IN THE LEAD-UP TO THAT ALL IRELAND FINAL, EVERYONE seemed to think it would be close, and yet everyone seemed to think it would be Kilkenny. Cork were too young to win an All Ireland final; Kilkenny were too good to lose another for the second straight year: that was the thinking at the time. It wasn't our thinking. Jimmy steeled us against the popular notion that 'you have to lose one to win one' and that we'd be back some other time by reminding us that '73 had been the optimum time for the county footballers to win an All Ireland before 'this machine', Kerry, came along. We looked at the Galway footballers of '98 who came up to Croke Park out of nowhere and won. We could do the same.

We also set ourselves a goal: not to concede any. That summer, Kilkenny had scored thirteen goals in three games. 'If we keep them goalless, we'll beat them,' I told the lads the week of the match. It wasn't going to be easy, with D.J., Carter and Brian McEvoy having the summer of their careers and their rookie, Henry Shefflin, already showing signs of greatness, but if any defence was going to shut them out it was ours.

The day of the game, Landers had another motivational master card ready for us. In Dundrum, he had told us that the backroom team couldn't win the All Ireland for us, but now he reminded us that we could win it for them. He showed us a photograph. It was from the 1982 All Ireland final, with the two captains, Jimmy Barry-Murphy and Brian Cody, shaking hands at the toss. We all knew how that day panned out for both of them; it was one of Jimmy's worst days as a player. We had the chance now to make this one of his best days. Jimmy and Cody would be shaking hands after the game.

One of them would be devastated, as Jimmy was in '82; one of them would be holding the Liam McCarthy Cup, as Cody did in '82. We had the power to decide this time the victor and the vanquished.

If Landers made it clear just how much Jimmy meant to us, Jimmy then made it clear to us just how much we meant to him. He came over to us one by one and presented each of us with our jersey with a shake of the hand first then a hug. It was simple, spontaneous, special. Fourteen years after playing that demonstration game out the back of the primary school for him and Mr O'Neill, now here I was receiving an All Ireland jersey from him.

Then his lieutenant, Teddy, had a few words. 'Brian Corcoran has carried us on his shoulders for long enough!' he announced, thumping the tub in the dressing-room. 'Let's carry him on our shoulders today!'

Now, at the time, I picked up Teddy's words the wrong way. I thought he was inferring that I was nearly on my last legs, and I said to myself, 'Hey, Teddy, I plan to have a say in this thing today!' Others told me later, though, that right away they knew what Teddy was getting at, and that it added to the whole upbeat, focused vibe there was in the room.

But then someone mentioned that it was 'feckin' lashing' outside. In the bad, sad old years, when we'd routinely lose first day out to either Clare or Limerick, it had a tendency to be lashing outside.

I stood up. 'Hey, it doesn't matter a shit if it's raining! I'd prefer to win in the rain than lose in the sunshine. It's an All Ireland final. There's only one thing we're here for, and that's the cup. It'll be a battle now, and we'll win that battle. It's heads down and fight to the end.'

I was on John Power, a wiry, fiery, brilliant centre-forward. The mood I was in, though, it didn't matter if I was on John Power or Mick Power or Mick Mackey; I was going to stand in front of him, get out in front of him, read the play and play the ball.

A minute or two into the game, Kilkenny had their first puckout. My old Midleton CBS colleague, Ronan Dwane, who was a sub and hurley carrier for us that day, was down behind the Kilkenny goal and could overhear their selector and former goalkeeping great Noel Skehan instructing James McGarry. 'Loft it straight down the middle. See how Corcoran gets on with Power hanging off him.'

It would be a standard policy of Kilkenny's under Cody to try to weaken an opposing team by instantly attacking their strengths. So, McGarry knocked it straight down the centre. I caught it. And the strange thing about it was that Power had tried to catch it too. A few months later, I would listen to Cork 103 FM's commentary of the game, which my mother had taped. The co-commentator was Ger Cunningham, and, after that passage of play, he said he couldn't believe that Power had tried to catch the first ball instead of just pulling on it.

It was a scrappy first half. Conditions were miserable. The rain eased, but the pitch was slippery and the ball was wet and heavy. Both sets of forwards would be heavily criticised for shooting more wides than scores (34 to 25), but that was more due to the weight of the ball that day; it was like trying to hit a rock.

Scores were at a premium, but, by the mid-point of the second half, Kilkenny were finding them handier to come by. Then, Charlie Carter had a goal chance with no one on him. Instead, the ball skidded off his hurley and skidded over for a point. Reading his book, it's obvious that Charlie still can't believe that miss, and, at the time, I couldn't believe it either. But it still put Kilkenny four up, and, on a day in which every score seemed to be chiselled out of granite, that was a big lead.

I started to picture going around Paddy Barry's Corner on

the open-top bus the following night. Would we be turning that corner and seeing a sea of people with our thumbs up, or a trickle of faithful supporters with our heads down like in '92 and '93? It couldn't be like '92 and '93.

And then, everything seemed to change. Seanie scooped up a ball with that little wand of his and fired over a point. Things hadn't really fallen for Seanie in the first half, and a few of the selectors had suggested taking him off, but Jimmy said no; he had put his faith in the players, he had picked a bunch of hurlers, and Seanie personified that philosophy. That faith would be rewarded. After further points from Timmy, Ben and Joe, Seanie drew us level. Then Joe and Ben put us two up. Now we were the ones in the lead – and defending that lead as if our lives depended on it.

Ben came back down the field to stem one attack, but on another Shefflin pointed a free to leave just one in it.

Then they attacked again. I won a ball over in the right corner, down by the Canal End, under the Cusack Stand. But once I cleared it I felt I hadn't an ounce of energy left to drag myself back to man the centre. But somehow, from somewhere (the thought of Paddy Barry's Corner, most likely), I got this lease of energy.

The ball came in again. We drove it out again. Then the ball broke around midfield, on the ground. The ref, Pat O'Connor, seemed to signal with his hands for a foul ball. Our dugout seemed to think he was signalling for full-time. And when they ran onto the field, Pat seemed to take that as the signal for full-time.

Next thing, he was blowing that whistle.

It was over.

The match, the final, the wait, the quest.

I looked around, and the first person I saw was D.J. We shook hands.

Then we were hit by this deluge of subs and mentors.

Jimmy ran over and we hugged.

'Thanks, Brian,' he said.

And I said, 'Thank you too, Jimmy. Thank you too.'

It's actually happened. I can't believe it's actually happened.

I wanted to savour everything, and I did. It helped that the spectators couldn't come onto the field. It mightn't have been as spectacular or as popular a sight as most post-All Ireland scenes, but it was special, being free to see and embrace teammates out on the field, rather than waiting till the dressing-room to salute them all.

As long as I live, I will always remember and treasure the lap of honour. Landers, with the cup in his hand, insisted I come to the front and carry it around with him. We ran down by the Hogan Stand, towards the Canal End. I noticed our local parish priest, Fr Kerry Murphy O'Connor, running across the pitch. Then I looked over and saw my uncle D.D. hanging onto the wire. I left Landers and the lads and dashed straight over to D.D. Tears were streaming down his face, and yet I'd never seen him so happy. I stretched out my arms, clasping his hands, and then I made my way back to the lads, waving and smiling to D.D. as I did. I was lagging a bit behind them now, but it was just as well for the view I would soon see.

As I was walking halfway down over by the Cusack Stand, the lads were already down by Hill 16, which was just one mass of red and white.

Then Landers climbed up onto the railings and raised the cup in one hand above the wire, the cue for a wall of sound. It was one of the sweetest sights and sweetest sounds of my life.

For years, I'd watched All Irelands and seen players and supporters take over that field and thought, God, I'd love to know what that feels like. Now I knew what they felt like.

Now I knew what they meant by 'actualisation'. This was actualisation. This was nirvana. This was heaven.

Back in the dressing-room, the inner glow remained. I stepped under the showers with this big smile on my face, and nothing could wipe it off. We were walking on air. Jimmy told us how proud he was of every one of us and that it was the best day of his life. Afterwards, during an RTE interview in the Cusack Stand, I just looked out at the pitch below, and the sun finally coming out to shine on it, and wondered at how beautiful it was.

And that's how I was for the rest of that day, for the rest of that week. I don't think that smile ever left me. It was there when our bus noticed Sonia O'Sullivan and her family just around the corner from Croke Park and stopped to let Sonia put baby Ciara in the cup up the front. It was there when we walked through a sea of people out in the reception area of the Burlington Hotel and I finally got to see and embrace Elaine. All day, all night, all week, I was just floating. I didn't touch a drop of alcohol, because I didn't want to miss a thing. Just small, special things, like being beside Wayne Sherlock at the private pre-reception for just players, partners and officials, and us basking and sharing in the feeling of having actually done it; like walking into the function itself and 2,000 people on their feet to salute the All Ireland champions; like Ger Canning presenting me with the RTE Man of the Match award, crystal, and tickets and five-star accommodation for the football final two weeks later.

Ray Cummins and John Fenton came over to pay respect. That meant a lot. Now I was part of all that, of what they'd done and won. I was now welcome to that club.

The following evening, we returned to Cork, and, after we stopped off briefly to receive a rapturous welcome in Mallow, I slipped away from the singing and joking and drinking to do something I'd waited six years to do. Standing between the two carriages, just opposite the toilets, and with no one in sight, I put the Liam McCarthy Cup up to the window as we passed Kilcully graveyard and just said a little prayer for an old friend. 'This is for you, Kid. This is for you.'

It was meant to be a private moment, but, as I closed the window, the county chairman Brian Barrett came out of the toilet and was puzzled about why I was standing there with the cup. A few hours later, we were both on a stage in the Grand Parade, and Brian was telling the whole of Cork about my tribute to Kid. At the time, I'd rather Brian hadn't mentioned it, but the following week I got a lovely letter from Kid's niece, thanking me for remembering him.

Kid had told me something else on that train up in '93: just how special it was to turn around Paddy Barry's Corner the Monday after winning an All Ireland. And it was. To come around McCurtain Street and then onto Patrick's Hill to look down at Patrick's Bridge and Patrick's Street, with people all lined up on the streets and hanging off lamp posts and outside shop windows, waving their red flags, was the ultimate high.

And then, after the speeches from the stage, we went to a reception in the Imperial. Outside to greet us and walk in with us were my parents, Nuala and John. They hadn't gone up to the game on Sunday, as Dad was feeling a bit under the weather, but now he looked a million dollars. You wouldn't have known there was anything wrong with him.

And you wouldn't dream that, only two months later, at sixty-five, he would have passed away.

It's the hardest thing in the world to describe, the last time I saw my father, probably because it was one of the hardest things I've ever had to endure. Dad always had a smile, and now he couldn't smile. Dad always looked strong; now he had hardly any strength at all. Dad always had a kind word; now he could say no word at all. 'Don't worry about it, Brian,' he'd say to me when I'd be down after some loss. 'We'll do it the next day.' And now, for us, together, there wouldn't be a next day.

Christmas was always a big thing in our house, but that Christmas there was no tree, no crib, no lights, no telly. It was the worst Christmas of my life. At that stage, 1999 was the best and the worst year of my life.

I married the girl of my dreams, and I won the cup of my dreams, but I lost my father, the most gentle man of all gentlemen.

And that was hard, very hard, to deal with.

But the way I looked at it was this: thank God Dad was there to meet Elaine and see us married; thank God he was there to see us win this holy grail we'd all been after for so many years; and thank God I shared that phone call with him and Mam on the bus just after the game, hearing the tears and the joy in their voices and the cheers from the neighbours in the distance.

And even now I still hear him. I always have and I always will.

CHAPTER TWELVE

A SUNNY DAY
IN THURLES

'Munster final day is an occasion that's impossible to duplicate around the globe. This is Cork versus Tipp. This is Semple Stadium. This is the pitch where Seán Óg Murphy and Martin Kennedy did battle long before the phrase Hell's Kitchen was invented and where Dinny Barry-Murphy was a hero before Jimmy's da was even thought of. This is us. This is our game'

LIAM GRIFFIN, *SUNDAY TRIBUNE*

TUESDAY, 6 JUNE 2006

Tonight was my first night back in training since the Clare game, but, by the time I got out of work and got through traffic, I was half an hour late. I was annoyed about that. It was a beautiful evening out in Carrigtwohill, and I could have done with the full session as I'm going to be in Italy next week.

I noticed Declan Kidney, the coach of the Munster rugby team, up on the bank, watching on. We didn't get to talk to him or congratulate him on their brilliant European Cup win the other week, though; by the time we'd finished up, he had gone.

He'd have seen a smart, well-planned but simple session. A lot of it is just concentrating on the basics. We have very few games in training. Again, it goes back to O'Grady's time. I couldn't believe it in 2004 when we weren't playing any games of backs and forwards or full-scale A versus B games, especially when you'd be hearing reports of Kilkenny and Waterford flaking lumps out of each other every night. Instead, we were just standing around hooking and blocking, working on our first touch and striking. But, when we destroyed Antrim in the All Ireland quarter-final, I realised the method in his madness. It wasn't just the way the backs had closed Antrim down; it was all the hooking and blocking our forwards were doing, too. It was automatic. It was systematic. It had been drilled and instilled.

When we do have a game in training, the two teams bear no relation to the actual team or positions; some nights, I could be with Sully, and he's the one in the forwards. It's only 12 minutes – with a series of conditions. For the first four minutes, we just pull on everything. For the next four, there's still no soloing, and if you receive a hand-pass you must give a stick-pass, and vice versa. The last four minutes, we just play freestyle.

Personally, I don't understand the logic of the first four minutes when we're doing nothing but ground hurling; in real matches, we do virtually no ground hurling. I can see the logic of the middle four minutes, as it is intended to promote support play. But, if it was up to me, we'd just play freestyle for the 12 minutes.

THURSDAY, 8 JUNE

Going training tonight was even harder than usual.

The two girls have been suffering with chest infections for the last couple of days, and while on my way home this evening Kate came on the phone.

'Daddy, I want you to come home!'

I told her I'd play with her tomorrow night. But, for a five year old, tomorrow night might as well be next year.

'But I want to see you, Daddy!' She coughed into the phone. 'I'm feeling sick. I'm very sad.'

So I rushed back from Cashel to see them before training, but, just as I was about to head out the door again, Kate was wrapped around one of my legs, and Edel was hugging the other.

'Don't go, Daddy! I don't want you to go!'

I pulled their arms from my legs and left them, and I left Elaine to look after them – again. It played on my mind a lot, but ultimately that's what commitment to the three in a row involves. It comes before everything else.

The other day, unusually, I was able to collect Kate from school. Her teacher commented on what an advanced reader Kate is for her age. 'What are you doing?' she asked. 'You must be doing something special.' And I had to answer that it's probably because every night her mum reads her plenty of bedtime stories. What I didn't mention is that it's never her dad. Her dad is out playing hurling.

Kate is five now; Edel will be four in October; Ewan is ten months; and yet the amount of time I've actually spent with my kids is shameful. There have been weeks when I don't see them from Monday to Friday between work, training and meetings. Even on Saturdays, I'm still no good to them because I'm conserving energy for training or a match the next day. A family day is virtually off-limits during the summer, as I have to recover from a frantic week and hydrate.

Elaine is the most unselfish person I know. Her goal for the past three years has been the same – that Cork win the All Ireland. She had no interest in hurling before she met me, but, because it's important to me, it's important to her, and she'll do all she can to help me achieve it. After Ewan was born last August, I was the one sleeping in the spare room, to ensure I didn't miss a night's sleep ahead of the All Ireland.

Am I being fair? No, I'm not. So why do it? I can live without hurling; I certainly did during my retirement. I cannot live without my family. And yet, I leave them practically every night of the week to play hurling. I'm sure I'll come to regret all that lost family time. I probably already do. But there's an inner drive that I just can't ignore. It's like an addiction, and I'll do whatever I have to do to feed the habit. The addiction isn't to hurling, as such. I wouldn't miss the muck and the slog in the dark, the belts and the bruises, the hectic schedule, not even the games. It's the quest for the holy grail, for sporting immortality. Winning an All Ireland has been my goal, my drive, my destiny since I was old enough to hold a hurley. Everything I have done in my life has led me to this challenge, prepared me for this quest. It is who I am, and everything I am is intrinsically tinted with my lust for gold.

History and madness.

WEDNESDAY, 14 JUNE

Greetings from Sabaudia, one hour south of Rome. It's very nice and easy to look out at the view from the beach here, but, as I learned this morning, it's not so nice or easy to run on it.

My flight got in late last night, so I waited until eight this morning to find out where I could train. I jogged along the beach for a few minutes in the blazing heat before settling for this quiet stretch away from the hotel. Then I picked up four stones and set them twenty metres apart, to form a Fartlek course, and set my mobile phone to count down the three minutes.

The first one was very tough, with the sand being so soft and deep, and for a moment I thought about knocking the second circuit down to two minutes. Then I thought of Seanie and all the lads at home. This week, he will be putting the lads through their toughest week of training this month. He doesn't believe that you just keep 'ticking over' between matches. The week after, say, a Munster semi-final, we'll go easy enough, but then for the next week we'll dig deep into what he calls 'the well' to build ourselves up for a Munster final.

So, I pushed hard for those three minutes, jogging the sides and sprinting the diagonals, and then, after a minute's breather, pushed hard for three minutes more. By the time I'd done my warm-down, I was soaking wet. I thought about just sitting there and admiring the ocean, but instead I decided to shower, have breakfast and then come out and relax for a few hours before the meeting with my Swiss and Belgian colleagues.

The meeting was mostly presentations, and the small talk was mostly about the World Cup. Michael Jordan's old college coach, Dean Smith, used to tell his players if they were nervous before a big game to relax; a billion Chinese people couldn't care how the game went. It's like that here. On Sunday week, 55,000 might pack into Thurles, but here in Sabaudia nobody will know or care.

THURSDAY, 15 JUNE

I got back tonight, but while I had the stop-off in Heathrow Con texted me from Páirc Uí Rinn, wondering if I'll play tomorrow in the UCC Golf Classic in Cork Golf Club. Apparently there was a discussion about whether we should be allowed to play or not. Eventually it was decided we could, but the whole thing reminded me of a run-in I had years ago with Frank Murphy.

Back in 1994, when Johnny Clifford was coach and Frank was a selector, the club was scheduled to play a league game against Blackrock the same night as Cork training. We'd been told with Cork that we wouldn't be released to play for the clubs, but on the day of the game Martin Bowen called me while I was doing my work experience in Kinsale. The club was stuck. Only 13 lads were available to play. If myself, Colman Dillon and Timmy Kelleher, who were also on the county panel at the time, didn't play, the club would have to forfeit the game.

The following day, I got a call from Páirc Uí Chaoimh instructing me to attend a meeting before training on Thursday. As I walked up to Frank's office, I met Colman coming out after getting a bollicking. Timmy had received the same treatment. The selectors had employed the old divide-and-conquer approach, and I was going to be the next they'd try to isolate and bully.

I sat down. All the selectors were on the other side of the desk, including my own clubman P.J. Murphy, but Frank did all the talking. We had been instructed not to play with the clubs, and the three of us had breached that instruction.

I decided I was going to stand my ground. 'Well, what were we supposed to do? The club wouldn't have been able to field a team, and you'd have been the ones fining the club. We keep hearing that club is the bedrock of the GAA, and here we are being criticised for playing with the club when it's in trouble.'

Frank changed his tack. 'Actually, I'm wondering about your attitude lately. I hear you're playing a lot of golf.'

I wasn't buying that red herring. For one, I was playing hardly any golf, being down in Kinsale. Two, even if I was, it was irrelevant. 'I don't see what that's got to do with anything.

This is the first I've heard that playing golf somehow equates to having a bad attitude. Golf has never affected my hurling. For what it's worth, I played golf the day before the '91 [All Ireland] minor final.'

I looked at Frank.

I decided to keep going.

'And, while I'm at it, I played nine holes the day before the '92 senior final!'

Frank was nearly falling out of his chair.

'As far as I'm concerned,' I added, 'playing golf has nothing to do with hurling.'

And, from that night on, Frank and myself have never crossed each other.

Frank has got a lot of bad press in his time, but the man is a great resource for Cork. The way he runs off all those fixtures in a dual county; the way he knows every rule and regulation; his speed of thought in argument; it's incredible. If I was charged with murder in the morning, I'd go straight to Frank to defend me. He has a brilliant mind. Back in my days playing minor, we'd have a meal in the Imperial Hotel after the last training session before a championship game, and Frank would give this stirring speech for ten minutes without taking a breath, without consulting a note.

He had to change his ways, though. Cork GAA had to change its ways. The strike proved that. It wasn't that Frank was the problem, but he was at the head of the organisation that disrespected players and backroom members.

The first time I met Seanie McGrath, the trainer, was when Larry Tompkins had him in to do some tests with us at the start of '98. That spring, we played Kildare in the league, and Seanie wanted to go up with us to Newbridge. Larry had to tell Seanie he couldn't go with the team. Seanie ended up making his own way and paying his own way into that game.

We also had a character called Mick Curtin with the

footballers back then. He just showed up at training one night in Ballygarvan in the pissing rain, and soon he was a regular feature, putting out the bollards and cones, and helping with the gear and water and whatever else had to be done. It was great to have him around, but he didn't have any official status. The day we played Kerry in Killarney in '98, we sneaked Mick into the dressing-room. The board wouldn't give him a pass to go out on the pitch, and as he had no match ticket Mick had to watch the match from outside the dressing-room door at the very far corner of the ground.

Fringe players were treated particularly shabbily. In 1999, Eoin Fitzgerald was on the training panel, though not the panel itself. The Thursday night before the All Ireland semi-final, he went up for his tickets. Tom Cashman had to tell him none had been left out for him and that he wouldn't be travelling with the party on Saturday. Poor Eoin's face said it all. After training all that summer, not only was he not travelling with the team, but the board couldn't even swing him two tickets.

Those of us who did manage to get tickets for that year's final were also disappointed. Elaine shot a tape of the day with her camcorder, and you could tell she was barely able to see over the dugout in front of her. My brother John found himself over at the corner flag by the Canal End. These were so-called prime tickets for the players.

Things have improved now, though they could improve some more. We now don't have to fight for gear. We now have gym access. Mick Curtin now drives the equipment van for the footballers. We now tell the county board where we go on holidays, instead of them telling us where we can afford to go. We can fund-raise the holidays ourselves, and we organise the holidays ourselves. But we still have to fight for tickets, especially good tickets. We still have to request every improvement. The county board grant these improvements because the current players are strong and because they're winning. If the next generation of players is not as strong, I'm not convinced the concessions will be so forthcoming.

All the changes that have been made in recent years, though, can't have been easy on Frank. In the past, he'd be in the dressing-room and dugout before and during games. These days, the only time we see Frank is on the bus from the Burlington to Croke Park when we have a game in Dublin. The rest of the time, we only see him after games. The morning of the 2003 All Ireland semi-final against Wexford, Frank entered the room when the panel were having a meeting, and O'Grady asked him to leave. And for a proud, powerful man like Frank, that must have been hard.

He seems to have adjusted. At times on that bus to Croker, he must wonder how the hell having Al Pacino and Eminem playing from the speakers can help a Cork team win an All Ireland, but after the 2004 final we shared a bear hug in the dressing-room. There's a great photo of us that day, with Frank hanging off one of my arms and our treasurer, Pearse Murphy, hanging off the other.

And, if we win in September, we might share a moment like that again.

FRIDAY, 16 JUNE

I played that round of golf. I was with Con, Niall Ahern from Sars and Hero. I wanted to save energy for training tonight, so I hopped in the buggy between shots, as well as taking loads of water. Hero walked, though, and Con did most of the time too. Once Ger Cunningham saw them tonight, he knew by the red necks and red faces that they'd been golfing. But I slipped under the radar. Hero probably thought I was being the real old man with the buggy, hat and collars up. Now you know, Hero.

I enjoyed training, and I enjoyed the golf too. It was only my second round all year, and conditions were suited for a good score. On the par-five eleventh, there's a plaque to mark how far Seve Ballesteros drove this massive drive in an exhibition game with Liam Higgins in 1981. I haven't heard of anyone who's outdone it, but today I felt conditions were ideal to have a cut at it. I hit a beautiful draw, and it skipped on and on. I hopped into the buggy, dying to see how far it had gone. Ten yards short. It just made me fully appreciate what an incredible drive Seve's was, considering the equipment he had back then. But I got close today. Next time, Seve. Next time.

TUESDAY, 20 JUNE

The alarm goes off at six in the morning. I keep it close to me so I can silence it after the first beep; I don't want to wake Elaine and the kids. I lie for a few minutes, not wanting to get up, but then find the drive to drag myself out. Last night, I shaved and laid out my clothes so I can get out quickly today, and by six forty I'm in the car.

I get the end of the *AM Kelly Show* on Today FM and the first hour of Ian Dempsey's. When they play a song I don't like, I play a track from the CD I've just compiled – some Nirvana, AC/DC, Guns 'n' Roses, Billy Idol, with a bit of Billy Joel and the Boston Symphony Orchestra thrown in.

By eight, I'm in Cashel and sitting down to work. It's as busy as ever, but there's a good buzz around the place this week. A lot of people are travelling to work from Cork, Limerick, Kilkenny, but there are enough locals from Tipp to have some banter about the game. I go for a snack, and when the girls in the canteen see my order of porridge, brown bread and yoghurt, they joke how they must pass this info on to Babs. 'Maybe that's why ye're winning! The porridge!' It's good-natured, harmless stuff, but I don't want to be going in there next Monday or Tuesday having lost.

I leave work at half four. I get down to the Park for quarter to seven. The rest of the lads are already there. Some of them have been here from as early as six, to get a rub, or just to get the scandal. The small talk is a lot like the kind in Sabaudia – the World Cup – and a lot of the lads seem to fancy Argentina's chances.

Then we get down to business: how we're going to play against Tipp, how we're going to play against Eoin Kelly. The man is phenomenal and seems to have brought his game to another level this year. Against Limerick, he scored fourteen points, nine from play. In his last game, against Waterford, he scored 2–9. Tonight, John tells us that, if Kelly goes in full-forward, Sully will pick him up there; if he goes centre-forward, Curran will take him up; and if he goes to either wing or either corner, he's Brian Murphy's. We all feel good about that. There mightn't be a better forward in the country than Eoin Kelly, but Eoin will know there isn't a better man-marker than Brian Murphy.

He's one of the unsung heroes of this team, Brian. On the field, he's so quick and so sticky. Off it, he's very low-key, almost shy, but you couldn't meet a sounder or more dependable guy either. The ultimate Silent Pig.

On holidays in New Zealand 18 months ago, we were all stuck in this long line at the airport in Auckland. Sometimes at airports, they fast-track families to the top, but that wasn't in vogue here, and Elaine and myself were at the back with all our luggage and two tired, cranky girls in the driving heat. Brian was on the other side of the labyrinth of rope.

'Jump in ahead of me there, look,' he said.

So he lifted the rope for us and pulled through our bags, and, instead of being at the back, we were now near the front. Elaine, who was ten weeks' pregnant at the time, still talks about how thoughtful Brian and his girlfriend Annette were, but some of the lads behind us in the queue didn't appreciate it as much. They were all single. They didn't understand. Brian was single, but he could understand; he could relate. And it's that kind of ability to read a situation, it's that kind of honour and emotional intelligence that makes me believe he's the one to hold Eoin Kelly this year.

THURSDAY, 22 JUNE

Seanie wasn't happy tonight. He said our sprint times weren't anything like as sharp as they should be. Last Sunday morning, in Ballinlough, he was raving about them and our first touch, but tonight he felt we were too giddy and sloppy and that we need to seriously pick it up.

I actually didn't do the sprints tonight. On Tuesday night, I asked Deccie to give me a rub because my back and hamstrings felt stiff and sore, so he pulled me from the sprints that night and again tonight. I've never had such a disruptive build-up to a Munster final before, but I'll be able to do some speed work tomorrow night.

FRIDAY, 23 JUNE

Seanie apologised for what he said last night. I don't think he had anything to apologise about. If he sees something wrong, he needs to say it.

The one thing is, we do try to keep things positive the week of a game. John's a big believer in that. The other night, he made a very good point, then qualified it. 'Lads, this is our fourth Munster final in a row. Now, this is the only negative thing I'm going to say all week: if we lose, we'll be the 50 per-centers. For a team of this quality, two out of four isn't enough.'

He also kept up the tradition of handing out a few individual awards at the last training session before a big game. First up was the T-shirt for the style award. 'This man doesn't need any management,' John said. 'He turns up, does the business, goes home, no fuss about him. He's a class player. He's a stylish player. Joe Deane.'

We all give Joe a big round. The way he's been playing, he'll be winning a lot of individual awards this year.

'The next award goes to another special man,' says John. 'In 2002, people were saying Cork hurling was in the doldrums, that it would be years before it would turn around. But here we are, the defending All Ireland champions, about to play in our fourth Munster final in a row. One man made all that happen, because one man had the courage to stand up and be counted. The Silent Pig award goes to Mr Donal Óg Cusack.'

It might seem strange to categorise Donal Óg as the Silent-Pig type, but in training that's just what he is. Himself and Anthony Nash and Martin Coleman all just head down to the other end of the field and do their drills, and it's all business; we can barely hear a peep from them.

Tonight, though, we needed to hear from Donal Óg and Pat Mul, over in the corner of the field for our customary players' talk.

Pat spoke about when he was a sub for the 2004 All Ireland final. After ten minutes, he just knew there was no way we were going to be beaten by Kilkenny, because we were just so focused and hurt from losing to them the previous year. 'Lads, we need to remember that Tipp lost last year's Munster final. We're playing a team who have that fear of losing.'

Donal Óg agreed; we're going to be in for a battle. But first, we must be the ones who'll bring the battle to Tipp. We are not defending our Munster and All Ireland titles; we are *pursuing* Munster and All Ireland titles. 'Lads, Clare were so psyched for Cork they thought they were going to come and blow us away.

But we didn't let them. We were even more determined than them. We have to bring that same intensity now on Sunday. We are the hunter, not the hunted.'

And he's right. Everyone's making us out to be clear favourites, but this is Cork and Tipp. It's like Cork and Kilkenny; there are no favourites. It's not like being favourites puts any scores on the board. It's 0–0 to 0–0. It's not about the favourites; it's about work rate, it's about attitude, it's about intensity.

It's about being the hunter, not the hunted.

SUNDAY, 25 JUNE

Four minutes into the Munster final and we're four points down, the sun is shining and Semple Stadium is shaking. Lar Corbett has just buried a goal, and Donal Óg has had to pull off a save to stop Diarmuid Fitzgerald getting another.

I'm not worried. We've got early goals against Waterford, and by half-time they've been ahead; vice versa. There's a long way to go. Sixty-seven minutes, to be exact. Tipp aren't going to win any Munster final with a score of 1–1.

They're on to everything, though. Once Kelly pointed the 65 from Donal Óg's save, Babs was behind the goal with the umpires about Donal Óg switching the sliotar from an O'Neill's to a Cummins. The umpire handed Donal Óg another O'Neill's, but Donal Óg just threw it away again and launched a Cummins. It's a lighter ball, and we agreed during the week that with the first few puckouts we're going as long as we can straight down the middle.

Now another Donal Óg puckout is coming down. It goes beyond me and Paul Curran, but Jerry is on to it and knocks it over.

Curran's going to be tough to beat today. He's strong and he's quick and he has skill. I beat him to the next ball, though, making a run across goal from right to left. For a second, I try to take him on, but in the corner of my eye I see Joe slip in, so I hand-pass the ball into him. The pass is a bit high, and Joe mis-hits his attempted bat, but I've continued my run, and, as the ball trickles across to me, I bury it in the net. I'm looking straight into the Tipp end, and they're still and they're silent. Now it's our crowd's time to roar.

I'm feeling the heat, though. During the warm-up, I was thinking of taking off the helmet but opted to leave it on because Donal Óg's first few puckouts would be aimed down towards me. But now I'm just after blocking and banging into Curran down in the corner, and, as the ball goes out of play, I'm gasping for air. That's it. I have to take off the helmet, fast, and I give it to Davy Pyne, running along the sideline.

It takes me about ten minutes to get my breath back, but in the meantime the lads put together a goal that takes everyone's breath away. Brian wins a ball down in the left corner. He plays it to Curran, who drives a low diagonal ball out the right wing to Ben. Ben turns and passes it to Timmy. Timmy plays it along to Tom. Tom then feeds it on to Ben again. And then Ben blasts it past Brendan Cummins in by the near post.

It's a special goal, a lot like Argentina's 24-pass goal last week in the World Cup. We can't celebrate it like they did, though. Just like Corbett's goal wasn't going to win Tipp the game, Ben's isn't going to win it for us either.

Now it's Tipp's turn to come back at us. John Carroll manages the nearly impossible by scoring a point off Seán Óg, we concede the odd careless and unfortunate free for Kelly to tap over and they're on to every break around midfield and their half-back line. A minute before half-time, they're only a point down when they win a 20-metre free. Any second now and we could be two points down.

We're not. Thankfully, the Tipp management have told Kelly to take his point and he's obliged. I think it's the wrong call. A goal just before half-time would have been a huge boost for them. But, as it is, they're going into the dressing-room with a spring in their step and their crowd on their feet.

As we go off, I have a word with the referee, Dickie Murphy. I've had four belts to the head since taking off the helmet. One time, Curran hit me across the face. He didn't mean it, but I turned round and stared at him. 'Keep the feckin' hurley down, all right?' Another time, I got a clip down the back of one ear, and another time a little nick down the other.

'Keep an eye under the dropping ball there, Dickie. There's a lot going on and no frees being given.'

He waves me away. I leave it at that. There are other things to be concerned with now.

In the dressing-room, Donal Óg comes over to me.

'What do you think?'

'You mean with the puckouts?'

'Yeah, we're in trouble.'

For starters, Donal Óg thinks Tipp have tightened the pitch. He tried to find Jerry with one puckout, and it went over the line. Cummins hit one over the line too. Cummins knows Thurles like the back of his hand. No way would he do that if the pitch was the usual width.

Tipp have also dragged their half-forwards back into midfield and placed their midfield right in front of our half-forwards, seriously reducing the chances of Donal Óg picking out Timmy and Cian and especially Niall.

'Well, Gardiner's free, and you haven't given it to him,' I say. 'Maybe you need to puck a few short ones to him, to keep them honest and draw them back. If he gets it then, he can bypass their half-back line.'

Donal Óg nods. 'That's what I was thinking. We'll try a few short ones, so. Keep them on their toes.'

John and the selectors come in. There's no change in personnel, but there's to be a change in attitude. Tipp have outscored us six points to one in the last fifteen minutes.

There's no need to panic, though. We haven't played well, we're making a lot of mistakes and yet we're still level. We just need to pick it up and keep it simple at the back, instead of taking that extra pass.

We get back out, and Donal Óg varies his puckouts. He becomes the first right-handed keeper to puck out left-handed, to Pat Mul in the right corner. He hits another to Gardiner, and another to Seán Óg, to open up the play. At the other end, Ben picks off a nice point. Then he wins a ball out on the wing. I call for it, and he cuts it back straight into my hand. Then I cut it straight over the bar from a forty-five-degree angle from about forty-five yards to put us two up.

It's not all plain sailing, though. Tipp are tenacious, hard and mostly fair but not always. We're finding it hard to win a free. Eventually, we get one when Cian is fouled by Paul Ormonde. Initially, Dickie is reluctant to give it, but in the end Dickie books Ormonde. He runs out, and as he passes he says to me, 'I think it was an accident.'

'If it was an accident, Dickie, why did you book him? There are a lot of accidents happening.'

Soon, Tipp go level again when Kelly comes out to the 45 and shoots over his shoulder for his first score of the day from play. Semple quakes again. The home crowd sense victory, an upset.

Then Joe shows his class by getting out in front of Declan Fanning, making that shimmy of his and pointing off his left out on the left wing. Curran and Gardiner grab a few missiles out of the air and then launch a few of their own. It's real backs to the ropes stuff, but, like an old veteran heavyweight champion, we just about keep holding the tenacious contenders at bay with the odd jab.

Then, with three minutes of normal time left, they get the chance to deliver a clear body shot. Kelly has the chance to equalise but instead goes for goal. Donal Óg stops it, controls it and clears it. Fraggy comes on and, with his first touch, winds up to shoot. I'm shouting for him to slip it to me, but he goes for it himself and drives it over the bar. We're two up now and into injury-time. Joe taps over a free, and it's now three. Tipp launch one last attack, but the ball drops around the back, and it's cleared. Dickie blows the whistle, and we raise our arms. Then Pat goes up into the stand and raises the Cup. It looks good. Every winter and spring, you try to picture your captain with a cup, especially the Liam McCarthy Cup. Pat looks the part. He looks the leader.

That's what got us through today: experience and leaders. It's probably why John gave the team talk he did out in Dundrum. He went through everyone on the panel, from Donal Óg Cusack to his brother Conor Cusack, talking about how they were leaders and how they'd need to be leaders today. It was excellent. Ger Cunningham tells me it took John four hours yesterday to prepare that talk. Every minute of it was well spent, because every bit of leadership and encouragement was needed today.

Donal Óg showed it by making those saves from Kelly and Fitzgerald and changing the puckouts. Brian Murphy showed it by keeping Kelly to one single point from play. Curran again was incredible. Ben's only three weeks back training and scores 1–1 in a Munster final. Joe's just scored eight points in a Munster final and hasn't shot a wide all year. And Fraggy's response to not starting for the first time in two years is to come on and score a match-winning point.

We clasp each other's hands and arms, exchange the odd embrace, but no one is jumping up and down. If Tipp had won, this pitch would be a mass of blue and gold, but for us, this year, Munster is just a stepping stone. Two or three years ago, Donal Óg would have been on the lash after a Munster final, win or lose. This evening, back in the hotel, he's sipping water with his meal.

We'll have to improve. We generally do when we hit Croke Park, but after the Clare game we'd thought we had the magic formula for Munster too. Maybe Seanie isn't that far off when he goes by the times of those 20-metre runs. I'm after talking to him there, and he was really worried earlier this week that we'd gone over the top. He tried to take that comment back on Friday because he didn't want us to have any doubt in our minds today, but deep down he had that doubt, and he's determined not to have that feeling again.

Right now, I'm feeling shattered. A friend's just called me here on the bus, saying he saw me on the telly and that after the final whistle, as I walked through the crowds, you wouldn't think I'd won. Well, inside I was smiling. But I also felt relieved. Wrecked. Hunted.

CHAPTER THIRTEEN

AFTER THE GOLD RUSH

'Burnout: the psychological, emotional and physical withdrawal from a formerly pursued and enjoyable sport as a result of excessive stress over time'

ELLIS CASHMORE, *SPORT PSYCHOLOGY: THE KEY CONCEPTS*

A FEW HOURS BEFORE WE PLAYED TIPP IN THE 2000 Munster final, I was standing outside the front of our match-day retreat, Dundrum House, when I spotted a tall, familiar figure out on the golf course. It was Ray Cummins, getting in a round with a few friends before heading to the match. When they looked over at us, a part of them probably wished they could be us. I looked out and wished that I could be out there with them. Instead of going out in front of 55,000 in Thurles to defend our Munster title, I'd rather have been out there on those quiet fairways of Dundrum.

At least I would have got to hit a few balls. More and more around that time, I was finding that opposing teams were deliberately bypassing me by either pucking the ball down the wings or putting some hare in at centre-forward for me to chase. Ivan O'Mahony from the Barrs was one of them. The club played them in a city championship game in Ballinlough, and, running out on the field that night, I just knew that Ger Cunningham wasn't going to puck a ball near me. I ran and ran for miles chasing Ivan that night and didn't touch one ball from a puckout. As I drove home, I said to myself, 'If this is the way hurling is going to be for me, then I don't want to play.'

I would be just as frustrated after that 2000 Munster final. While I was glad for myself and the team that we had repeated our success of '99, I also felt a bit cheated. OK, I had come to Thurles first and foremost to win, but I had also come to play, and that hadn't happened. I was on Eddie Enright, and while Eddie had hit very little ball I had hit little too. That day, Tipp devised the tactic of Eddie pulling from the centre out to the wing and Brian O'Meara drifting in from the wing to the centre to try to capitalise on his height advantage over Wayne Sherlock. These days, our three half-backs would stay in their own zones and swap men as they ran over, but back then we just followed our men. And that was disheartening, running and knowing neither Eddie nor I was going to touch the ball.

The commitments of the previous winter were catching up on me too. It seemed I was out at a function or going around with the Cup or presenting medals every night. Years later, when I came back and won All Irelands in '04 and '05, I had learned to say no to the clubs and societies I just couldn't fit in, but back in that winter of '99 I hadn't. I didn't want to let anyone down, so I'd go and do my best to please everyone. It meant I didn't have a night off to myself from September to December.

Any player who has done that circuit knows the drill: because you play inter-county, it's assumed that you should constantly be available as either a great public speaker or a half-decent comedian. With the kids, presenting medals, I'd go the public-speaker route and talk about the need to 'practise, work hard and enjoy it'. With adults, I'd try my hand at the comedy, with mixed success; invariably the men would enjoy the husband–wife jokes, but sometimes the women would not. But ultimately the whole circuit was exhausting – and very questionable. You might have to be there at seven o'clock and, being guest of honour, shake hands, have a word with everyone (invariably about hurling), stand in for photographs, make a speech and stay there till half-one in the morning, for a voucher for a restaurant you'll never have the time to visit and to promote a GAA that you have to fight tooth and nail to get recognition and rights from.

Before I knew it, it was January, and it was as if I'd had no escape or break at all from the whole scene. The thought crossed my mind to pack it all in, now that I had my All Ireland, but I figured I was just tired, so I went back. A couple of months later, we were playing Waterford down in Walsh Park. There was a huge crowd at it, yet, before the game, I was on the treatment table, getting a rub from our then masseur, John Allen, not wanting to play and thinking that maybe I should have quit over the winter.

By the time the championship came around, my competitive juices had kicked in, and I had a very good first half in the Munster semi-final against Limerick. But even that day the body was feeling the effects of all those nights and, possibly, all the years. With about 20 minutes to go, the man I was marking, Ciaran Carey, bent over, gasping for air. Ciaran was only a few weeks back on the Limerick panel, but I wasn't feeling much better.

'It doesn't get any easier, does it?' I said.

'Wait till you get to my age,' said Ciaran.

A couple of months later, I was again struggling – this time in Croke Park, and this time I had no old adversary there to empathise with me.

An ankle injury caused me to miss three weeks' training going into that All Ireland semi-final against Offaly, and on the day it told. I won the first ball that landed between myself and Gary Hannify, and when I won the second I put the ball on my stick and ran. But, as I got to their 45, I tried to flick the ball over the head of Johnny Dooley, who had tracked back, and Johnny caught me in the chest. I dropped to my knees, choking for air, and it took all I had to get up and run back. Normally, when I'd get a belt like that, I'd find a second wind; in years to come, Seanie McGrath's warm-up routine would be programmed to find it. But that day that second wind never came. In the previous year's All Ireland semi-final against Offaly, I came off the field feeling I could play another match. Now, exactly a year on, I was shattered after ten minutes.

I finished the match. Whether I should have is another thing. After half-time, I was beginning to come more into the game, but then I was whipped out to wing-back. Hardly any ball came down there, and then, with ten minutes to go, I was shifted into the corner. At that point, it was like the '95 football semi-final against Dublin all over again; it would have been better if I was taken off. Tony Considine would write that in the *Examiner*, and he was nearly lynched in Glounthaune and Cork for saying it, but he was right.

Worse, the whole team was floundering. In the first half, we had played all right, with Joe in particular on fire at full-forward, but in a perverse way the few points he'd got before half-time might have been the worst thing that could have happened. Jimmy had tried to guard us against complacency. The public had virtually written off Offaly after they had been destroyed by Kilkenny in the Leinster final and had barely beaten Derry in the All Ireland quarter-final, but Jimmy reminded us that Offaly had troubled us the year before and had won the All Ireland the year before that again. And fellas were maybe subconsciously thinking, 'Yeah, it'll be harder than people think, all right.' But that still meant fellas assumed we'd be fine, and, at half-time, being 0–12 to 0–10 up was in total keeping with that script.

But then, when Offaly hit a purple patch, the script went out the window, and so did our game plan and composure. We started to panic; we started to go for goals when points would do, just like Na Piarsaigh in the '92 county final against Erins Own. That was rooted in complacency. Fellas had never envisaged being three or four down with fifteen minutes to go. Otherwise, they would have just kept taking their points; otherwise, they'd have kept their heads; otherwise, they'd have played low ball instead of high ball into Joe; otherwise, five or six of them would never have been up at one o'clock the previous night playing cards.

The fallout from that defeat was severe. Jimmy decided to walk away. In some articles, there was an inference that I should too. Justin McCarthy had given me a lot of favourable write-ups through the years, but after that game he didn't even refer to me by name when declaring that the time had come to release Diarmuid O'Sullivan to centre-back. Some other *Examiner* writers said I mightn't be finished as an inter-county hurler but I was basically finished as a centre-back. It fired me up to go out the next week and play one of my best games ever with Erins Own in the club championship, and the following January I was determined to make up for an All Ireland I felt we had left behind. For the first winter in my career, I cut out the snack bars and fizzy drinks, got down to 13.5 st. for the first time since '92 and trailed only Seán Óg and Mickey O'Connell in the laps around the tunnels of Páirc Uí Chaoimh. Donal Óg wondered if I was on drugs.

That enthusiasm, though, would not be sustained. Before the league started, I came on in a challenge match against UCC and got a knock that broke my finger. I was back for the league game against Wexford, but, as we travelled down, I didn't want to be on that bus. I was in even worse form on the way home. If any game turned me off hurling, it was that game in Enniscorthy. Wexford were all pumped up to impress their new manager, Tony Dempsey, and their crowd were baying for blood as well.

The first ball I caught, Paul Codd came thundering in to shoulder me in the chest. No free was awarded, and, after I got my breath back, I asked the ref why not.

'You turned into him!' he said.

'It doesn't matter!' I said. 'You can't shoulder charge into the chest!'

But the ref was not listening, and I knew then the kind of day we were in for. A while later, a ball came down the wing. Codd was out in front of me, and, as the ball bounced waist high, he had plenty of time to pick it up, but instead he let the ball run past and then pulled straight across me. That was another finger broken. Then, shortly after I had to go off, poor Mike Morrissey from Newtown was stretchered off, face down on the stretcher and his foot facing the sky. I sat in the bus that day and said to myself, 'This isn't hurling. This isn't fun.'

Neither was training. There were nights when I stayed on in work to avoid it. Then, in February, Kate was born, and I resented being dragged away from being with her. And then, in April, I learned my mother had cancer.

Mam had been in hospital since January because of the pain in her leg, but they couldn't diagnose what the problem was. Further tests showed that the pain in her leg was a secondary form of her cancer. I was in the car when Ann called with the bad news. I turned the car around and went straight to the hospital, where Mam was sitting up in her bed, smiling and laughing with her sisters. I didn't know if they had told her how severe the cancer was, but she had a great attitude from the start. The following day, I asked one of the doctors if it was terminal. He said it was. I asked how long we had. He said it was hard to know, but probably six to nine months.

WE DID IT
With the Liam McCarthy Cup after the 1999 All Ireland final
(courtesy of *Irish Examiner*)

DREAMWORLD
Celebrating with Jimmy Barry-Murphy after the 1999 final
(courtesy of *Irish Examiner*)

EYE ON THE BALL
About to clear a ball in the 2000 Munster final (courtesy of Sportsfile)

GET OUT OF MY WAY
Clearing the line against Tipperary in the 2000 Munster final
(© INPHO/Patrick Bolger)

ON YOUR KNEES, BOY!
My championship comeback started with this point against Ollie Moran
and Limerick in the 2004 Munster semi-final (© INPHO/Tom Honan)

BROTHERS IN ARMS
The forward line that delivered Cork two All Ireland and
two Munster titles (courtesy of *Irish Examiner*)

FRIENDS FOREVER
With Dr Con Murphy, Donal Óg Cusack and Jerry Wallis in the
background on our team holiday to South Africa in 2006

REBEL YELL
Celebrating the point, win and comeback with Joe Deane at
the end of the 2004 All Ireland final (courtesy of Sportsfile)

PRIDE AND JOY
Edel and Kate after the
2004 All Ireland final

FACE-OFF
D.J. and myself were part of Club Energise's marketing
campaign ahead of the 2004 All Ireland final

ON THE RUN
Some of our greatest battles and wins have been against Waterford
and Fergal Hartley and Tony Browne. On this occasion, we beat them
in the 2005 Munster semi-final (courtesy of Sportsfile)

PRIZE IN SIGHT
Running out on All Ireland final day in 2005 for the
biggest prize in hurling (courtesy of Sportsfile)

THE CORCORAN CLAN
With Edel, Kate, Elaine and Ewan
(photo taken by our builder, Liam Dunlea – thanks, Liam)

I was stunned, and then, about half a minute later, I was even more stunned when he asked me how hard Cork were training. Maybe he'd become that desensitised and accustomed to death, but I wasn't. I looked at him, but he continued to talk about how important and healthy hurling and sport were.

'There's more to life than sport,' I snapped and walked away.

At that moment, I wanted to walk away from hurling too. If my mother had only six months to live, I didn't want to be wasting it three nights a week out training and being away playing a game at the weekends. But, as the championship was only a few weeks away, I decided that I would play.

A few weeks before that first-round game against Limerick, I broke another finger in the dying seconds of a club championship game against Sars. After putting in probably the hardest winter's training I had ever done, I was now in danger of missing our first – possibly our only – championship game of the season. The weekend before the game, though, I was able to train, and on the Monday night I told our manager, Tom Cashman, that I could hurl and was fit to start. The following night, Tom approached me.

'We're not going to risk you on Sunday,' Tom said. 'We're going to save you for Waterford.'

Teddy Owens followed him over. 'Are you all right about that?'

And the first thing I said was, 'I just hope there's going to be a Waterford.'

Waterford might have been already through to the Munster semi-final but we weren't. We had to beat Limerick first. We'd been complacent in 2000 against Offaly. Surely we weren't going to make the same mistake now in 2001 against Limerick?

Pat Mulcahy was a good man to have come in at centre-back, though, given how well he had played there for Newtown and how good his form that year was with Cork. Pat would ship a lot of criticism for that game against Limerick, but I thought he was unlucky. When Moran drifted out, Pat rightly decided to hold the centre, but when Ollie scored a few points from loose play, Pat was switched back into the corner, and I was brought on at half-time. I felt rusty out there, but when Sully scored a monstrous point from over a hundred yards and Alan Browne broke through for a goal, we were back to within a point of them and had the crowd and momentum on our side.

But Limerick held their nerve, and when Landers drew us level, Barry Foley cut a sideline ball over the bar. We should have had a few more minutes of injury-time to try for the equaliser, but the referee, Pat Horan, didn't play them. Our summer was over, and as I sloped off the field that day I knew my inter-county career was over too. That was the infamous day on which the Garda escort never showed up at Páirc Uí Rinn, and we had to drive through the traffic ourselves to get to Páirc Uí Chaoimh, and now, after the game, we were having to wade through the crowds again and endure the Limerick crowd tapping on our window and cheering. Landers, Donal Óg and myself got out of the car in Páirc Uí Rinn, and the lads asked me if I was going into town. I declined. Instead, I drove straight home.

Later that summer, Erins Own played UCC in the county championship, but I was in no mood to play. Their big full-forward, Eamon Collins, came out with the ball, and I hit him a shoulder on the side that knocked him to the ground. Eamon hopped right back up, but Joe O'Leary blew for a free in. I nearly exploded. 'What's that for?'

'You hit him in the chest!'

'If I hit him in the chest, he'd still be on the ground!'

The more the game went on, and the more UCC increased their lead, the more bad calls Joe gave against us, and the crankier I got. Before, I'd never get cranky. Just the previous year, in a profile of me for the Munster final, our then club chairman Michael O'Connor spoke of the only time he saw me ever react negatively to a referee's decision: when I was wrongly called for over-carrying and I snapped the ball to the ground. But now incidents like chasing Joe were becoming too common.

We played Imokilly in the 2000 county championship semi-final, and I was in for a clash ball with Landers. Diarmuid Kirwan threw in the ball, I pulled and Landers stuck his leg out. I ended up hitting him on the ankle, and Diarmuid gave a free in to Imokilly. I went berserk.

'If he puts his leg out, that's his problem! He knows that! You throw the ball in, and we pull! That's how it works!'

If anyone else had protested like that, they'd have been booked. I know, because when Timmy Kelleher joined in, Diarmuid showed Timmy a yellow card.

And so, here I was playing UCC, playing my last hurling game for Erins Own, a tired, angry man. How Joe put up with my hounding I don't know. A few weeks later, after the county minors won the All Ireland, I spotted him outside the Imperial Hotel, went over and told him that, while I thought a lot of his calls were wrong, so was my reaction. 'I was out of order, and I don't know how you didn't send me off,' I said.

I walked away that day, anyway. When Joe blew the final whistle, Martin Bowen's son, Alan, came running over, and I handed him my hurley. 'You can keep that, Alan. I won't be needing it.' A few weeks later, my uncle D.D., a selector with the club that year, called, asking if I was available for a league game down in Cloyne. 'I'm not, D.D. I'm not playing any more.'

And I didn't play again, not for another two and a half years. I waited until the New Year to decide for sure, and I was sure. Nothing could persuade me back, not even the club's offer to play me in the forwards, not even a call from the new Cork manager Bertie Óg Murphy. I was sick shit of hurling. I was burned out.

A few months after we won the 2004 All Ireland final, Donal O'Grady spoke about burnout at a GAA coaching seminar at Dublin City University. O'Grady stated that if Brian Corcoran was the classic comeback story then Brian Corcoran was also the GAA's classic burnout study. A friend even used me as a case study for a sports-psychology college paper on burnout. And, when you read it, you'll find that my case validates nearly every theory there is on burnout.

Of course, it was the culmination of the years; of course, it was 'progressive by nature'. I look back through the scrapbooks Mam lovingly kept, and I wonder at the number of games I played in certain periods and at some of the quotes I was giving to reporters before I was even 20.

In 1991, between club, college, county and division – hurling and football – and minor, Under-21 and senior, I played for 14 different teams. That summer, there was a week when I was a sub with the county seniors against Tipp in the Munster final on the Sunday, played full-back for the county minor footballers against Waterford on the Tuesday and then played midfield for the county Under-21 hurlers against Waterford on the Thursday.

The following month, I played for Cork in that All Ireland minor semi-final against Donegal on the Sunday, for the club minor footballers in a semi-final on the Tuesday, an All Ireland Under-21 hurling semi-final on the Sunday, the club minor football final on the Monday and a club junior football semi-final on the Wednesday. 'At times, all right, my legs get very tired,' I told the *Examiner*'s Mark Woods before that year's All Ireland minor football final, 'but I don't mind all that much, really.' All I could see was the next ball, the next game, the next trophy.

That applied to Railway Cups. I missed a few hurling

Railway Cup weekends because they clashed with some club or football national league game, but in 1996 I finally managed to get my hands on a hurling Railway Cup medal. I had missed the semi-final, but the curtain-raiser to the final in Ennis was the football semi-final. So, as I came off the field after playing for the footballers in our win over Connacht, the hurling selectors asked me to stay on for the hurling final against Leinster. And, with about 20 minutes to go, I came on and scored 1–1.

I didn't mind the occasional double bill like that, but I look at some of the other games I played and question my judgement. When I was at college, I would not compromise my studies. If Cork were training one night, I'd stay in the college until the labs and library closed the next night to make up for it. Fitzgibbon training would often be held from one o'clock to two o'clock, but often I wouldn't go because I didn't want to miss any of my lectures either side of training and be taking notes that I could barely make out from someone else. Games were hard to resist, though, and in my first year out there we won basically every freshers' trophy going. The night before the freshers' hurling league semi-final and final, I got injured playing for the club and could barely walk into college the next morning. Noel Collins persuaded me, though, to go to Limerick anyway, where I was dropped off at the regional hospital to get my leg X-rayed while the lads played the semi-final. A few hours later, Noel came back to collect me. They'd won, and we were playing our rivals UCC in the final that afternoon. I had to play! Now, while the X-ray showed that nothing was broken, I still couldn't walk. 'That's all right,' Noel said. 'We'll strap that leg up, and you can come on if we're in trouble.' With about ten minutes to go, we were in trouble, so I was thrown in at full-forward. I got two points to draw us level, and then we won a twenty-metre free over by the corner flag. I put it over and we won, but I could barely walk off the field. Looking back, I should never have played, but a part of me was pushed, and the other part would have pushed myself regardless.

In that paper on burnout, it says there are three characteristics that make people susceptible to burnout: being other-orientated, lack of assertiveness and perfectionism. There were times when I was assertive: I showed it that time I stood up to Frank over playing with the club in '94; I showed it by not playing for the club senior side until I was 18; and I showed it when I continued to play football when the club's 'knife in the big ball' brigade were urging me to focus just on hurling. Then there was the time I said no to football. In 1997, the division, Imokilly, qualified for the county football semi-final. The set-up was very casual, though, and, after training something like 160 nights in 270 days with the not-so-casual set-up that was the county footballers that year, I opted to go on holiday to France with Elaine rather than play the semi-final. The day after I informed them of my decision, one of their selectors was on the radio and in the papers ranting about my 'disgraceful' decision. But I wasn't changing my mind, and I would never play football for Imokilly again.

But there were plenty more examples of when I wasn't assertive: training and playing games when I felt I shouldn't; attending functions that I didn't want to because I couldn't say no. I was too other-orientated. I'd be training nearly every night with either the county footballers or hurlers, and then the club would call, 'We haven't seen you in a while.' So I'd go down the next night, and there'd be an agreement I'd just join in for the hurling, not the hard slog, but inevitably I'd end up getting stuck doing all the laps too.

As for perfectionism, I was out practically every night training and playing. I wanted to achieve. I was obsessed with winning All Ireland medals and I'd train however hard it took to win one.

That was a big part of the problem. In that college paper, a theory called the negative-training stress response is considered as one of the leading models on burnout. Basically, burnout is a product of excessive training. 'Far too many coaches, through improper reinforcement and motivational techniques, make sport into drudgery and work,' says a sports psychologist called Henschen. 'When this is the perception, athletes become bored, stale or burned out. "No gain without pain is a myth."' When I came back to play for Cork, Seanie McGrath's training programme made training interesting – at times, even enjoyable – but with Larry in the '90s, no pain, no gain was the law.

Even in the hurling, that creed became increasingly fashionable. More and more in the winter and spring, the training would be unrelated to hitting a ball with a stick. As a kid, as a teenager, in my early 20s, I'd loved hitting a ball with a stick, but now I'd show up for 'hurling' training and not even hit a ball. It was laps of the tunnel in Páirc Uí Chaoimh and road running along the Marina.

Then there was the weights. We'd go in and pump iron for three or four months over the winter, and I'd play league games feeling as strong as an ox. But when the evenings started to get longer, we'd be out on the field all the time and never go back into the gym, leaving all that hard work over the winter to go to waste. Much of the strength gains were lost by the time summer came. That used to baffle me. I wouldn't blame the trainers, though. Back then, we didn't have access to private gyms and the only facility available was Páirc Uí Chaoimh, which would be locked up the nights we weren't training.

The biggest cause of disillusionment, though, was the system. In that same college paper, a guy called Jay Coakley is cited. He maintains that the biggest cause of burnout is how a sport is organised. And, once again, my case study validates his point. When I look back on it, the old championship structure, the old way of playing the league before Christmas, was farcical.

With the league before Christmas, it meant we basically had no off-season. Even if we weren't training for some of those league games, hurling was always 'there'; mentally, there was little time for recovery. But, if we had too many games in October and November, we had too few in the summer. The reality is that, in five of the ten summers I hurled for Cork from 1992 to 2001, we had only one championship match. In two of those ten years, we had only two championship games. From 1993 to 1997 – five years – I played six championship games. In 2006 alone, the Laois footballers played seven championship games without even reaching the All Ireland semi-final. They got a fair shot. They got to pack a whole career into a year. They got to bloody play. Even if we were a bit off All Ireland standard in '94 and '95, we at least deserved another chance, such as getting to play in an All Ireland quarter-final, like teams do now.

But that was the system at the time, and I had to live with it. And that was so tough. I don't know how many trips to the States to play hurling I turned down to play some football league game in October. I remember after we lost to Clare in Ennis in the football in '97 questioning my sanity. Friends like Ronan Aherne and Tony Hickey were off in Australia for a year, enjoying themselves, enjoying life, and here I was killing myself for eight months to play possibly only seventy minutes in the summer.

The breaking point, though, was Limerick in 2001. There I was, after training harder than ever over the winter and spring, rushing back not once, not twice, but three times from breaking a finger, and for what? Thirty-five minutes in Páirc Uí Chaoimh.

There's a thing called the Maslach Burnout Inventory, which measures burnout. And it is frightening how high I would have scored in that questionnaire if I'd had to fill it out in 2001. It consists of three parts. The first is your level of emotional exhaustion: 'I feel mentally tired before beginning a training session.'

I was tired the morning of a training session. I didn't even want to play games, like that 2000 league match in Waterford and that one down in Wexford in 2001. Suffice it to say, a tick for emotional exhaustion.

The next part is your level of depersonalisation. And yes, I was even becoming depersonalised, when you think of questions such as: 'I find myself treating others impersonally and feel less sensitive and more hardened towards others,' and 'When things go wrong, I am less tolerant and tend to blame others more than I used to.'

Hounding Joe O'Leary that day against UCC; hounding Diarmuid Kirwan in that game against Imokilly: again, tick, tick. I had become more depersonalised.

And then there's the last category, sense of diminished personal achievement: 'As a hurler, I don't feel that I am accomplishing as much as I used to,' and 'When I began as a player, I felt I could make more impact than I feel I do now.'

And again, I could tick all those boxes. Chasing Eddie Enright in Thurles; Cunningham not giving me a puck in Ballinlough: I wasn't in control like I used to be. I was training harder than ever, I was fitter than ever, yet I wasn't getting to play. I wasn't enjoying the game any more.

So I quit. I was no longer a hurler. It was no longer fun and I had too many other things to do and be. I was the son of a mother who was dying. I was a father to little Kate. I was a husband to Elaine and now free to have the time to look for a new house. And, if I wanted to hit a ball, I could be a golfer.

When I walked off that field against Limerick in 2001, I had absolutely no idea or intention that I'd be back playing against them five years later in an All Ireland quarter-final.

CHAPTER FOURTEEN

LIVING ON THE EDGE

'A game ebbs and flows. The rhythm constantly changes. And with these changes you have to be in tune. The best teams and players impose their tempo on the opposition. There's a time to quicken to the pace of the game, a time to slow it down, a time to tackle, a time to hold off, a moment in a game where someone needs a wake-up call – a bollicking – or some words of encouragement'

ROY KEANE

FRIDAY, 7 JULY 2006

I turned up tonight feeling nearly too tired to train, yet when we finished at 11 p.m. I didn't want to go home. You can put that down to Roy Keane.

Before training, a few of the lads were speculating that he might be coming to see us, as John had called a players' meeting and Keane had been in town earlier to promote the Guide Dogs Association. Sully had brought his copy of Keane's autobiography and Donal Óg his Celtic jersey, just in case. Others weren't so keen. Kelly thought Roy was wrong over Saipan. 'Will you walk yourself if Roy is here?' I asked.

'I don't know,' said Peter, shaking the head.

By the end of the night, though, even Peter was a fan. Quite simply, Roy's one of the most fascinating people we've ever heard speak.

Roy watched most of our session tonight. And, judging by what he said later on, it was a lot like Manchester United's: incredibly simple. He laughed about how some of his buddies from Cork found United's training a huge anticlimax and couldn't believe that the players just ran and kicked the ball around the place. The same could be said of us. We concentrate on two things: the basic skills of the game and speed, for, as Seanie always says, 'speed is king'.

The hardest part of tonight's session was the usual 12-minute blowout. After two three-minute shuttle runs with the ball, it was into the grids with two teams of three: one with the ball, the other with body pads. The team with the ball had to make six successful passes while the other three pummelled them with the pads. I decided when I had the ball that I'd be the aggressor and the one to drive into them. Some of the lads must have thought I'd lost it, but I wanted to raise the tempo.

Roy's talk was the highlight of the night, though. He just sat down as we pulled our chairs around in a circle, and for the next few hours we were riveted. At the start, he seemed almost embarrassed, uncomfortable, but once he began talking he was at his ease. He told us he wasn't going to preach to us but if we had any questions about his experiences and career he'd answer them as honestly as he could. He was true to his word. He spelt out who were the 'bluffers' and 'muppets' he played with and who were the warriors. That's what it came down to for him. The real test of a player was Arsenal at Highbury. When he stood alongside Vieira, waiting to emerge from that tunnel, he wanted a certain calibre of competitor lined up behind him. That tunnel in Highbury was his trench, and he only wanted certain players in it.

The training ground was another measure of a player for Roy. The odd player, like Mark Hughes, could be a carthorse during the week and a thoroughbred on Saturday, but, as a rule, it was the guys who put it in during training that you could depend on come match day. It galled him to see someone turning up late for training and then skipping the warm-down at the end.

Saipan obviously frustrated him as well. Joe asked what was so bad about it. 'Well,' said Roy, 'imagine ye go up to Dublin three days before the All Ireland final and on the Friday there's no gear or sliotars, and when you complain to the manager he shrugs and says, "A fella let me down."'

I asked him about his attitude before he tore his cruciate in that tackle with Alfie Haaland in '97. 'You said there, Roy, that it refocused you. You had very high standards after that, and you'd get on to people if they didn't match them. But, before that injury, were there any Roy Keanes getting on to you to cop yourself on?'

He grinned. Yeah, there was. At Forest, Stuart Pearce would be constantly on to him to leave that last drink and head home. But Roy wouldn't listen; he had to learn the hard way.

There was no question he avoided.

'When do you go into the zone, Roy?'

'Five to three.'

'When will you go into management?'

'October, maybe,' he smiled. 'There's been no offers yet, but a lot of fellas get sacked in October.'

And on he went, about the genius of Brian Clough ('My first night with Forest, he just said, "Roy, when you get the ball, give it to a red shirt and move." I've made a career out of that.'), about how he finished with United, about the offers he had from abroad towards the end of '99, about how to deal with distractions and handling tickets, because things like that can drain your energy.

And the one thing that really stuck was what he had to say about the three in a row. 'Embrace the challenge,' he said, 'don't fear it.' Whenever United won something, he was already looking for the next trophy. When they retained the Premiership in 2000, he was instantly looking forward to making it three in a row.

'It's there for ye, too. I've always seen Cork and United as the same. The standard-bearers . . .'

We could have listened to him all night. And Roy looked as if he could chat away all night. Finally, after two and a half hours, John said, 'Roy, I think we've taken up enough of your time.'

Roy nodded.

I went up to shake his hand and thank him for his time.

'No problem, boy.'

A driven man. Even more reason for us to be *Corcaíoch*.

SUNDAY, 9 JULY

We'll be playing Limerick in the All Ireland quarter-final. Some people will think that's a handy draw, but I don't. They reached the league final and were only narrowly beaten by Kilkenny in it and then by Tipp in the Munster championship. If you take away their disastrous qualifier game against Clare in Ennis, they've a very good record this year. They had a tough game up in Offaly last week and won well. They've turned things around now under a new management team, led by Richie Bennis, with Gary Kirby as a selector. They've nothing to lose against us. It's a tricky, dangerous match.

Another worry is that Jerry's looking doubtful. He pulled his hamstring the other night and is getting physio twice a day. Coming from the Limerick border, he'll be mad anxious to play.

We trained in Páirc Uí Rinn this morning. It was hard and it was long, but it was really enjoyable. Sully in particular was in great form. During a short game in which only ground hurling was allowed, he let rip from 60 yards to send it flying to the top corner of the net, just like John Fenton's immortal strike against Limerick in '87. Cheers and arms went up, and even in the warm-down Sully was still talking about it.

Roy Keane wouldn't mind having Sully in the tunnel in Highbury with him. I know I wouldn't want another full-back. People say put a fast forward in on him and he's vulnerable, but those people don't seem to realise that he's one of the fastest guys on the team. And, of course, physically he's so strong. One day with the club, we were playing Cloyne in a junior football championship game when a bit of a melee broke out near the end. One of our fellas instantly went in looking for their biggest guy. That meant Sully. I knew that wasn't a good idea, but, by the time I arrived, Sully was already holding our man up to his chest with his two hands. For a second, I thought Sully was going to hit him, but instead he just caught the Erins Own jersey and ripped it straight down. You couldn't have cut that jersey with scissors, yet Sully made it look as if it was a piece of paper as we watched the bravado in our teammate's face deflate like a pricked balloon.

I had a run-in of my own with Sully back in Carrigtwohill while playing Cloyne in the league. I was going hell for leather for a ball when I caught sight of Sully charging towards it from the opposite direction. I knew he wasn't going to back down, he knew I wasn't going to back down and the crowd waited and winced as we ploughed into each other at full speed. Every bone in my body shook, but we continued to fight for the ball. The next night at training I saw Sully. 'I'm still aching all over, Sull.'

'I'm glad you said it,' he said. 'So am I.'

Sully fits the hard-man image – no helmet, wrists strapped up, the verbal and mind games with opposing forwards – but then you see him with kids or with the latest gizmo, such as a flashy new mobile phone, and realise he like's a kid himself. He was the same when he scored that goal this morning.

The first time I met him was when he was about 13, and he'd go behind the goals in Cork training, pucking the ball back out to us. All these years later, and that love of the game, the kid in him, is still there.

THURSDAY, 20 JULY

We had our rehearsal and players' meeting tonight. It might be a Thursday, but the game is on Saturday, so everything moves forward a day. There was another difference tonight: I spoke at it. I was in two minds all day about whether to say anything, but I decided I didn't want to have any regrets on Sunday morning, wishing I had said something.

The theme of it was that word 'complacency'. John's done his best to guard against it all week. He cut out last Monday's *Examiner* and read out Jim O'Sulllivan's report of the Cork footballers' surprise win over Kerry in the Munster final replay. 'Lads,' John said, 'I'm going to take the liberty here of swapping the Kerry footballers for the Cork hurlers, and the Cork footballers here for Limerick. Headline: "Limerick blossom as Cork wilt." "The manner in which Limerick triumphed so convincingly contrasted sharply with the way that Cork struggled, confirming the view that another All Ireland title was beyond them. Limerick's success was essentially a reward for having the greater appetite."' Then John folded up the paper. 'I don't want to be reading that on Monday morning.'

And yet, for all those warnings and all the Lombardi quotes up on the dressing-room wall, I've noticed a kind of casualness in training this last week. The game isn't in Croke Park but Thurles, and there isn't the normal kind of build-up or vibe for a game there in the Munster championship. I've taken measures to stay fresh by cutting out the commute and working from Cork this week, but I still felt issues had to be addressed tonight: like the fear that fellas mightn't be steeled for a tight game. My good friend Dave Keating, the golf pro in Charleville, lives on the Limerick border, and he told me yesterday that the Limerick fellas around there are very confident of catching us on the hop. That's why tonight I stepped forward into the circle.

'Lads, people are doing a lot of talk about the three in a row. Well, before we have a chance to do that, we have to do something no Munster team has done in over sixty years, and that's get to four finals in a row; we have to do something that's against the odds. There have been great teams before us who have failed. Kilkenny played in six All Irelands in seven years from '98 to '04, but they didn't get to four in a row. We have to ask ourselves the question: why don't teams do it? Is it because they come up against a better team? Is it because they run out of luck? Is it because they get complacent and get caught by a team that's inferior to them?

'Limerick have nothing to lose on Saturday. It's going to be a battle, and, lads, it'll probably be a battle with ten minutes to go. We can't be in a situation where we're two down with ten minutes left and fellas are going, "Shit, what are we going to do?" We have to be ready to click into the zone, like we did against Clare when they went six points up. People say Cork don't do panic. Well, we did do panic: in 2000, against Offaly. I know the team has changed since then, but you all saw it. A lot of us were there. And that day we feckin' panicked because we weren't mentally ready for it. We never envisaged being three or four down in the last fifteen minutes; we never thought that could happen to us.

'You might think, "Ah, sure, we were only a bunch of young fellas then." Well, in '99, every game went down to the wire, and we won them all, yet a year later we panicked and started going for goals. And I'm convinced that's because we thought we'd be five or six points up with fifteen minutes to go. That, lads, is complacency. So, whatever happens on Saturday, don't have this regret on Sunday morning: "God, if only we took them more seriously." I'm saying it right now: take them seriously.'

Pat then talked about Limerick pride and how they'll tap into this Munster rugby attitude of 'Stand Up and Fight'. He's right. It's going to be a battle.

SATURDAY, 22 JULY

This is a battle, all right. We're in the closing minutes here in Thurles, and there's only a point in it. We're the ones ahead, but we're the ones being hunted. Limerick have scored six of the last seven points. It can't end here – the year, the career – not in this bloody rain, before we even get to Croke Park.

It can't be to Limerick either. Not with the way they've gone on today. While the ball's been in play, it's been as clean a game as I've known, but when it's been dead or down the other end of the field there's been all kinds of cheap shots going on. T.J. Ryan just ran into Gardiner with his hurley up and knocked him to the ground. On the line, their manager Richie Bennis has had a run-in with Jerry and even John Allen himself. 'I don't want to have to go into their dressing-room after this as the losing manager,' he told us at half-time. I don't want it either.

I've had a strange tussle here with Stephen Lucey. For

the first ten minutes or so, any time I watched what was going down at the other end and turned around, he was there to hit me a shoulder. I'd walk around him and he'd ram me again. Eventually, when I turned round and he caught me again on the shoulder, I just looked at him and half-laughed. And with that he just said, 'All right.' And he hasn't shouldered or bumped me off the ball since. Their dogs-of-war mentality might suit some of their lads, but it's not Lucey's game, his mentality; all that crack at the start was distracting him more than me. The other minute there he accidentally stood on my toe, and he said, 'Oh, sorry about that.'

I can't lose this game. No way. Too much is at stake. I presented a scenario like this on Thursday to the lads. Now I have to do something about it.

I see Niall out the field. So often he's been the one who's pulled us through when we've been in stormy waters. The first half of the 2003 Munster final, the first half in Killarney in 2004, the second half of the All Ireland in 2004, last year's Munster semi-final against Waterford: in all those games, it was Niall who gave the lion's roar.

I go out towards the 40. 'Niall! Niall! We're still winning this feckin' game! We need to fight for it now!'

Niall nods. 'Yeah, we need to lift it.'

I go over and shout the same to Tom. He nods too. Yeah, we need to crank it up a bit.

And I stay there for a minute or two, urging lads on. No ball is coming in towards us, so I might as well do something constructive.

Now a ball finally comes to me. There's only one thing to do with it: turn and run. I look up. There's no runner, but there's a gap. There's a goal. I'm going to take this now as far as I can and bat it in.

Next thing, I'm on the ground, on my shoulder. I struggle

to get my breath, when Mike O'Brien appears above me. 'Get up, you fucker, you! You shouldn't even be playing! You must be nearly 40 years old!'

I get up. 'What's your name again?'

Now I'm hearing this tirade of abuse from someone along the endline. I look over. Gary Kirby is there, but that wouldn't be Gary's form. The culprit is one of their water-carriers. But as soon as he sees me glaring at him he stops and looks away, like a kid caught messing in school.

The whole place seems to be going crazy here. Sully is coming up the field to take the penalty.

'Ref, did you see that?' someone shouts.

I look back. Sully's on the ground. Someone's wrestled him on his way up.

'Look, ref, look! He's trying to use a new ball!'

Eventually, a Limerick man is booked. John decides that Joe should take the penalty – and a point; we're two up with about four minutes to go.

Joe puts us three up. But then Andrew O'Shaughnessy knocks over a free, and Mark Foley scores a monstrous point from inside his own half to cut it back down to one. We need something special again.

Ben delivers it, scoring his fifth point of the day. They quickly respond with a point, but then Niall cancels it out with a huge point of his own. Now he's the one giving us all the lion's roar – and a two-point lead.

From the puckout, O'Brien scores a point, but it's too late. It's over. We've won by a point. We've won the battle. We've survived.

I raise my arms. So does Joe. We hug. It hasn't ended here. It has for Lucey. I feel sorry for him. Good player, good guy, and we shake hands. Kirby comes over, and we do the same. And, in a way, I don't blame some of their colleagues for going on like they did today. It's a ruthless game, trying to win

Munsters, trying to win All Irelands. If you don't win, the only thing you're guaranteed is abuse, and they weathered plenty of it after the Clare defeat.

But again, rather them than us. On Thursday night, Donal Óg declared in the huddle that we were fighting for everything we believe in. Bennis had come in and had ditched the bananas and psychology and support game and gone back to old-school ways. If Limerick had beaten us, then the whole of hurling would have been saying that our professionalism and set-up were a load of baloney. We pride ourselves on those things. This morning in Dundrum, John used Clive Woodward's term: the critical non-essentials. What others deem non-essential, we deem critical, the difference between winning and losing – such as hydration, the puckout strategy, the logistics, the stamps, the slogans, everything.

But we need to review the critical essentials and non-essentials, and maybe add a few things to the list. Today, we did not abide by Every Single Ball. We thought when we were five up at half-time and again midway through the second half that we were home. We became the very thing we said we wouldn't: complacent. We didn't get the ball into the full-forward line quickly enough either; Joe and I only got a point each from play today.

We need to have a good look at our warm-up as well. After the Munster final, a few fellas were saying they were struggling during it. We're meant to do it all together, in one line, but some guys are going too fast and skipping the gears that Seanie always talks about. Even Tom says he felt knackered during the warm-up. That can't happen the next day.

But at least there is a next day. That's a huge relief. I'm glad I spoke up on Thursday and went out the field to give the lion's roar to some lads.

Finally, we're back in Croke Park. As much as I love Thurles, Croker is the place to be if you're a hurling man.

And yet, oddly enough, I only went there once when I was retired.

But that once made all the difference.

CHAPTER FIFTEEN

TIMEOUT

'In the space of four years, I became a man. I married
my wife, had beautiful children, won championships,
lost my father and walked away from the game I love.
Before, I had been playing a kid's game and leading
a kid's life. By the time I retired, I was a man leading
a man's life'

MICHAEL JORDAN

WHEN JIM WILLIAMS CAME IN TO SPEAK TO US IN THE
Rochestown Park in February 2006, he spoke of the importance
of attitude, of taking responsibility for your attitude, of
choosing your attitude. He shared anecdotes from his own
career and from those he knew and saw. It resonated with me,
because I've seen plenty of examples myself. But just about the
best exponent I know of the power of positive attitude would
be my mother, Nuala Corcoran.

When I retired, I had much more time with Mam. It wasn't
easy leaving her sometimes, knowing she'd struggle that
night to sleep. And yet, throughout her sickness, she never
complained about the cancer. She never even talked about it or
death. One man I know, when he heard he had only months

to live, died the next day. Mam was told she had six to nine months to live, yet lived for twenty months. The way she saw it was, while she was alive, she might as well live.

They moved her into St Patrick's Marymount Hospice. Normally, when you go in, you don't come out. But, after six months, Mam returned home. Throughout her life, she was brilliant with her hands, yet, before she got sick, she had never painted. In Marymount, though, they ran art classes, and after she was released from there she'd still go up there once a week for her day care and for her art class.

She loved seeing Kate, and when John got engaged in August '02 she was talking about what dress she'd wear at the wedding the following March. Mam didn't make it to John's wedding. That October, she passed away. And when she took her last breath we were all there, holding her hand.

Twelve days after Mam died, our second daughter, Edel, was born. In one sense, it would have been great if my mother had seen her, especially as Edel is the image of her, but maybe it would have made it even more difficult for her to go too. I'm still very grateful that she got to see Kate. And, in a way, she's still with me. In a way, herself and Dad always will be. But their absence is always there too.

In the space of three years, I had gone from being a single, inter-county hurler with no kids and two parents to a married, retired player with two kids and neither parent. Life had changed, but so much of the change was good. Not playing hurling meant playing with the two girls. It meant having time to buy a new house and returning back to Glounthaune. It meant time working on my golf swing and playing every Sunday morning, where at least I knew I was guaranteed to hit the ball and have no one else to blame.

I didn't miss hurling one bit. I didn't even lift a hurley in those two years; I didn't even go for a run. In March 2003, the new Cork manager, Donal O'Grady, called, asking me if

I wanted to come back, and I said no. He then asked would I mind if he called again in the summer, and I said he could but he'd get the same answer. O'Grady didn't call back, and I was just as glad. I was happy being a mere spectator.

I wasn't even that, really. The only club game I went to was Erins Own's 2002 first-round match against Castlelyons. I watched all Cork's games that year on telly; getting in a game of golf and spending time at home was more appealing then being stuck in traffic and some pub in Thurles with the odd know-it-all saying I 'should be out there'.

Then, the following September, I decided to go to one game. As an All Ireland winner, I was entitled to two tickets to that 2003 All Ireland final, so I headed up to the match. And I really enjoyed the whole experience. Walking into the game, I bumped into old teammates and opponents, such as Kilkenny's Dick Dooley, who I'd marked as a 15 year old in the '88 minor final. The game itself was both pulsating and frustrating. Cork shot a litany of wides in the first half, but when Setanta scored that goal and Niall Mac scored that point, it looked as if they'd still pull it off. But then Henry Shefflin stepped up, scored a point or two and set up a goal for Martin Comerford, and before my other old adversary from '88, D.J., lifted the cup, I was already walking back towards O'Connell Street.

As fate would have it, though, I had parked the car that day at the Citywest Hotel, where the Cork team were staying that night. I decided to stay around to offer my condolences, and, after saluting them in the foyer as they trooped in off the bus, I was persuaded by Tom Barry, the organiser of the team's post-match function, to stay for the drinks reception. Then Tom asked me to stay for the dinner. Jimmy McEvoy insisted that I sit at his table among all the players. So I went out to the car and changed out of my Cork jersey and put on a shirt.

It was four o'clock in the morning before I left the Citywest to be at work in Cork for eight. And, that Monday evening after work, I headed over to the train station and then the Imperial Hotel for the homecoming in Cork. And on those two nights, back around the guys I soldiered with in '99 and mixing with the young guns like Setanta and Gardiner, something inside me was stirred. It was as surreal as it was sudden. There wasn't a minute in that game when I wished I was out there playing. Elaine asked me that question when I called her after the game, and on the Monday in the Imperial John Allen also wondered if I missed it at all. And I didn't. John found that hard to believe, but it was true. In the Citywest, a supporter who was in my vicinity for much of the night would often interject when there was a break in conversation, 'You should have been out there! You have to come back!' And I told him he was wrong, that I was happy where I was and as I was. But, by the Tuesday morning, I was starting to think that maybe I should be out there for '04. Maybe I should come back.

I was already out of the stadium when Donal Óg had called them into that famous huddle in the pitch and vowed, as Setanta wiped away his tears, that they'd be back to win it in '04. From talking to them and seeing them those two nights in the Citywest and Imperial, though, I knew that they were going to be true to their word. Cork were going to win the 2004 All Ireland final. I could sense the hurt, the sense of purpose from just seeing Donal Óg sitting down on the floor in the reception room in the Imperial, with his legs out, staring at the floor. I could also gather they had a coach who'd learn from this defeat. 'You'd love the set-up now, Brian,' Donal Óg said. 'O'Grady's unreal. The days of the hard slog are gone; it's all scientific now.'

I'd always liked O'Grady. Back in '99, Jimmy had brought him in to do a few sessions with us backs, and he was excellent. As a man, I liked what I knew of him too. The Thursday before that 2003 final, I had left a voice message, wishing him good luck, and as he walked into the foyer of the Citywest that Sunday he saluted me when I caught his eye, and he said, 'Got that. Appreciated it a lot.'

So now there were a few carrots. The biggest one was to win another All Ireland. But the idea of playing under O'Grady appealed to me too – and of playing with Tom. I'd known him ever since he was a kid, and in 2001 I'd slag him to hurry up, that I wanted to play with him before I quit. The idea of teaming up with Setanta also excited me. He had lit up that summer, with his strength, speed, skill and audacity, and at only 19 was only going to get better. Then there was the new Croke Park. The '99 final had been the last match in the old Croke Park, and, while I'd been up there again in 2000, that was the same summer that Trevor Giles rightly described the place as a building site. By this time, it wasn't a building site; it was one of the most impressive grounds in Europe. And the thought of playing there in the 2004 All Ireland final kept racing through my head that Tuesday and Wednesday.

Come Wednesday evening, I was sitting with Elaine, in front of the TV. 'I'm thinking of going back playing,' I said.

'That's great,' she said. 'I'm sure the club will be delighted.'

'Actually,' I said, 'I mean going back with Cork.'

CHAPTER SIXTEEN
SECOND COMING

'I'm back'

MICHAEL JORDAN, MARCH 1995

THE NIGHT AFTER THAT CONVERSATION WITH ELAINE, I walked into the gym of the Silver Springs Hotel, gear-bag in hand. It was time to get back to the gym anyway. A few weeks before going up to that final, I was buying a pair of jeans in Merchant's Quay. All along, my waist size had been 36", but this day 38" was too tight. I refused to buy those jeans. I was going to work out and get back to a 36. Now I had a bigger reason to work out: to win an All Ireland medal.

There were no guarantees when I started the comeback that night. The previous evening, myself and Elaine thrashed out all the possibilities and agreed there were five potential scenarios. I could go back with the club and never get the call from the county. I could get the call, try out with the county and be a disaster. I could get the call, do reasonably well and make it onto the panel but not the team. I could make it onto the starting 15 but still fail to win the All Ireland. And I could make it onto the starting 15 and win the All Ireland. I had to be willing to accept all those scenarios. I had to live with the idea that this might not work out – that, if you considered the odds, it probably would not work out. But the one thing we concluded was that I could live with all those scenarios a lot easier than staying in retirement and watching Cork win the All Ireland without me.

There was also the Stuart Anderson factor: even though I would be thirty-one in 2004 and hadn't hurled in over two years, I still believed that I would make it back onto the starting fifteen. And I had just as much confidence in the rest of the lads that they'd win the All Ireland. I would joke with Elaine over the next few months that it would be great to find a clairvoyant who could tell for sure who'd win the 2004 All Ireland, but my own gut instinct was telling me that it would be Cork, and over the years my gut instinct had usually been right.

When I was doing my Leaving Cert, I had put accountancy down as the number-one course on my CAO form. The authorities were slow getting back to me, though, which made me doubt whether they had ever received it. In the meantime, I had changed my mind, so I sent away another form, with computing as my number-one option instead.

The following week, I got a phone call. Which course was my number one? And I went with my gut: computers, even though I knew nothing about them.

In 1992, I had completed a two-year cert in Computing. I had to decide whether I would move to the degree course or not. At the same time, Justin McCarthy offered me a job selling oil with Tedcastles. A job with a company car in the early '90s was very attractive, while Justin had made a good first impression on me that time I met him down in the Mardyke. His hurleys were polished and taped to the nines, and he had this gear-bag that was more like a toolbox, with its tape and band and tools to doctor any hurley. I couldn't get over how someone who hadn't played inter-county in almost 20 years was still so caring and meticulous about his hurleys. But again my gut told me to go back to college and get my degree, just like my good friend John Walsh was doing. Then I met Danny Culloty, who had been in the oil game himself for a while, and he said that it was a grand job if I wanted to talk hurling and football all day. I didn't.

So now, again, I followed my gut. But did I really, really want to go back to this routine of going out the door and togging off and training three or four nights a week? I pressed on and togged off. And then, as I walked in the gym door, the first person I walked past exclaimed, 'Are you coming back?'

I laughed it off. Coming back? You must be joking! Have to lose a bit of this belly; you know yourself.

That night was the start. Every journey starts with a single step, and that night I took a few thousand, on the treadmill. I was puffing after ten minutes, but I was still running after forty. And, over the next few months, I'd pop out there three nights a week at about nine o'clock and get an hour in, not telling anyone why.

After Elaine, the next person I confided in was Martin Bowen. He called down one day that autumn, telling me he was going to be manager of the club senior team but he needed a coach. I told him I wasn't interested, and I could see by his face that he was disappointed. 'I'd prefer to play, Martin,' I added. And after that he was only too happy to give me the keys to the club's ball alley.

That first night up in the alley it was as if I'd never hurled before. My eye was out; my touch was gone. I didn't let it get me down, though. It was always going to be that way. The only thing to do was to practise and practise, and slowly but surely the touch and eye would return.

I was coming along in the gym, too. I have Donal Óg Cusack to thank for that. Every night I went up there, he'd already be there. In the first few weeks, we'd often talk for a few minutes, and then he'd carry on with his workout and I'd go about mine. One night, as I passed, I noticed he was struggling with one weight. And, as anyone who lifts weights knows, a helping hand, or, often, a helping finger, is the difference between progressing and not progressing. That night, I stopped to give Donal Óg that extra help, and he asked me if I wanted to join him. Then we started competing with each other, lifting weights, doing sit-ups, running on the treadmill. It was just what I needed. Before, when I was on the treadmill, I'd be going at a reasonable pace, but my own pace. When I saw the rate with which Donal Óg was pushing himself, I figured that if I was to be an inter-county player again I'd have to be somewhere close to where he was.

I have always got on well with Donal Óg. The night before the 1995 Harty Cup final, I phoned to wish him good luck, him being captain that year and me being one of the class of '88. We had played together with Cork in 1999, 2000 and 2001, and won an All Ireland and two Munsters together. But really we had only been friendly, not friends. Over those few months up in the Silver Springs, we became friends. That November, I confided to him that I was thinking of going back with the club. He started emailing. 'Didn't see you there last night. Are you still training?' One week, I was abroad on the job, and when I got back there were a few emails there. 'Still alive? The training that hard?'

Over those months, I was beginning to be spotted more and more in the ball alley and the gym. I kept denying all the speculation about a comeback, but by Christmas I let Donal Óg in that I would be back with the club all right.

'Delighted to hear that,' he emailed. 'Look forward to playing against you – and maybe with you as well.'

*   *   *

MY FIRST MATCH BACK WAS AGAINST OUR OWN UNDER-
21s, down on the pitch in Caherlag. 'You better play well now,'
smiled Ronan Aherne that morning. 'A lot of these young
fellas can't even remember you playing!' I went in full-forward,
scored 1–5 from play and a couple of frees. It was nothing
to get too excited about – I must have had half a foot on the
Under-21s' full-back – but it was a start.

Over the next few weeks, then, we played a series of challenge
games outside the county. And again they went reasonably
well. I was playing centre-forward, rather than my preferred
position of full-forward, but that was fine; the extra running
was like extra training for me.

The first real night back was a floodlit league game in Páirc
Uí Rinn. About a thousand people showed up to see us play
Killeagh, including all the county selectors bar O'Grady. Eight
months later, John Allen would admit to me that they hadn't
been overly impressed. I know a few balls had dropped out
of my hand, and I'd struggled with a few on the ground too,
but I'd scored four good points from play and five from frees,
and, while my marker and old friend Mark Landers hadn't
been at his fittest, I still wasn't either. It had been hard to
make out the ball at times, as it went from being pucked out
in the light to sailing through the dark.

I'm sure O'Grady was the one who fought to bring me back.
And, one Saturday that April, the phone rang. I knew it was
O'Grady, because I had stored his number from his call the
previous March.

'I told you I'd call you back,' he said. 'It's maybe later than I
said I would, but here I am.' He said he knew I was back with
the club; how did I feel about going back with the county?

'Well, I'd love to try,' I said. 'The mind is willing. Not sure
yet if the body's able.'

There was only one way I would know, we agreed: to come
back and see how it was. If I felt I was up to it, great; if I didn't,

I could always walk away. But I'd get fitter back training with Cork now than not training with Cork.

'We'll be training probably next Wednesday,' he said. 'I'll call you on Monday to let you know where and when.'

The call ended at that, but within seconds I was on to him again. I'd forgotten to tell him something. I had no interest in chasing rabbits again.

'Just checking one thing with you there, Donal. If I do come back, where would you be thinking of playing me?'

Donal played the *an muinteóir* routine, about how we'd see, that he had no specific place in mind.

'Well, which end of the field would it be?' I asked. 'Because, to be honest, I have no interest in coming back as a back.'

'No, no, it would be as a forward we'd be considering you. Now, it could be any of the six forward positions . . .'

I was happy enough with that. But I was still apprehensive. Would I fall flat on my face? Would I be stepping on someone's toes, taking somebody's place? How would those fellas feel about my return?

I got an email from Donal Óg that Wednesday morning. 'Any word from Grady?'

'Yeah. Rang me on Saturday. Asked me to go back training tonight.'

'Great news. Will we see you there?'

'Not too sure. Part of me thinks I'm mad. How do you think the other players would feel if I came back? I don't want to cause hassle or step on any toes.'

It took a bit longer for his next response, but it was that response that made all the difference.

'To a man, I have no doubt and know that your return would be a great boost for us all. We have a tough job ahead of us this year in our quest for All Ireland. We don't want Kilkenny winning three in a row on our watch, especially when we know we are as good as them. I know you'll enjoy and relish putting your shoulder to this wheel.'

Five minutes later, I was on the phone to O'Grady. 'Donal, Brian Corcoran here. You were supposed to call me about training tonight?'

'Oh, yeah, sorry. Forgot. Down in the Park for seven o'clock.'

I was down there by twenty-five to. I didn't want to be entering a full dressing-room at ten minutes to. I got out of the car, and right away there was a beep from another. I turned around, and Tom Kenny and Eamon Collins were waving at me. When I got inside, all the lads came over, and it was great to see them all. It was a pity that Setanta wasn't there. I was delighted for him when he got that Aussie Rules pro contract the previous December but disappointed for myself that I wouldn't get the chance to play with him. Everyone else was there, though, and all of them made me feel at home.

For O'Grady, it was just business as usual. When he called us in to the huddle, he didn't even acknowledge I was there. Then, a few minutes into a drill, he told me I was holding my hurley the wrong way. That's right: at 31, I was still holding the hurley the wrong way. The heel of the hurley should always be closer to the ground than the toe, he said. My sin was, when I was going to control a ball coming at my left side after controlling one on my right, I was moving my arms across instead of twisting them to keep the heel closer to the ground.

'I know it's 20 years of bad habits,' he said, 'but I want you to change.'

Then, when I went to bat a ball, he told me my hands were in the wrong position.

O'Grady was a believer, though. Shortly after that first night back, the club played UCC in the first round of the championship. I was at centre-forward, on Kilkenny's John Tennyson. Apart from my free-taking, I didn't impress, but at least we won.

Walking out that day, some punter saw O'Grady: 'Corcoran won't do at all for Cork!'

'Don't be fooled by that,' said O'Grady. 'We have something different in mind for him.'

THE FIRST MATCH BACK WAS A LEAGUE GAME AGAINST Waterford down in Páirc Uí Rinn. A few hours before the game, the selectors had even considered starting me, because of a few injuries. In the end, they decided it might be too much pressure too soon, but John Allen came over to me in Jury's Hotel to say that I should expect to come on in the second half. I did, with 15 minutes to go, to a big cheer from the crowd. Only two balls really came my way: one that I won over by the wing before being half-blocked, and another that I pulled out of the air before being pulled down for a penalty. We ended up blasting that penalty over the bar and were beaten by a point, but again it was another step down the road.

There were other milestones along the way. I was sick for our last league game against Clare but was introduced in the closing 20 minutes of a challenge game against Tipp in Fermoy. I scored a goal off Philly Maher, and afterwards O'Grady told me he was pleased with my performance.

I came on in our first-round game against Kerry in the Park to score that batted goal and a point, plus win a penalty, and in the warm-down I felt full of energy. I was sure now that I was good enough for the panel.

I was fine with being on the bench, though, for our first real test of the summer – Limerick in Limerick – even if I found out afterwards that Dr Con had told the selectors I wasn't. 'I wanted to get them thinking,' he'd later tell me. At half-time, we were behind, like we would be so often over the coming three seasons, but then, just as I got word to warm up, a Ben O'Connor free from out the field fell through the raised hand of poor Albert Shanahan. We were back in the lead, and, a minute or two after I ran in at full-forward, we would add to it.

I was standing just behind Ollie Moran when this high ball came in. I went out to contest it, hit Ollie a fair shoulder and caught the ball. But, just as I went to turn and shoot, I slipped and ended up on the ground. I rose to my knees. I had never taken a shot in such a position before, but instinctively I knew that if I waited to get up I'd be blocked by Ollie. So I hit it and watched as it sailed over. The crowd went mad with that one, and the next day so would some of the papers, but I couldn't get too excited about it; I was still only number 22. The important thing was we'd won and were back in the Munster final.

Two weeks later, we played a game that changed my year. O'Grady had organised a challenge game with Clare in Ennis and, while we were in that part of the country, a weekend retreat in Killaloe. The club had also organised a challenge game for that Saturday, just up the road in Gort, so I called O'Grady a few days in advance, wondering if it would be possible for me to play one half for Cork and then go up and play another half with the club; I could do with the match practice.

'And what makes you think you won't be playing the full match with us?' he said.

'Well, it's just I haven't played one so far. I assumed I'd be coming off the bench again.'

'Mmm. No, I don't think that'll work out at all. Go all the way up to Gort? No, you'd be better off staying with us for the full day.'

I knew then that I'd be starting and that, if I took this chance,

I'd be starting in the Munster final as well. And, even though that game in Cusack Park was played behind closed doors, I was as focused as I am in front of 50,000.

I was on Lohan, and, as you'd expect, it was physical. With the first ball that came between us, we both pulled hard, and I broke my hurley. With the next one, he broke his too. You get nothing easy off Lohan, but that day I managed to score three goals and a point and hold him off to set up a few scores for others.

Later that evening, then, we headed up to Killaloe, where we did a series of team-building activities at the University of Limerick's adventure centre and stayed in the Kincora Hall Hotel by the beautiful lake there. In Christy O'Connor's *Last Man Standing*, Donal Óg would say I was in great form. It was that weekend that the lads knew I was really back.

JUST WHEN I THOUGHT I WAS BACK, I WAS ALMOST gone again. A few days after I was named to start in the Munster final, but a few days before the game itself, I picked up a chest infection. On the Saturday, I was very bad. I actually togged out and went into the back garden, and, after doing a few laps, I was choking for air. No way would I last in Thurles. The following morning, when we met up in the Silver Springs, I headed straight for Jerry Wallis and informed him that my heart rate was very high.

O'Grady and Seanie were consulted, and it was decided they'd wait to see how I went in the warm-up. So I ran onto the field in Thurles that day not knowing whether I'd be fit to start. It was a tricky one. After all that hard work, I wanted to play, and, after all that work, I didn't want to fall flat on my face either. I couldn't let my heart rule my head. But the Deep Heat that Con rubbed on seemed to work, and I decided to block out the idea I was ever sick, except to use the time the ball was at the other end of the field to get my breath back. And it worked for that first half. I scored two points and a third that was called back for a free, which Joe pointed. We played some great hurling in that first half. Waterford couldn't cope with the pace of Ben and Tom and Jerry, and, if we had gone for goal on a few more occasions rather than settle for our points, we'd have been ahead by more than 1–14 to 2–8 at half-time.

Then, a few minutes after half-time, John Mullane was sent off. Instead of just being three up, we were now a man up too, playing with the wind. And, subconsciously, we eased up. While we might have got away with this against previous Waterford teams, this one, instead of being deflated by Mullane's dismissal, was galvanised by it. Paul Flynn and Ken McGrath came thundering into the game, while Michael Walsh and Seamus Prendergast seemed to be on to every break and puckout. What really did for us, though, was how we made such poor use of the ball. I hardly got a touch of it after half-time; instead, I spent the whole second half chasing balls over the line or watching them sail either wide or into the hands of their keeper, Stephen Brenner. The next thing, a Flynn free sailed into Donal Óg's hand, the ref blew for full-time and the whole pitch was flooded by a blue and white tsunami. Waterford 3–16, Cork 1–21. There I was all winter and spring thinking Cork wouldn't be beaten all summer, and now they'd already been beaten in Munster. Playing our part in a classic was no consolation whatsoever. There was only one consolation, and the following Wednesday I zoned in on it.

That evening, we had a players' meeting upstairs in Páirc Uí Rinn. John Allen, as the players' liaison, was the only selector in the room. At the start, an important decision was made: everyone in the room had to say something, otherwise it would just be the usual suspects. So everyone did. Fellas spoke about how we had gone away from our game plan and just started lashing the ball aimlessly when they had started to claw back. Just before it came round to me, Mick Byrne from Killeagh pointed out that we had four goal chances in the first half but took our points instead. I reiterated Mick's point: we hadn't been clinical enough.

'Lads, we've lost Munster, but I didn't come back to win Munster; I came back to win an All Ireland. There are fellas in this room here – John Gardiner, Martin Coleman – who were beaten in the 2001 Munster final but won the 2001 All Ireland final. Now, every one of you knows that they won that All Ireland, but I'd say a lot of us had forgotten about that Munster final. And it'll be the same this year if we win the All Ireland: no one in Cork will care that we didn't win Munster. I know I won't. Is Gardiner's All Ireland cheapened by the fact he doesn't have a Munster from the same year? I don't think so. Winning Munster is nice, but it's a separate competition from the All Ireland. That All Ireland is there for us, and I'll have no problem winning it without winning Munster.'

Yet, at half-time in our next game, we were in trouble again. We were four points down to Tipp in a do-or-die qualifier game in Killarney, and, as I looked around the dressing-room, I was wondering to myself where the Cork team I'd seen on the telly last year had disappeared to. I was 35 minutes from going into retirement again. O'Grady was 35 minutes from oblivion, and everything he and the strike stood for was on the line.

O'Grady knew it too. 'Fellas, last September you vowed in the middle of Croke Park that you were going to learn from that hurt and be driven by that hurt and be back there 12 months later. If we lose here, there is no Croke Park! It's very easy to say "Next year, we'll be back." Lads, as someone once said, commitment is doing the thing you said you would do, long after the mood you said it in has left you. Fight for your inches and honour your commitment.'

Normally I'd be relaxed at half-time, but that day I was riled to the hilt. Heading out the door, I threw off my helmet. From here on in, there could be no more distractions, no more inhibitions.

And, at the start of that second half, everything seemed to click. In the first half, little ball had come in to me, so I decided to roam out the field. Philly Maher followed me, leaving this big gap that Timmy McCarthy ran into to hammer the ball past Brendan Cummins. It was a brilliant finish, the kind that a fortnight earlier we wouldn't have gone for. Cummins would admit later in *Last Man Standing* that he had done less shot-stopping in training before that game, because we usually settle for our points. But we'd learned from Waterford. Timmy had listened to Mick Byrne. And, after that goal, our backs blotted out their forwards, our midfield and wing-forwards started scoring from out the field and then, with five minutes to go, Niall McCarthy drifted into that middle and whipped a ground shot past Cummins. We'd won. We'd honoured our commitment. My second retirement would have to wait.

As pleased as I was for Niall that day, I was especially delighted for Timmy. He hadn't started that game and had shipped an incredible amount of ill-informed criticism after the Munster final, but about 20 minutes into the Tipp game he had come on and answered those critics. I saw his mother outside the dressing-room afterwards and went over to say hello. Someone passed us and said to her, 'Timmy did great today.' And Mrs McCarthy, with a tear in her eye, said, 'Yeah. But he tried as hard the last day as he did today.'

That's what I've always admired about Timmy. His work rate never dips. All the running, all the space he creates for others, all the times he prevents some of the best wing-backs in hurling clearing their normal share of ball often go unnoticed, but they don't go unnoticed by his teammates. The fact he's come up with big scores and big performances in the big games is often forgotten too. It was Timmy who scored that late match-winning goal in the 1997 Munster Under-21 final that probably set the whole momentum for '99 in motion, Timmy who scored three points in that crucial game against Waterford in '99 and Timmy who scored another three points in the All Ireland final in '99. Never, though, did he make a more important contribution than the one he made in Killarney.

That game, in hindsight, was a watershed, both for us and for Tipp. After that game, they would fail to make the All Ireland semi-final for the next three seasons, while we would reach the All Ireland final those three seasons. In our next game after Killarney, we came up against a team coached by a passionate Tipperary hurling man, Dinny Cahill, but some of Dinny's passion ended up backfiring on him and Antrim. The Tuesday before that All Ireland quarter-final, Dinny not only declared that Antrim would win the All Ireland but proclaimed that I was 'finished' and that Niall McCarthy, our best player in Killarney, wasn't an inter-county hurler. Whatever chance we had of being under-motivated and complacent vanished after that. Before the game, O'Grady was as passionate as he had been at half-time in Killarney. He took out some of Wednesday's newspapers. 'This is personal. Look at what this man said about two of our players. There's only one answer to that.' Then he rolled the clippings into a ball and threw it to the ground. 'Destroy them.' By half-time, I'd scored two goals, Niall was flying and we were sixteen points up. Game over.

In the semi-final against Wexford, it appeared all over at half-time too, but O'Grady assured us it was not. The five minutes after Tom Kenny's 30th-minute goal had been 'the worst performance I've seen by any team I've ever been associated with'. We'd started 'showboating', and getting 'sloppy'. 'This is an All Ireland semi-final!' he shouted. 'It's 70 minutes. You go to the last.' So we went out for the second half with the mentality that the score was 0–0 to 0–0, instead of 1–13 to 0–4, and in the end we won by 18.

He was a brilliant coach, O'Grady. Even in those few sessions with the backs in '99, you could tell that his technical knowledge of the sport was unsurpassed. He showed us ways of hooking and blocking that nobody had shown us before, and yet it was so simple. Most players make the mistake of tracking the opponent's hurley when attempting to hook him, but O'Grady's attitude is that, if the hurley goes up, it must come down, so stick your hurley in, wait for his to come down and it'll hit yours. At times in 2004, I thought he was overemphasising hooking and blocking, especially after the Munster final defeat, but the following month after we beat Antrim I could see his whole philosophy paying dividends.

He had this natural authority and presence. Although players were encouraged to have their say, he could be dictatorial at times. His style was a bit like Brian Clough's. One time, a reporter mentioned to Clough his reputation for not listening to his players. 'That's not true,' Clough countered. 'I invite them in here all the time, ask them for their opinion, and, after they tell me what it is and I say what I have to say, we all agree that I was right.'

It wasn't just his players who got to see the school teacher in him that summer. After the game in Killarney, two officials on behalf of the Irish Sports Council entered the dressing-room to conduct a random drug test. Donal Óg and Seán Óg were selected, and, as the four of them went into the toilets to conduct the urine test, O'Grady came in.

'What's going on here?' he demanded.

The lads from the Sports Council explained.

'Can I see some documentation?' ordered O'Grady. The two lads produced a card and a form. O'Grady creased his brow and pointed to some initials in small print. 'What does this mean?'

'I don't know,' one of the two lads confessed, like a schoolkid back in O'Grady's principal's office. 'It's my first day doing this.'

'What? You're in here, drug-testing my players, and you can't tell me what this means?'

It was all mind games with O'Grady. In the 2003 final, the lads had got little protection from Kilkenny's occasional tendency to tackle high by putting the hurley around the neck. Before the 2004 final, O'Grady went to have a word with the referee. In training that week, we'd been practising a puckout situation where Sully would run in and take the puckout and pass to Donal Óg. 'I'm just clearing that with you, Aodán [Mac Suibhne]. There's nothing illegal about it, so there's no need to blow up for it.' Mac Suibhne nodded, and O'Grady headed away, but then he turned around for a brief second. 'And by the way, Aodán, you might watch out for the high tackle too.'

We were going to have to fight for every inch that day. Kilkenny were going to be the ultimate test.

We wouldn't have wanted any other kind. After the win against Antrim, we caught the first half of the other All Ireland quarter-final in Heuston Station while waiting for our train. Clare had Kilkenny on the rack, and the Cork supporters in our company were all urging on Clare. 'Christ, if Kilkenny are beaten, we have a great chance,' said a guy beside me. But, privately, every player was willing Kilkenny to win that game. We didn't want anyone else doing the dirty work for us; we wanted Kilkenny all to ourselves.

Before the final, the press made a big deal of the fact that, if Kilkenny won, they'd overtake Cork in the roll of honour. To be honest, it hardly registered in our thinking. The same applied to our supposed desire to stop Kilkenny completing the three in a row; although Donal Óg had referred to their target in that email to me back in April, it was more as a reminder of Cork's scarce return in that time. The way we were looking at it, half the team had yet to win an All Ireland and the other half hadn't won one in five years. We weren't out so much to prevent Kilkenny winning three All Irelands in a row; we were out to make sure we didn't lose two. We had to atone for the pain and the hurt of the previous year.

Three weeks before the final when we walked into training, we found a series of photographs, images and headlines that Eddie O'Donnell had put on the wall. They were all from the 2003 final. Gardiner on his knees, his head in his hands; Setanta with tears trickling down his face, with a devastated Sully by his side; Joe and Donal Óg staring into the ground: those clippings stayed there for two weeks. But then, the week leading up to the game, they were replaced by positive images and headlines. We needed to play to win, not just play to avoid losing. But, as much as the desire to win was vital, so was the fear of losing. The morning of the game itself, I was up in my bedroom, flicking through the channels, when I came across the *Final Moments* documentary of the 2003 season. Normally on match day, when I'd see anything related to the match, I'd flick it off, but this time I couldn't. The footage was so real, and Gardiner's hurt and confession so sincere and heartfelt. I couldn't bear to see him or any of us like that again in five hours' time.

The occasion and wet conditions meant it was a tight, scrappy game, and, with three minutes left before half-time, we had yet to score from play. I went out the field again. It was just something that evolved that year. O'Grady's last instruction before I went on against Limerick had been to stay around the square, but when I started to roam against Tipp and Wexford he hadn't disapproved. So, again, I made a run to the wing, and again my man – Noel Hickey – followed. A ball came our way, and Hickey and myself jockeyed for position. He pushed into me; then I pushed back into him to create the room to pick up the ball. I got it into my hand, saw the opening, ran, and then cut across to hit it over the bar. And when the umpire raised the flag, I gave the lion's roar by punching the air. We were back on track now, only a point down. This was still our All Ireland for the taking.

At half-time, I reiterated the point, calling the lads in before we went back out. 'Remember the pain of last year. Remember we're the best team in the country. I know it.' Then I spotted Sully and I hit him on the shoulder. 'And you know it.' And I practically went around the whole team. 'And you know it, and you know it and you know it. But, lads, there's no point in us knowing it if they don't know it out there. There's no point in meeting in a huddle in 40 minutes' time saying that we didn't do it today; we'll do it next year. You made a promise last year; today's the day to deliver it. So we decide now how we want to feel. Do we want to be crying again in the middle of the field or are we going to be collecting that cup having shown everyone we're the best team in the country?'

In the second half, we gave the country our answer. Kilkenny, boasting two of the greatest forwards in the history of the game in D.J. and Shefflin, were held scoreless from play. When they did link up, with D.J. offloading to Shefflin, Henry's shot was saved by Donal Óg, who coolly rolled it up, slipped the ball to Sherlock, who hand-passed off to Jerry O'Connor, who picked out Niall McCarthy, and then Niall drilled it in to Joe, who was upended by James Ryall. That free pushed us four up, and then another Joe free, a point from Fraggy and a brilliant point from Tom cutting through the centre extended the lead to seven, entering injury-time.

Con would later tell me that, of the 18 All Ireland senior finals he'd been involved with since the footballers' success in 1973, 2004 was the first one he could actually enjoy and savour in the closing minutes. Out on the field, I wasn't thinking that way. Instead, I was thinking of how Offaly had scored two goals in forty seconds to steal the '94 All Ireland off Limerick. If any team could repeat that, it was Kilkenny. So, when a ball broke out by the wing in the closing seconds, I literally adopted the mantra of fighting for every single ball. I managed to flick the ball away from Ryall and into the corner. Then I picked it up, and, as Hickey came towards me, I sidestepped him. For a moment, I thought about crossing it, but then I looked up and shot at the posts. I fell as I hit it and, for what seemed like an age, was there, on my knees, watching it hang in the air. And then it curled in, and then it went over, and Croke Park erupted. So did I. I roared, raising my arms in the air, and the next second Aodán was blowing for full-time and Joe and the rest of the forwards and subs were sprinting down towards me.

If we all have one moment in time, then that was probably mine. The point, being on my knees, the Rebel Yell, the lads flooding towards me; it was a great, great moment, the ultimate way to finish the game, the year, the comeback. Because, all year up until then, there had always been some doubt – doubt whether I'd make it back onto the panel; doubt whether I'd make it onto the team; doubt whether we'd bounce back after Waterford; serious, serious doubt at half-time against Tipperary; doubt after going the first half-hour without a score from play in the final; doubt even about being seven up in injury-time. But all along there had been even more belief, and now that belief had been vindicated, and all that doubt was no more. My prophecy had come true. We were the 2004 All Ireland champions.

And then we went on and became the 2005 All Ireland champions.

Now what matters is that we become the 2006 All Ireland champions.

CHAPTER SEVENTEEN
INCHES

'Life's a game of inches. So is football. Because, in either game, life or football, the margin for error is so small . . . The inches we need are everywhere around us. They're in every break of the game, every minute, every second. On this team, we fight for that inch. On this team, we tear ourselves and everyone else around us to pieces for that inch. We claw with our fingernails for that inch. Because we know, when we add up all those inches, that's gonna make the fucking difference between winning and losing'

THE 'INCHES' SPEECH, FROM OLIVER STONE'S
ANY GIVEN SUNDAY

TUESDAY, 25 JULY 2006

Donal Óg rings me at work today. He's concerned. We need to raise our game, otherwise we won't beat Waterford. He's phoned a few other players and wants to have a talk after training tonight. John isn't available, so there won't be a full-scale team meeting until Friday, but this year's and last year's reps should bounce a few ideas together about how to approach that group meeting.

So we meet. I say that what brought us two All Irelands isn't going to bring us a third; we need to do something different. Cunningham noticed how on Sunday night after the draw was made all the commentators were saying that Waterford must be happy they got us rather than Kilkenny. We're seen as the softer touch, as a team that perhaps are getting tired, that don't have the old hunger. There's no doubt about it, if we play like we did against Limerick, and Waterford play as they did against Tipp, we will lose. We have to come out a different animal to the one that was in Thurles last Saturday.

I suggest that we start Friday's meeting by showing the last five minutes of the 2004 Munster final. There's nothing like a dose of reality to stir the fire within. The lads concur. Donal Óg will organise that. John will open Friday's meeting, and then Seán Óg, Donal Óg, Joe, Pat and myself will all talk. We're to speak with more passion than ever. The real big push has started.

FRIDAY, 28 JULY

We have all been notified by text to be at Páirc Uí Chaoimh for 6.30 p.m. I arrive with ten minutes to spare. Already, most of the lads are congregated in the main hall and Donal Óg is pacing up and down.

We all sit around in a large circle. John starts the DVD of the final minutes of the 2004 Munster final. Prendergast's point. McGrath's catch. The final whistle. Their crowd flooding onto the pitch.

John presses the 'stop' button, then asks me to start proceedings.

'I don't know about the rest of ye,' I say, 'but it sickens me to relive that again. I don't want to have to relive it on Sunday week. We can't do anything about the past, but we can do something about the future.

'John got a bit of stick after the Clare game for saying something publicly that I have said many times within this group. The only team that will beat us is ourselves. How do we do that? We do it by not being mentally ready, by not preparing properly, by not having the right attitude. We got a scare against Limerick, but there are no second chances now. We had a meeting like this after losing to Waterford in 2004. It turned our season around. We need this meeting to do the same again.

'In coaching, in sports psychology, they talk about "deserving victory". You have to feel that you *deserve* to win. I have no doubt that Waterford believe they deserve to win. Why do they think that? Maybe it's because some of their players have been around for a long time and haven't won an All Ireland. Maybe it's because they believe that they are better than us. The reality is that they have had plenty of chances and haven't taken them.

'Now, why do I believe that we deserve to win? No other team has made more sacrifices than us over the last few years. No other team has been as professional as us. No other team has our team spirit. We are going for three in a row, four finals in a row, and we still haven't got the credit for it. People say that we are lucky. Luck doesn't win 12 championship games in a row. People say that we have only two forwards. You don't win back-to-back All Irelands with two forwards. The reality is that we are going to have to take the credit ourselves.

'Waterford hate our guts. They are sick of losing to us. They would love to stop us. We can't let that happen; we can't give them that satisfaction. Last year, in the quarter-final, with about 10 minutes to go, Tony Browne won a free. He jumped up into the air clenching his fists, turned around and eyeballed me and roared, 'You can fuck off back to Cork, Corcoran! We have ye today!' I scored the goal a couple of minutes later, and, as I was running out, I looked over at Browne. He was bent down, with his head in his hands. I want to see him like that again on Sunday week.

'The thing is, when that goal was scored, there were still six minutes left and only three points in it. They gave up. We wouldn't do that. We fight to the end. This game will be spoken about in years to come. Make sure that we can look back with happy memories. It's up to everyone in this room, and it has to start when we hit the field tonight.'

Joe's next. He asks us to think about how we'll feel for the next four weeks if Waterford are preparing for an All Ireland final instead of us. Then Seán Óg goes into the middle. 'Sorry now for standing up,' he says, 'but I want to stand up.' Then he talks about the need for all of us to stand up on Sunday week, to start playing with a bit more aggression, with a bit more of a chip on our shoulder.

Sully then speaks, with passion. So does Donal Óg. No notes, just straight from the heart. I've heard him give so many speeches, but I'm listening here as if it's the first time. He links in some history and quotes other guys in the room to make everyone feel included. He speaks about not underestimating the opposition, not underestimating the prize at stake and not underestimating the calibre of individual that we have going into battle with us. Then it's time to go onto the field, and you can just feel the energy within the group.

Just before Seanie starts the session, I say one last thing. 'Everything that was said in there was valid, but talk won't win the game. As Seanie says, it's what happens between the white lines that will decide it.'

It's a great session. It's intense, game specific, real. It has to be. Since the Clare game, I've played three competitive matches in the last ten weeks: the Munster final, a club championship game against Douglas and the Limerick game. Up to this week, we haven't played any matches in training, just that twelve-minute conditioned game in which the first four minutes with the ground hurling is a virtual waste of time. I know the policy is probably one of the reasons we've had so few injuries these last few years, but we've been going into matches in Thurles this year basically playing from memory. It's very hard to develop an understanding with Joe in the red heat of championship when you haven't been playing together in training; it's very hard to get shots off in championship when you haven't had someone in your face in training. When I won the penalty against Limerick, I had a posse of fellas on my ass. I never had that in training; even hearing their footsteps was all new.

I mentioned it to Seanie on Tuesday night. He was setting up this drill where we run out to a ball played in to us, control it and hit it over the bar. 'Right,' he said, 'you have to imagine now that there's someone breathing down your neck here.'

And I said, 'Seanie, can we put someone in there, so? It's one thing imagining it, another thing having someone hanging off you.' And Seanie agreed.

So we do that tonight, and we also play a match for 15 minutes. I'm finally on Sully, with me the forward for the first seven and a half minutes, before we're meant to swap around. It's good, intense stuff. Then I run out towards the wing, and Sully takes the legs from me. I go down awkwardly on my ankle, and, for a second, I fear the worst. But Deccie comes over and says it'll be fine but to give the rest of tonight's game a skip.

The lads finish up soon afterwards, anyway. Seanie comes over to wish us all good luck. He and Susan were married on Wednesday and fly out on their honeymoon to Bali tomorrow. It'll be the first time in four years he's been away from the team. We wish him good luck. We're going to miss him over the next week. The best present we can give him now is to make sure he has an All Ireland final to prepare for.

Tonight can't be his last night training us this year.

TUESDAY, 1 AUGUST

Everything's gone to another level. The past few months, when we'd been warming up and stretching, you could hear fellas talking and, the odd time, laughing. Not now, not since last Friday's talk. Everyone's focused; everyone's all business. No one strolls over to get their water and strolls over to the next drill; fellas run over and run back. There's a greater urgency and purpose there now.

We play another match among ourselves. Again, the pace is blistering. Sully's marking me, and, while the ball is at the other end of the field, we comment on how things have picked up. Young Cathal Naughton in particular is flying out on the wing.

I turn to Sully. 'I'm surprised he hasn't seen any action yet.'

'Same here,' says Sully. 'I was only saying it to Fred Sheedy the other night. Imagine being a corner- or wing-back and have him come running at you with 15 minutes to go. Your worst nightmare.'

All the subs are really tuned in at the moment. In fairness, their attitude has always been very good. They all drink their water and energy drinks on the bus; they all apply themselves in training. I got a text from Kelly on Wednesday. I had been onto him earlier looking for a business card.

'Sorry for delay,' his message went. 'In pool for recovery session. Must get the edge over our opponents!'

You look at his face in some of the team photos before games and he is as tuned in as if he's about to start. After the way John Browne was suddenly unleashed in the 2004 final, everyone feels they could come on at any time. This Sunday, it could be Kelly. It could be Cathal. It'll take a panel effort, which is why Jerry Wallis stands in front of the cameras until every one of the 30 is in frame. It's all for one and one for all.

We're making a big deal of that unity this week. Waterford are a serious outfit, one of only two teams in the country who really believe they're better than us. But we see them as a bunch of individuals, while we're a team. You pick up the *Examiner* on a Monday morning in September or October and there always seems to be a melee in some club game between Mount Sion, Ballgunner or Lismore. This past week, John and the selectors have been consulting John Carey, the performance coach, to help with the mental preparation, and now there are more pictures and slogans on the wall.

There's a photo of Justin McCarthy and Tony Browne embracing each other after their win up in Croker against Tipp, with the headline below it, 'Bring On Da Rebels!'

We have a poster, which reads:

> OUR WORLD:
> Winning
> Discipline
> Professionalism
> Team spirit
> Unity
> Positivity
> Performance
> Taking responsibility
> Setting standards
>
> THEIR WORLD:
> Losing
> Fighting
> Blaming others
> Playing for oneself, not the team
> Relying on luck
> Bringing down others to their level

Which world do you want to live in?
Now is the time to fight for it.

Exactly.

THURSDAY, 3 AUGUST

The Subbuteo board is out again. Tonight, the agenda is puckouts, long-range frees and the game plan.

John is worried about our return from long-range frees. He's consulted the stats Eddie O'Donnell has kept this year, and our return is below standard. He says that it's up to Jerry O'Connor to decide. If he feels he can score, he'll take it. If not, one of the half-backs will play it down the channel, instead of going for the score.

John also says that we'll play Dan Shanahan the way we played Eoin Kelly in the Munster final, only this time Seán Óg will be the man to take him up if he goes to either wing or corner. Dan's 'The Man' at the moment, just like Eoin was in June. Again, we couldn't have a better man for the job than Seán Óg.

The big thing tonight, though, is puckouts. So far this year, we've only used two signals, and about 80 per cent of our puckouts have been improvised, while last year we had six signals, and all of the puckouts were pre-planned. We're going back to the six puckouts now, as Waterford won't be expecting it.

We go through it on the board. Then we go through it by all standing up in our spots in the room. Then we go downstairs and go through it out on the field. John blows the whistle, Donal Óg signals, fellas make the runs, and, a few seconds after the ball lands and is played on, John blows the whistle again for the next puckout. Anthony Nash and Martin Coleman hit out a few, too. If Donal Óg gets injured on Sunday, they'll need to know exactly what to do.

FRIDAY, 4 AUGUST

Friday night, rehearsal night, and we go through the signals and puckouts again. It means another deviation from our usual routine – Niall Mac has to train with us.

Traditionally Niall doesn't train on the Friday night; he just gets a rub and stretches. I don't think anyone gets more rubs or stretches than Niall. He goes to all these extra, quirky lengths to get right for match day. He has this thing for salt water and ice water. He's constantly on to Kelly, even when it might be freezing cold and lashing rain. 'Come on, we'll go down to the beach in Inch.'

When we got out of Killarney in 2004 with that win over Tipp, I told reporters that Niall was the heart and soul of our team. He still is. At centre-forward, he's so critical to our puckout strategy. He's especially critical on Sunday. We reckon Ken McGrath isn't going to follow Niall out, so we'll be targeting him early and often. He's going to be the main outlet: at least 50 per cent of Donal Óg's puckouts will be for Niall. For another 25 per cent, the room he creates for others will be vital.

So tonight, Niall takes a break from his rub and joins us for the puckouts, wearing a pair of runners. Then, when we're done, he runs off again, back to the table and Davy, the masseur. We don't want him to change old habits at this stage.

Some other people have changed their ways, though, and tonight that is recognised. After presenting Jerry Wallis with the fashion award for all the extra work he's doing in Seanie's absence, John hands out the Silent Pig award to one Mr Diarmuid O'Sullivan. As John says, he was far from a Silent Pig three years ago. Three years on from ripping his hamstring running out for the All Ireland final, he'll walk out of that tunnel on Sunday.

We also had our players' meeting. Pat covers everything. He

speaks from the heart – about standing up for our world, our way, our dream. He hands over to Donal Óg.

Donal Óg just waves his hands. 'Enough said.'

SATURDAY, 5 AUGUST

We have just pulled out of Kent Station, and the first two Cork hurlers to join the GPA aren't happy. I don't have my golf magazine. I always buy a golf magazine in the station, but the terminal's changed, and now there are no magazines sold in the new shop! Donal Óg Cusack, the most meticulous man on the planet, has forgotten his iPod. Eventually we each come up with a plan B. I get the brainwave to phone Ben, who'll be getting on in Mallow, to buy me my *Golf Monthly*, and Donal Óg borrows Sully's iPod.

While I read about how Tiger and Nicklaus compared to each other when each player was 30, the usual banter is going on: the card game, the laughter, the roaring. Joe O'Leary hands out the traditional quiz sheet. What's the capital of Cambodia? How many All Irelands have Waterford won? Who refereed last year's All Ireland minor final?

The amount of cheating going on is unreal. Donal Óg is checking answers online with his BlackBerry. Everyone else is cogging or comparing answers. There's a tie, so the winner is decided by who has the best one-liner. Last year, it was your best chat-up line; this year, it's your favourite quote – but it must be your own, and it must be original. Donal Óg and Tom Kenny are disqualified, because judges Fred and Patsy Morrissey deem their answers to be plagiarised, and, by the time Fred and Patsy announce the winners, everyone else is looking for them to be sacked.

Tom is now listening on his phone to the Armagh–Kerry All Ireland football quarter-final. It's a classic, by the sounds of it. I'd like to be watching it. I plan to catch the second half of the Cork–Donegal game when we get to the Burlington, but, as I walk into the lobby, Donal Óg wants a word. Traditionally on match day up here, we all go for a walk around Dublin 4, and then, on our way back, Seanie says a few words around the corner from the Burlington that set the tone for the day. What will we do tomorrow? I tell Donal that I'll step in for Seanie if John agrees. John does, so I head up to catch the second half of the football.

It's inspiring stuff. Apparently the first half was poor enough and Cork even poorer, but the way Nicholas Murphy and Ger Spillane pull Cork back into it and then combine for that winning point at the end has me in just the right mood. You have to hand it to Morgan. There he is on that line, nearly twenty years on from winning his first Munster, ten years after our last game together against Kerry, and now he'll be facing them again in the All Ireland semi-final.

After mass, I meet some of the footballers, as they're eating in the room across from us. I congratulate Nicholas and Ger on their displays and have a quick word with my old friend Teddy Owens, who is training them now. Most of them are staying up to watch the hurling tomorrow. It's farcical that we're not on the same double bill and thousands of Cork people had to fork out for both days – another example of the GAA not applying common sense.

After a light puckabout around the corner with some of the lads, I get a rub from Chris, have a few sandwiches in the team room and head back up to the room to watch some golf. I'm on my own. It's a tradition now. Patsy has had the job of allocating rooms ever since I came back, and, when he found there was one single room because there were 29 fellas on the panel, he told me it might as well go to the oldest fella. I don't know if it was that or just maybe that some of the lads had complained about my snoring. I have to admit, I'm a snorer. I'm not the worst, though. I roomed with Cunningham on holidays in Tenerife in '94, and every night it would be a race to get to sleep first. The bastard beat me every night. He'd put his head on the pillow and, two seconds later, be snoring. Then I'd have to get my pillow and put it over my ears.

Another night, it was my turn to keep a teammate awake. Brendan Walsh from Killeagh was over in Inverness with me in '92 for the Under-21 shinty international against Scotland, and we got talking about a murder case that was in the papers that week. Some fella had woken up in the morning to find his wife next to him, stabbed to death. Police found that it was his fingerprints on the knife, but he claimed he knew nothing about it, that he must have been sleepwalking or something. Then I told Brendan I was partial to the odd bit of sleepwalking myself. That next morning in Inverness, I woke up, opened my eyes and there was Walsh, his two eyes wide open, looking at me. 'You bollix, Corcoran. I couldn't sleep a wink all night!'

That can't happen to me tonight, so I'm going to leave the phone off the hook. Before last year's semi-final against Clare, it rang at ten to four in the morning. I stretched over.

'How's it going, Brian!'

Who was this? Why were they calling me at ten to bleedin' four in the morning? How did they know my name?

'Oh, sorry there, Brian! Mixed up the time. We're calling from America, see.'

The next morning at breakfast, everyone was asking the same. Did you get a call last night? From some fella claiming he was in America?

Nearly everyone had.

I doubt if anyone will take that chance tonight. Too much is at stake tomorrow.

SUNDAY, 6 AUGUST

Three hours to the biggest battle of our hurling lives; it all comes down to today. We've just stopped at Seanie's wall on our traditional stroll. It's time for me to speak.

'Seanie normally does this, but I have been asked to do it today. At this stage, Seanie is always talking about being nice and relaxed, so I'm not going to do any shouting and roaring. Everyone here owes a lot to Seanie McGrath, so the least we can do for him is to let him enjoy his honeymoon and have an All Ireland final to look forward to when he comes back.

'We have spoken a lot already, but I want to say this. During the week, a lot of people have said to me that Waterford will be very hungry and we won't be able to match it. I don't accept that. What is hunger? To me, hunger is a state of mind, an intensity, a desire to win. You choose your hunger. It's about the future not about the past.

'I don't know how many of you saw the British Open last week. In the last pairing of the final round, Tiger was paired with Sergio Garcia. Tiger had won ten majors, two British Opens. Garcia had won no major, no British Open. If the logic that I have been hearing all week applied, Garcia would have eaten Woods alive. But he didn't. He was beaten on the first tee, such was Woods's intensity and desire. And that's in a game where there's no physical contact.

'So why was Woods so hungry? The reason is that he has a goal that is greater than Garcia's. He is chasing Jack Nicklaus's record of 18 majors. He wants to be the best player of all time. He is playing for history; he is playing for greatness.

'Waterford are playing for greatness within their own county. We are playing for greatness within the history of the game of hurling. Our goal is greater.

'Let's go out there today and show them how hungry we are for that.'

*   *   *

266

INCHES

HALF-TIME IN THE BIGGEST BATTLE OF OUR HURLING
lives and it's level, eight points apiece. John comes in with
some of Eddie's stats. His talk is positive. The conditions out
there might be wet, the pitch might be ridiculously slippery,
but we're controlling the controllables. Seven of our points
have come from play. Only three of theirs have. It's frees that
are keeping them in it. We're doing fine. It was always going
to go down to the wire.

I had it in my mind all week to take Tom Feeney on whenever
I got the ball into my hand. But, when I intercepted a pass
of Feeney's there a few minutes into the game, I remembered
Sully talking last Friday week about fellas taking the wrong
options and the wrong shots against Limerick. So, when I
caught a glimpse of Tom Kenny flying up on my left, I passed
it off, and Tom scored a point. With the next two balls, I shot
over my shoulder out on either wing, one on the left, one on
the right, and they both went over.

I'm playing well, so if I get the ball in this half I'm going
to run at them.

We go back out, and the first thing they do is run at us.
Eoin McGrath shoots, Donal Óg saves, but Eoin Kelly buries
the rebound. Then, Prendergast scorches through for a point.
It's like the Munster final, though; it's like last year's game
against them. Four down with over half an hour to go is
surmountable.

We're making little road into that lead, however. They're not
pushing on, but they're not giving way either. God, maybe
they do have us today. We need someone to do something.
Timmy steps up. He gets on to a break, bursts past three of
them and splits the posts – then punches the air with his fist.
His reaction surprises me. Timmy's the kind who just runs
back out to his position, but he must sense someone has
to give the lion's roar. And it works. All of a sudden, I feel
re-energised. We're still in this. We can still win this. Jerry

Wallis runs in to tell me to urge on the lads, just like I did in the Limerick game.

We need something more now. Curran and Seán Óg are hurling up a storm at the other end, but so is Browne in front of me. Then John Allen finds that extra something and unleashes it. When play stops for a Gardiner free with 13 minutes to go, Cathal Naughton comes on for Neil, who has broken a bone in his hand. The first thing I think of when Cathal runs on is that he'll forget what's supposed to happen now. We agreed during the week that for these long-range frees the corner-forwards would come in towards the goal, break off me and sprint to the wings. I'm worried that Naughton's not going to remember that, just coming on the field in front of 62,000 for his first inter-county match. I can't shout anything in case the Waterford lads hear, so I'll make the run here myself. Wait, no need. Naughton's making the run. He controls Gardiner's pass dead, shoots over his shoulder and bangs it straight over the bar. He remembered. Incredible. Another lion's roar.

And then we're in the lead. I get dragged out the field looking for the ball and slip and fall to the ground. I look up, and all I can see is Ken McGrath's ass and Ken about to pick up the ball. But I can still see that ball, that inch, between his legs, and I can still get to it. I poke it away from Ken. Joe's on to it. He takes it on. I'm sure he's about to take his point, but then he slips it in to Naughton. Clinton Hennessy is coming roaring out of the Waterford goal to smother it. You've taken too much out of it, Cathal. But again he amazes me. Again, he's done the right thing. He just takes this short but powerful swing to the side of Hennessy, and the ball is in the net. Cathal leaps into the air, and so does nearly every Cork man, woman and child in the stadium.

But this time Waterford don't hold their heads in their hands; this time they don't give up. They sweep downfield and score a point. We come back up, then they go back down again. As the game enters injury-time, Hennessy over-hits a ball out to McGrath, and McGrath slides in and bumps Joe out by the touchline. It's the ultimate pressure free. We're a point up, but the ref's bound to give them another chance or two to reply. Joe hovers over the ball. It's drizzly, the crowd are booing and I know, from the second I see the ball swerve in the air, that he has the heavier, wetter O'Neill's ball. And yet it goes right over the black spot.

But it's not over. Mullane pops over another point, and the gap's back down to one. Then a ball breaks around their 65, and the referee awards them a free. I don't know why. I walk past the ref. 'What's that for?'

'A knee in the head.'

I didn't see it, but I decide to keep my mouth shut. It's one of those games people will say neither side deserved to lose, and all the ref is looking for now is an excuse to move the ball up another 13 metres.

This is going to be the last play of the game. There's no point in staying around our full-forward line. Better being back around our own goal and crowding it as much as possible. I run past the 21, towards our square.

'Get out!' roars Sully, like I'm a stranger trespassing on his land. If the ball is going to drop between himself and Shanahan, he wants room to go at it full tilt. So I move to the left corner, in case the ball breaks out there.

McGrath is standing over the ball. It's 90 yards out, but that's within his range. He bends down, lifts, strikes and the ball sails through the air. Is it going wide? Is it going over? Shit, it's going over. It's going over by a good two feet.

And then Donal Óg puts up his hurley. There's an old rule in goalkeeping never to challenge a ball that's going over the bar in case you bat it straight down and gift a goal. But Donal Óg's challenged every assumption about goalkeeping, and so he does what he's done so often in training and bats it out to the side.

I'm on to the break. I pick it up. Normally now I'd just flake this down the field, but I can't here. McGrath is still out there, and he's not going to miss a second time. I try to work it out, create space for a hand-pass, but I can't. Prendergast is blocking me. I sidestep him and tap it on my hurley, but there are bodies everywhere. I have to get rid of this thing quick now or the ref's going to blow for a free. So I swing, and I'm hooked, but I'm glad to be hooked, because at least the ball is still at my feet, instead of down with McGrath and him lining up the equaliser. I throw my body at it – everyone throws their body at it – when, seconds later, down in the very corner, the ref blows it up.

I raise my arms and turn around. Curran's there, and we smile, and we hug. I run back down to the corner to clap the Cork supporters on the Hill. Then I spot Brian Murphy on the ground, on his back. 'Brian, are you all right?' I ask. No answer. 'Brian, are you all right?'

He starts to shake his groggy head and looks up at me. 'Did we win or lose?'

We won, Brian. And the difference is the difference between day and night. You just have to look around. John Mullane's on his knees, his face staring down at the ground. I exchange a handshake and a small hug with Prendergast, like you would in front of a coffin. Because that's what it's like. No one has died, but a dream has died, and it's real and it hurts.

But our dream is still alive, and it's some high knowing it and sharing the feeling with the lads.

Timmy's sitting up from me back in the dressing-room. 'God, Timmy, you were fired up today!' He winks. 'It must be living close to the border there, was it?'

'Something like that,' he smiles.

A big cheer goes up. Donal Óg has won the RTE Man of

the Match. Only right. His control, his touch, his focus today were sensational. It goes back to the Ali quote, though, about the fight being won far away from witnesses.

A few minutes into today's game, McGrath launched a high ball into our square that Dan tried to pull on and Sully went to bat. Both missed, but both were practically on top of Donal Óg when the wet ball skidded in front of him. He had only a microsecond to see that ball, let alone touch it. But he caught it below his knee and danced out with it. Why? Maybe because last week he had Cunningham and Nash raining balls from 40 yards on top of the square, while Martin Coleman swiped at them to try to put Donal Óg off. He also had Nash pumping ball and, as it was landing, Cunningham throwing another six sliotars in front of Donal Óg, and still Donal Óg would focus on and claim the first dropping ball. And it was the same with that last free of McGrath's. All year, and all last week, Donal Óg had been swinging balls down from the crossbar and swiping them to the side. On a team that prides itself on fighting for that inch, he's the ultimate inch fighter. Surely they can't deprive him of an All Star this year.

I've been talking to him there, and he's just told me about how the sliotars worked today. There were two young fellas behind the goals designated to hand them out. So Donal Óg went to one of them, 'Do you play hurling?'

'I don't.'

He went to the other. 'Do you?'

'I do.'

'Right, you're my man. You have a bag of Cummins balls there. I want those. I don't want any of the others.'

Your man agrees, so Donal Óg doesn't go near any of the O'Neill's until after half-time, when his young friend tells him all the Cummins balls are gone.

'Right,' says Donal Óg, 'you're going to have to go up to the other end to get them, so. There's no problem with it; there's nothing illegal about it. The other keeper doesn't want to hit them, he wants the O'Neill's, so you take those up to him, bring me down his Cummins and I'll give you my jersey after the game.'

Somewhere in Dublin now is a young fella going around with the jersey of today's Man of the Match.

Donal Óg fought for that inch, but I have to fight for some more now. In the warm-up room, I have a word with John Allen. 'What are we going to do with the club games next week? Are we going to try to get them off?'

John says we can always ask. I say we need to do more than ask. But first I need to put it to the rest of the lads. John agrees, before being called away for an interview. I tell the lads that, personally, I think we have only one shot at this three in a row and we'll lose two weeks' valuable training if the club games go ahead. Donal Óg asks does anyone disagree. No one does. History demands 'no compromise'.

On the train down, the mood is good. I'm sitting next to Cunningham. He dials a number on his phone and hands it to me.

'Seanie?' I say.

'Who's that? That's not you, Ger!'

I tell Seanie who I am, and he tells me where he is. He's the happiest man in Bali, just back from hiring out an internet café at midnight and listening to the match on 103FM with Susan and this bemused local.

'Inches,' he says. 'Inches.'

Today, an irresistible force met an unmovable object, something encapsulated by that play in the corner at the very end. Yet something had to give, and it wasn't going to be us. Because we fought for every inch. Only an inch divided us, but we found that inch because we clawed for it, because it was there everywhere around us. It was there when Donal Óg, who isn't exactly 6 ft 5 in. with a 45-in. hurley, refused to let that ball go over the bar. It was there when I poked that ball away from McGrath (although O'Grady's just said there, 'That was from all the snooker you played as a young fella!'). It was there when we spoke about our long-range frees and Gardiner playing it down the channel so that someone, a Cathal Naughton, maybe, might come out and score that point. We fought for every single ball.

We had to. I've said some things about Waterford here, but, while I'm still glad it was them, not us, who lost today, I do feel for them, especially Ken McGrath. I see him now and I see myself as I once was. I genuinely hope some day he finds what he's looking for – just not in my time, not on our beat. He always performs; he always give it his all.

I'll say another thing about Waterford. Ever since this rivalry with them started with that league final in '98, it's always been a battle, it's always been epic and it's always been a game of ball; there's been hardly any messing. It comes down to this. We believe we're a better team than they are, and they believe they're a better team than us, so when we meet it's a case of let's just play and show who's the better hurling team. The odd time, they win. Most of the time, we win. Always, hurling wins. If we're Ali, then they're our Frazier.

Can't get sentimental, though. Can't get soft.

Next Sunday in Croker, two more hurling heavyweights clash, and Liston and Foreman are itching for another shot at us.

CHAPTER EIGHTEEN

IMMORTALITY BECKONS

'It's very difficult for me to say anything. I can only say this to you. Boys, you're a good team. You are a proud team. You are the world champions. You are champions of your conference for the third time in a row. That's a great thing to be proud of. But let me just say this: all the glory, everything you've had, everything that you've won, is going to be small in comparison to winning this one. It's not going to come easy. This is a team that's going to hit you. They're going to try to hit you, and you got to take it out of them. You got to be tigers out there. Keep your poise. You've faced them all. There's nothing they can show you out there you haven't faced a number of times. Right? RIGHT? OK, let's go. Let's go get 'em'

VINCE LOMBARDI

TUESDAY, 15 AUGUST 2006

So now we know. It's Kilkenny; they won that title eliminator with Clare on Sunday. We always sensed it would be them, that it was destiny. Two years ago, we stopped them doing the three in a row; now they have the chance to stop us. This will be my eighth All Ireland hurling final, and seven of them will have been against a side from Kilkenny. Thirty counties would have preferred any other pairing, but we wouldn't have wanted anyone else. Kilkenny wouldn't have wanted anyone else either. To be the best, you have to beat the best.

Before tonight's session started, John reminded us that we're going to be favourites but that it means nothing in Cork–Kilkenny games. Though Cork lead the roll of honour 30–28, historically we have a mixed record against Kilkenny in All Ireland finals; it's 12–8 to them. He reminded us of the night the big push started. We were 17 weeks away from the All Ireland final then. It's just three weeks away now. Nothing is to be spared. 'Our motto all year has been "Every Single Ball",' he said, 'but from here on in, you're competing not just for every single ball; you're competing against yourself.'

At the weekend, we'll be in Inchydoney for a retreat like the one we had last year. Tonight, before I headed home, myself and Donal Óg discussed some ideas for the players' meeting we'll be having down there. He thought that maybe we should play the 2003 *Final Moments* programme Dave Berry made, the one I watched on the morning of the 2004 final.

Maybe it'll make a similar impression on some fellas at the weekend. Just the other week for the Waterford game John showed the closing minutes of both the 2004 Munster final and the 2005 All Ireland quarter-final. Even the 2005 game stirred one of the lads. In the closing minutes, when it was obvious we were going to win, Ronan Curran was taken off. On the RTE commentary, Michael Duignan said that the selectors were making a point to Curran that he'd need to up his game the next day. I was two seats up from Curran when John played it, and I could tell by Curran's eyes that he wasn't going to allow Seamus Prendergast to outplay him again. He didn't either. Last Sunday week, when that game was on a knife's edge, Curran more than anyone made sure we won. He's been outstanding this year. But we'll need an outstanding team display to win this final. We'll need every inch and edge we can get.

THURSDAY, 17 AUGUST

Another night in the well, and I have the aches and pains to prove it. We battered the tackle bags tonight. We always do when we're in the well, but, with Kilkenny up next, we'll have to be particularly ready to give and take the hits. The hardest part in that drill is being in the middle, holding the pad. Volunteers are always scarce; invariably John has to tell someone to go in there. Tonight, I was that soldier. In the space of two minutes, I had twenty fellas, one by one, pick up a ball and drive into me. Some of them ended up standing on my toes; all of them tried to put a hole through the pad. I was glad to see the end of it.

We were all happy when training was over. With about 20 minutes left, black clouds gathered overhead like something from *Independence Day*. Then it started to spit hailstones, forcing everyone looking on to dash for cover. The downpour was so heavy we couldn't see what we were doing, but we finished out the session.

I was centre-forward on Curran in our game tonight. I'm not sure what the selectors are thinking, although Cunningham did mention on the train down after the Waterford game that they had considered bringing me out to the half-forward line at one point. I haven't played there since I came back, but if they want to throw something different at Kilkenny for a few minutes that's fine with me.

Donal Óg called another meeting after training. Tonight, myself, Seán Óg and this year's four players' reps – Gardiner, Pat Mul, Tom and Donal Óg – stayed on afterwards in the dressing-room. We talked again about our game plan, that we haven't been supporting each other on the field as we should and that we haven't been playing quality ball. We agreed that we need to go through this in detail on Saturday so everyone knows what has to be done.

On the way back to the car, I was talking to Killian Cronin about the plumbing job he's overseeing at our house, and then we got talking about the range of experience on the panel. Killian and Kelly have come onto the panel in their mid- to late 20s, while the likes of Niall, Curran and Tom are still in their early to mid-20s yet are now about to play in their fourth All Ireland final in four years. Gardiner has played five years with Cork and has played in a national final in each of those five years with Cork: the '02 league final and the last four All Irelands.

It's scary. Here they are, senior players, senior reps, leaders, yet it seems only a few years since Tom and his sisters Claire and Susan and his cousins Edward and Lisa were up in my hotel room the night before the '92 All Ireland final. I've known Tom since he was six. He'd spent a lot of his summers at his cousins' house just across the road from mine, and he'd join in our games of soccer, golf and hitting the ball against that old house by The Cross. He always had this likeable, personable way about him, a lot like his father's, and by the time he was 12 we all knew he'd make a top sportsman too. And that's what he is now, with those piercing runs from midfield and scores like that goal against Wexford in '04 and that point against Clare this year in Thurles.

It only seems the other day too when a baby-faced Gardiner stood in for a photo with me in the Burlington the day after the '99 All Ireland final. Two years later, I was the one coming up to Gardiner after an All Ireland. He was Man of the Match from centre-back in the 2001 minor final, and the following night I told him that his success was only starting and that mine was finishing. 'Keep it going,' I said to him. 'There's a number-six spot there for you.'

He's barely played there, of course, because of Curran, but he can play there and anywhere else. He's one of the best all-round hurlers in the game. He has everything you'd want: a great hand, anticipation, strength, speed, striking off left and right, heart and courage. Take that comeback against Clare last year in the semi-final; Gardiner instigated that. Take the Munster Final against Tipp in 2005 when he plucked ball after ball from the sky and set up so many scores. And, like all the other lads on the team, he is still very down to earth, a sound and solid guy.

I met him the night of the 2003 final in the Citywest, and he was devastated. 'Keep your head up,' I said. 'You're going to win two of the next three.'

I didn't know at the time I'd be back with him for those three tilts. After the 2004 final, he came up to me in the Burlington. 'We have the first one now, anyway,' he smiled.

Then, last year, he came up to me again. 'You were right,' he said.

I just hope now I wasn't too bloody right.

SATURDAY, 19 AUGUST

We were buzzing today. We went through the game plan down in Inchydoney this morning and then carried it out on the training ground this afternoon. If we move like we did today, then we will be very hard to beat.

John started the meeting by showing clips from the Kilkenny–Clare semi-final and then threw the discussion open to the floor.

Donal Óg kicked things off. 'We need to get back to our original game plan: support and quality ball.'

'I agree with that,' I said, 'but I think the full-forward line needs to play closer to goal. By the time we make our runs and get the ball, we're 30 or 40 yards out from goal. We're no threat out there. In '99, our aim was to keep Kilkenny goalless. We did that and won. In 2004, we did it and won. I have no doubt that our backs can keep them goalless, but it will make our job much easier if we can grab one or two ourselves. If the full-forward line stay in and the half-forwards and midfield are racing through on the overlap, it will be hard to stop us. We have plenty of pace, so let's use it.'

We talked about what we meant by support. Our whole philosophy is meant to be that you give the ball to someone in a better position and don't just pass for the sake of it. We've also looked at various scenarios, like what to do when a teammate gets the ball in the corner and who makes the run to support him or create an outlet for him. It was quite complex, quite detailed, but, judging by the training down in the nearby Ardfield pitch, well worthwhile.

After receiving a warm reception from the local club, St James, we had two fifteen-minute games. The ball was coming straight in to the full-forward line, and, whenever myself or Joe or Neil got a ball, either Timmy, Niall, Ben or Tom were thundering through for the lay-off. The pace and intensity were furious. Seanie wanted us to try out the game plan when we were tired, and we executed it. Again, the ball kept coming first time, and again the goals kept flying in. I think we're hitting top gear at just the right time.

SUNDAY, 20 AUGUST

J.J. Delaney is out for the All Ireland final. At first, when one of the lads mentioned it at breakfast, I was sceptical, but now that it seems true I'm disappointed. I know in theory it increases our chances of winning the All Ireland, but you don't want to win because one of their main men does his cruciate ligament in. It goes back to waiting for the train that time in Heuston in 2004, watching Clare–Kilkenny with our supporters – you want to earn it; you want to beat the best. It's cruel on J.J., to train all year long, and then, two weeks before the biggest game of the year, you're out. Cody now will use that to his advantage. They'll be mad to 'do it for J.J.'. It might seem a very simplistic motivational tool, but things like that can spur on a team.

It'll be a long way back now for J.J., but today I watched two other men who've bounced back from more serious setbacks. When he was a kid, Seanie McGrath had his leg amputated; now he's one of the leading sports scientists in Ireland. When he was 23, Seán Óg Ó hAilpín had his knee smashed in a car accident; now he's one of the true icons of Irish sport. And he handles that status so well. I've seen people approach him – plague him, really – on the street, and yet he'll have time and a smile for them all. When I phoned around the lads to wish them well a few days before the 2003 final, Seán Óg and I spoke for 45 minutes. My first night back training in April 2004, Seán Óg popped down to Páirc Uí Rinn after playing a football game for Na Piarsaigh. All the other lads had shaken my hand, patted me on the shoulder. Seán Óg hugged me. He's a man apart, class personified.

I was watching him with Seanie in the pool this morning as the pair of them went through in forensic detail the mechanics of the front crawl. I always thought Seán Óg was a great swimmer, but Seanie's like a fish. He was able to keep up with Seán Óg using just the one arm as he dipped underwater to study Seán Óg's technique. It was so typical of the two of them. Seán Óg so willing to learn; Seanie so willing to teach.

TUESDAY, 22 AUGUST

I missed training tonight, which was a bit of a disaster, but I couldn't do anything about it. We had American visitors in Cashel today, and I had to work late. On Sunday week, we might play in front of possibly the biggest sporting audience the world has known that weekend, but at the end of the day we're amateurs. We still have to work.

FRIDAY, 25 AUGUST

This afternoon, we had our press day. I didn't want to do it, but most of the lads didn't either, so I volunteered; somebody had to do it. I regret I did it now. I was there for three hours. Gardiner and myself had to do this interview for RTE. They tried to shoot it like the *Final Moments* series, with us talking to each other as if the cameras or Michael Lyster weren't there, but it was very forced, with questions such as 'If there was a transfer market in GAA, which Kilkenny players would you buy?' You don't want to give Kilkenny any ammunition, slighting some player you didn't name. Then, at five o'clock, there were sit-downs with the print media, along with Pat Mul, Curran and the management. In hindsight, I shouldn't have done both TV and print, and I ended up going to training feeling drained.

TUESDAY, 29 AUGUST

When I walked into the dressing-room tonight, Anthony Nash had a message from Seanie. None of us could go to the toilet because the drug testers were here. So we all sat around the dressing-room as the Sports Council guy explained that four of us were going to be picked randomly. They then produced a deck of cards and asked each of us to pick one. In the end, Jerry O'Connor, Tom Kenny, Kevin Hartnett and Donal Óg were the four selected. When I was in the shower afterwards, I noticed one of the testers was looking at us. 'What's this guy's game?' I thought to myself, but, as it turned out, Jerry had been too hydrated before training, and his sample hadn't been dense enough. It clicked with me then that the tester had been out on the pitch during the session too, obviously monitoring Jerry. It seemed a bit excessive, but, as long as Kilkenny have been tested this week too, I'm fine with it.

I'm more concerned with how we're going. We had another of those restricted 12-minute games tonight, and I felt it was lacklustre. In the second four minutes, one of the lads in midfield received a hand-pass and then fed a hand-pass to one of the other lads bombing through. The whistle went. Two consecutive hand-passes. OK, it was against the conditions of the game, but it was a good pass, in keeping with the principle of the game: offer support and use support. Next Sunday, in the same situation, we don't want fellas being hesitant offering or using that kind of support.

Everything tonight should have been positive and it wasn't. But I have to forget about it now and start thinking only positive thoughts myself. We are the Munster champions. We are the reigning All Ireland champions.

THURSDAY, 31 AUGUST

Tonight was my last training session with Cork. It wasn't something I announced, or even something I was thinking about until John presented me with the Silent Pig award in the dressing-room tonight.

John said a few words about my return to the team, about how, in his view, I was a beacon for Cork hurling in the dark years that were the '90s. 'If any man deserves to win the three in a row, if any man was ever the Silent Pig, it is this man. The Silent Pig award tonight goes to the one and only Brian

Corcoran.' As I went up to collect the award, the lads rose and gave a standing ovation. They must have sensed this was my last night too. As I sat down, I could feel a lump in my throat. I kept my head down, but I could tell by the applause that the lads were all still standing. And they must have stood there for another 30 seconds, clapping away.

Of all the honours I've received in my life, I don't think any was as moving or as appreciated as tonight's.

SATURDAY, 2 SEPTEMBER

I'm not wearing a helmet tomorrow. I didn't in the semi-final either, but that weekend I still brought it up in the train. I didn't today. I just feel more comfortable without one now. When I wear it, I also wear a sweatband, Björn Borg style, underneath, because I sweat so much. But, on hot sunny days in Thurles and Croke Park, your head expands with the heat, and, as the helmet and headband are pressing in, it gets very uncomfortable. I've tried everything, like using Vaseline instead of the sweatband to stem the flow of sweat, but it doesn't work. So now the helmet is gone.

It's strange, because for so long that helmet formed a big part of my hurling persona. Back when I was playing football, someone who wanted me to stick with the hurling used to say, 'Corcoran just doesn't look right without that helmet.' A few years ago, when we were living in Watergrasshill, a neighbour called over to say a lot of garden sheds in the area had been broken into the previous night. I went out to check ours, and everything seemed to be there, but a few hours later we got a call from the Gardaí to say they had recovered a battered black hurling helmet. So we went down to find an Aladdin's cave of lawnmowers and toolboxes, and, as it turned out, a certain manky, mouldy, bent helmet that was stinking out the Garda storeroom. In the shed that night, I'd had a lot of equipment – a lawnmower, barbecue grill, deckchairs – yet the only thing our visitor was interested in was that helmet. The lad had taste but obviously no sense of smell.

For me, putting on that helmet was like putting on war paint. It was like that ritual in *Battlestar Galactica* where Starbuck and the lads would go up into their fighter planes, and then they'd press a button and this glass shield would come down. Whenever I put on that helmet, all the fun and games stopped; it was time to enter the zone.

But then, over time, taking it off became the signal that we were in a real battle. It started with the '98 league final; it was fierce warm that day and I couldn't bear the sweat and heat. It was the same in the 2000 Munster final, and then when we were under pressure against Offaly the following month. In Killarney in 2004, I did it again – to hell with the sweatband and helmet and all restrictions and inhibitions. It was the same for the finals of '04 and '05. It'll be the same tomorrow. I felt much more comfortable warming up against Waterford last month without those bars distracting me. I know it's a risk, but we're so close to winning it all and need every edge we can get.

Kilkenny are going to be ravenous. The Cork public seem to think we're sure to win. It's surprising, considering they weren't so sure before the Waterford game and Kilkenny are a more proven team than Waterford. They are the reigning league champions and Leinster champions. They have yet to lose a game this year. On Thursday night, Donal Óg told us that, no matter how tired we are, we're to dig deep and find what ever bit of fight we have left, because we'll need it against these fellas. They've been sitting waiting for us for two years, and we're going to have to be ready to match that hunger.

The lads all look as relaxed and ready as usual, though. Again, a few of us went for our customary puckaround and walk; again, Seán Óg had an Aussie Rules DVD playing in the team room – this time a 'Greatest Hits' collection of all these unbelievable hits and tackles; again, a few lads headed off to the cinema. After the walk, I just watched some golf on the telly, after getting a rub from Davy.

It's all about routine now. Tomorrow, I'll get up and have my porridge. We'll go for our walk to Seanie's wall and listen to his words of wisdom. I'll get another rub from Dave or Chris, and then try to eat some chicken and pasta. Maybe I won't feel like eating it this year either; maybe I will. Then I'll sit on the bus with Sully, listening to Pacino. The nerves will be rattling around inside me, as will the thought of going home to Cork without that cup. But then I'll hit that warm-up room and start to feel relaxed and reassured by the familiar, hypnotic thud of ball meeting wall, ready for whatever happens on another Sunday in September.

CHAPTER NINETEEN
ANY GIVEN SUNDAY

Tony D'Amato: Never forget, on any given Sunday, you're either going to win or you're going to lose. The point is . . .

Willie Beamen: 'Can you take it like a man.' I got it, Coach.

D'Amato: Next year, I'm out of here. I'm not right for this any more. I want to start living again. But, you know, there was this great quarterback in the '70s . . . I ran into him a few weeks ago, we had a few beers and you know what he said? He said when he looked back, he didn't miss the cups or the girls or even the glory. What he missed were those other guys looking back at him in the huddle, every one of them seeing things the same way. Looking downfield. Together. That's what he missed. I'll miss you, amigo.

OLIVER STONE'S *ANY GIVEN SUNDAY*

THURSDAY, 21 SEPTEMBER 2006

Nearly three weeks on, and the pain is still there. Justin McCarthy once compared losing an All Ireland final to losing a bride at the altar. 'You feel passionate about something, you put your heart and soul into getting everything right for that one day, and then, at the final moment, it's taken away from you. It is not any game or girlfriend. A piece of you dies.' He's spot on. A dream has died, and a part of you dies with it.

I rang Donal Óg today, and he's finding it just as tough. We're brothers in grief, consoling, counselling each other. What's killing us is we're still convinced that Cork are a better team than Kilkenny, yet, as Cody said in '99 and '04, the best team always wins the All Ireland. In 2006, Kilkenny won the All Ireland, beating Cork 1–16 to 1–13, and that's a cold, hard fact I'm finding very hard to come to terms with.

At the start of the year, I said if I had a crystal ball that could tell that Cork would not win the 2006 All Ireland I wouldn't have played this year. How do I feel about it now? Part of me says I don't regret it – cementing friendships, the high after beating Waterford, knowing we tried, knowing at least I wasn't in the stands, watching Cork being beaten and regretting I wasn't out there. But the other part of me, the bigger part of me, says I could have done without it. If you told me at the start of the year we'd get to an All Ireland final and lose, I'd have had to pass on it, because I've already had that experience. I gave up a lot this year, with the commuting and time away from family and family events. I gave up a lot last year, too, but at least we achieved what we set out to achieve. This year, we didn't. Success this year was winning the All Ireland, anything less was failure, and we failed this year. There's no two ways about it for me. We failed, and that feeling of failure is a desperate feeling.

Am I annoyed about the pitch the day of the final? Well, it was a disgrace. Never in my career, not even in the winter, have I ever played on a pitch with the grass so high. But it was the same for both teams. It's not as if we play that much ground hurling anyway. That's not what's galling me. What's galling me is I don't think that was truly us out there. We didn't do as we planned to do. Instead, we played straight into Kilkenny's hands, by slowing up the play and allowing them to close us down.

For the past few weeks, I've kept hearing it was Kilkenny's 'hunger' that beat us. They were certainly hungry and played an intense, high-tempo game, but I don't accept the notion that they were 'hungrier' than us. I think we answered the hunger issue against Waterford. But when people see that Kilkenny had extra bodies onto the break, and had two guys surrounding one, they automatically say, 'That's hunger.' It was more to do with spacing and tactics. They had done their homework.

On the Thursday night before the final, Cunningham and Donal Óg called us all in and showed us on the laptop a clip from the Kilkenny–Clare semi-final. Just as Davy Fitz was taking a puckout, Donal Óg pressed pause to show us how Kilkenny were set up. And they were set up just like Tipp were in the Munster final: their corner-forwards pushed out to the half-forward line, their half-forwards pushed back to midfield and their midfield pushed back to crowd the half-back line. So we were expecting it, and we had talked about it, but we didn't counter it effectively. Maybe what we needed to do was take the odd short puckout to the man that was free and then get him to do a Forrest Gump and put it on his stick and run, Forrest, run. That would have created an overlap all the way up. All we would have had to do was try it out once or twice, maybe get a score from it, and Kilkenny might have fallen back to a more orthodox formation.

Jerry Wallis pointed out to me afterwards that our two midfielders tried to pull out to the wings for the puckouts, but they were being marked by Kilkenny's half-forwards, who had dropped back, so any time we knocked the ball there was a spare Kilkenny man waiting. The reason why Kilkenny won so many breaks wasn't that they had more hunger; it was that they had more men under the breaks.

I didn't have a good game myself. Ninety per cent of the ball that came in was up in the air, and that always favours a back. It wasn't as if Noel Hickey was catching ball over my head; he didn't even try to. Kilkenny are like that. They don't want you catching the ball, and Noel did a good job of making sure I didn't.

The one thing O'Grady and John have drilled into this team, though, is never to give up. And we never did. Even when Donal Óg was wrongly pulled up by the ref for giving a perfectly good hand-pass, we kept fighting for every single ball. Niall burst along the endline and fed it back to Ben, who rifled it home, and for a moment it looked as if we could still pull it off. But then the stewards started to line up around the field and you knew time was running out. And then it ran out. I turned to Hickey, we shook hands and my heart sank to the floor. Then I sat down on the pitch, watching Kilkenny men do what Cork men did last year and the year before.

A Kilkenny supporter made a break past the stewards, and suddenly there was an avalanche of black and amber onto the field. I stood up and waited for the presentation. And, as we did, people came over – Kilkenny lads, such as James McGarry, Derek Lyng and Henry Shefflin. Kilkenny and Cork supporters came up to say that we'd been great champions, great for the game. But, though it was gracious of them, at that moment in time I just wanted to either dig a hole or be parachuted out of Croke Park. You just want to disappear – you don't want to talk to anybody; you don't want to see anybody – while, when you win, you want to see everybody; you want to savour everything.

Back in the dressing-room, the difference between winning and losing was even more pronounced. Last year, that room was a haven of joy; this year, it was like a morgue. No one could talk, except a few RTE heads looking for someone to give them a few words. Every player just sat there, staring at the floor, not wanting to take off their jersey, not wanting to do anything, just wishing it was like last year.

Then Cody dropped in, and he was just as gracious and as dignified as he was in '99 and '04. I was in getting a stitch from Dr Con when he came in, and, as he was leaving, I went over to shake his hand. He just said five words, but they were genuine and succinct: 'I know how you feel.'

Today is the Thursday after the football final, and I see the Mayo lads skipped the homecoming, they were so devastated. I can tell you, if I had a say over it, I would have done the same thing. I would have hopped into a car straight after the match and driven either straight home to Cork or to the other end of the country to get away from it all. But I couldn't. Instead, we had to get dressed, throw the bag into the bus and head up to the players' lounge. I went over to congratulate James Ryall and John Tennyson. After a while, I headed back to the bus. Donal Óg was there, and I sat down beside him, just like I did 12 months earlier.

'Some difference a year makes,' I said.

'Yeah,' he sighed, and again we just stared at the floor, thinking of what was and what might have been.

Then it was back to the hotel for the reception and banquet. 'This is the start of a long, drawn-out torture,' I said to Joe. It's like what Justin says. When you win an All Ireland, it's as if you're all having this one big, happy wedding; when you lose it, it's as if your bride has fled but your family says you've paid for the meal and the band so you might as well go through with it. As we waited to enter the banquet, the MC introduced us as the Cork hurling team of 2006. Seanie was standing beside me and shook his head. The last two years, we'd been introduced as All Ireland champions. We no longer are.

And that's the thing. You win together, and you lose together, and you get through it together, trying to take it like men.

Kids help. When I saw Kate and Edel after the game, they were as full of life and innocence as ever. 'Why did you lose the game, Daddy?' The smile on their faces put a smile on mine.

The following morning, I got a text from Jerry O'Connor. A Garda colleague of his had asked him to visit someone, a Gerry O'Leary from Kanturk, in the Mater, waiting for a heart transplant. Jerry and John Allen were going up to visit him. Would I come along? And, again, the difference between this year and last year struck me. Last year, the three of us spent the Monday morning in the Crumlin Children's Hospital, and we were only too happy to be there. But now there was no cup to kindle anyone's eyes, and no twinkle in ours either. But I went, and I'm glad I went. Just to see Gerry there wearing his Cork jersey and this big smile on his face. You wouldn't believe what Gerry's been through this past year. Since December, he's been hooked up to this machine that's keeping him alive. He hasn't been home in nine months. Home now is this little room, with a window looking out at the sidewall of a building. But it's the classic case of one prisoner seeing bars and another seeing stars. Gerry sees stars. He sees the bright side of life. He chooses his attitude. So, as I left, I thought to myself, 'Brian, you can choose your attitude.'

And that's the way I've tried to see it since: the Gerry O'Leary way. But it goes over and back. At times, I'm still going, 'Feck it, we shouldn't have lost that match!'

I was talking to my good friend Dave Keating the Tuesday after the All Ireland, and it was like that scene at the end of *The Commitments*. The band have imploded, and Joey The Lips is trying to comfort a distressed Jimmy Rabbitte. 'Yeah,' he says, 'they could have gone on to make albums and sold millions and been "successful", but that would have been predictable. This way, it's poetry.' And Jimmy says to him, 'It's a load of bollix is what it is, Joey.'

Dave's been saying to me, 'It's been a fairy tale as it is. You've come back and played in three All Irelands, and won two of them. To win three would have been incredible, but life's not like that.'

And I'm saying to him, 'Of course it could have been like that! We were that close to the complete fairy tale.' But I know he's right. If someone had told me three years ago that I'd come back and play in three All Irelands and win two of them, I'd have bitten his hand off. But you get greedy. You want more. You want it all.

John has resigned as manager. We all suspected he would. He's been a great leader, and we're all better men for having worked with him and for him. Jerry Wallis won't be back next year either – another big loss. I don't know who else will go – maybe another member or two of the backroom team; maybe another player or two. There's a lot left in this Cork team, though, including a couple of All Irelands – if the structure and support in place stays and improves. It's a fear we all have now, that it might go back to the pre-strike days if the players don't stay strong. The Monday after the All Ireland, just before we checked out of the Burlington, a county board officer had a piece of paper for both Seanie and myself. I opened mine up, and it was a bill for €11.55, for some food ordered to the room. Seanie's bill was €2.25 for a 7-Up. A day after my last game for Cork and a day after possibly Seanie's last day training Cork and we're counting out coppers to pay for our sandwiches and a fizzy drink. The strike may be over, lads, but the struggle is not.

I'm back with the club now. Our team manager Martin Bowen told me to take the week off after the All Ireland, so I licked my wounds, drinking and eating crap, but I'm ready to give the county a rattle now. We're through to the quarter-finals. The symmetry with '92 is there. In my first year with Cork, we lost the final to Kilkenny, but I won the county with

Erins Own. Now, it's my last year with Cork, we lost the final to Kilkenny; maybe I'll win another county with Erins Own.

We'll have to wait and see. The talent and depth is there to win one. You could say we're the opposite of the team of '92. Back then, we had little underage success and the bare minimum to pick from; now, we've players who've won county minor titles and Under-21 finals galore but haven't yet made the breakthrough at senior level. And, the longer we go on without winning another county, the more the pressure mounts. The old team never seriously contended for county honours again, but then, in 2000, along came this group of minors including Tomas O'Leary, Cian O'Connor, Hero, Shane Murphy and Fergus 'Gusky' Murphy, and we reached that year's senior final. But we lost to Newtown and haven't been back there since, and it's hanging over the younger fellas' heads. Our coach Sean Prendergast often refers to the pictures in the clubhouse of the lads with their minor and Under-21 county titles and says, 'Yeah, ye were the best at boys' hurling, but ye've done nothing at men's hurling. If you ever do, then all the boys' stuff was brilliant, because the storyline's complete, but, if ye don't, it'll always be thrown back at ye: "Yeah, they won the boys' stuff, but they couldn't do it when it counted."' Maybe this year will be different. The younger lads have matured, and Hero is getting there.

One night earlier this year, when the Cork team were training down in Carrigtwohill, Kelly and Hero were talking about the good news that they had made the championship panel.

'We made it, anyway,' said Hero.

'Yeah,' said Kelly. 'John Allen came over to me last night to tell me.'

Hero looked a bit disorientated. 'Jesus, he never came over to tell me!' He paused and then grinned. 'I must have been a certainty, so!'

That's Hero. The ultimate Stuart Anderson.

I've trained and played more with Cork than with Erins Own over the last few years, but it doesn't seem too long ago when Erins Own were my social life, my hobby, my life. They were the days when we'd hurl all day for the fun of it. I played with lads I grew up with, was coached by neighbours and lived right across from the pitch.

We've packed a lot into our short history from the time my grandfather Tim Sheehan, along with the likes of my uncle D.D. Sheehan, Christy Twohig, Humphrey Collins and Charlie Nicholl founded the club in 1963. Through the years, I'd watch Tom Aherne, Mickey O'Connor and his brother Razor, the Murphys and the Bowens bring the club from junior level to intermediate and on to senior. I spent so many nights down at the pitch watching those teams training, retrieving balls from behind the goal and imagining that one day I would be training with them and we'd go the whole way.

The foundations had been laid. We had good, knowledgeable underage coaches in people like Humphrey Collins and Margaret and Colman Dillon Snr. Colman is still coaching the kids today. In 2005, he rightly received a lifetime achievement award from the club to honour his outstanding contribution over the years. But, though Colman may have got the awards, Margaret was the one with the reputation. She was renowned in east Cork as the woman to keep refs in check. When Billy Cody or Dan Kenneally refereed an Erins Own game, they'd have a running conversation with Margaret, standing on the bank. The match would have to be stopped on occasion, and the ref would have to shout out, 'Margaret, would you ever shut up!' She was so passionate about the games.

Eoghan O'Connor and Billy Hegarty were another two underage coaches that gave the club great service. Timmy Buckley was the man with the ash, and his love and knowledge of the *camán* is still evident today. Others like him, such as Timmy, Brendan and Michael Lambe, are the bedrock of Erins

Own. Thanks to the huge level of work and commitment from unsung heroes like Mickey O'Connor, Sean Twohig, Paddy Twomey and our good neighbour Denis O'Keeffe, we now have facilities any club would be proud to own.

But one man stands out from the rest: Mr Erins Own himself, Martin Bowen. Martin has been secretary of the club for the past 30 years and, in that time, has been the driving force behind every development in the club. I've never seen anyone give as much commitment to any cause.

After the All Ireland final in '99, he invited myself and Elaine to have some lunch in the Ashbourne Hotel with a few people from Erins Own. When we arrived at the function hall, it was full of all the faces I had known so well over the years. Later, he would also organise a function for the whole community to enjoy, and it was a night to remember. He had raided my mother's photo albums to put together a visual history of my hurling career, which he played on the big screen. He presented me with two pictures that I have hanging in my hall: one of me doing the lap of honour with Liam and Landers; the other a collage of the Cork team of the millennium. When I now look at that picture of me running with the McCarthy Cup, I think of all the people who were running with me in spirit, especially those from Erins Own who helped me there.

But now, it's nearly time for me to move on, so this is my last chance. I won't be playing with the club next year either.

I'll leave the game on good terms, though. I didn't the last time I walked away. I know I wanted the perfect end this time, but Dave's right: life's not like that. I was lucky as it was. If Cork had won the 2003 All Ireland, I wouldn't have been back at all, because that sense of mission and hurt the lads had wouldn't have been there either. I came back because I wanted to win and I wanted to play with the lads, and I've achieved that. You look at the psychology of comebacks and, for a lot of fellas, it's because they miss the buzz, the adrenalin and applause; they feel odd being known for something they no longer do. When Sugar Ray Leonard came back to fight Hagler, he claimed, 'This [the ring] is the only place I feel who I really am.' I never had that gap in my life in the two years I was away from the game. I didn't miss the game at all. But they say one of the other causes of a comeback might be a person's competitiveness. Sports people have been socialised, conditioned, to win, to meet challenges, and when they're away from the game, they begin to say to themselves what could be more challenging than a successful comeback? 'The joy of competition,' says Ellis Cashmore, 'lingers long enough to motivate a comeback.'

That's probably what motivated me to come back: the joy of competition, the competitor within. It wasn't the love of the game. It's a long time since I played the game for the love of the game. I've played to win All Irelands, and hurling has just been the medium to win them. If you told me in January I wasn't going to win one this year, I wouldn't have played. Other lads are different. If you told Donal Óg he wasn't going to win next year's All Ireland, he'd still play away, because playing hurling and playing for Cork is what he loves.

One of his favourite lines, one of his own, is 'It's the memories of matches and fellas you played with that you'll bring to your grave.' And there will be many of those memories for me: running out of that tunnel in Croke Park against Antrim in '88; Tony Sull throwing that ball out to me for my first point for Cork; coming out with a ball in front of Hill 16 in that '91 minor football final; Damien O'Neill raising the cup after the football Under-21 final in '94; the Canon's embrace after my baptism of fire against Tipp; Hennessy laughing; Cunningham snoring; D.D. crying after we won the county in '92; Jimmy's smile in '99; Morgan grinning, shaking his fist, looking right at me after beating Kerry in

Killarney; Cahalane grimacing as he squeezes Counihan and takes one shot for Cork; Sully strutting around the place, chest out, knowing Croke Park's his house; Con's laugh; Curran, Gardiner and Seán Óg bursting out with the ball; Ciaran, Larry, Morgan, Teddy Owens, shouting how much we have to win this one; Timmy and Joe and John Fitz leaning back against the wall, feet up on the bench, ready in their own good time; the bang on the door and the shout that it's 'Time, lads! Time!'; running towards the Cork crowd down by the city end, downfield, together, knowing that Roy Keane would be glad to have any of them with him in that tunnel in Highbury.

I've played with special teams, special men, none more so than the guys of '04, '05 and '06. There's a bond there that few teams have. We'll meet at weddings and funerals down through the years, and it'll still be there, the respect, the memory of when we were kings, the peace of mind of knowing we fought for every single ball. Joe O'Leary once said of the group, 'These guys will shoulder each other's coffins.' And I know I'll be honoured to shoulder or be shouldered by any of those lads.

But I have a lot of living to do before that. When I was a teenager, I didn't want to live beyond 35. What was I going to do beyond 35, if I wasn't able to play the games? But now I feel that life is only starting at 33. I'm going to miss training with my friends, playing with my friends, soldiering with my friends, but, at the end of the day, Elaine is my best friend. I'm looking forward to spending more time with her. I'm looking forward to the summer holidays, the birthday parties, reading bedtime stories to the girls, bringing them down to Fota, and some day maybe bringing them and Ewan to Croke Park and to Thurles, those fields of dreams.

Where I lived out my dreams.

POSTSCRIPT

In October 2006, Brian Corcoran and Erins Own did indeed reach the final of the Cork senior hurling championship. This match, against Donal Óg Cusack's Cloyne, had yet to be played when this book went to print.

BRIAN'S ROLL
OF HONOUR

AS A HURLER:

Three All Ireland senior medals (1999, 2004, 2005)

Two Hurler of the Year awards (1992, 1999)

Five Munster senior medals (1992, 1999, 2000, 2005, 2006)

Two National League medals (1993, 1998)

Three All Stars (1992, 1999, 2004)

One Cork senior county medal (1992)

Two Munster Under-21 medals (1991, 1994)

Two Munster minor medals (1988, 1990)

One East Cork Under-21 medal (1991)

One Harty Cup medal (1988)

One Railway Cup medal (1996)

Selected on Cork team of the millennium

Played for Ireland in senior shinty international (1995, 1996)

Played and won for Ireland in Under-21 shinty international (1992, 1994 as captain)

AS A FOOTBALLER:

Three Munster senior medals (1993, 1994, 1995)
One All Ireland Under-21 medal (1994)
One All Ireland minor medal (1991)
One Munster Under-21 medal (1994)
One Munster minor medal (1991)
One Cork county junior medal (1994)